Nonsense of a High Order

The Confused and Illusory World of the Atheist

Rabbi Moshe Averick

Tradition Reason Press

Tradition Reason Press

Published by Tradition and Reason Press, Inc.
2737 W. Fargo Ave.
Chicago, Ill 60645

Printed in the United States of America

Library of Congress Reg. Number: TXu001691634
ISBN 13 - 978-1456445942
ISBN 10 - 1456445944

Cover and Book Design:
Devorah Haggar Graphic Design

Visit Rabbi Averick's website at:
www.RabbiMaverick.com

This book is lovingly dedicated
to the memory of,
and for the *zchut* and
aliyah of the *neshama* of,

Moshe ben Ze'ev Halevi

— Manfred Hart —

Table of Contents

Acknowledgements:

"No Man is an Island"

A project such as this one is not possible without the help of many people. First and foremost my parents, *Dr. and Mrs. Nathan J. Averick*, my brother and sister-in-law *Dr. Rauvan and Judy Averick*, who have always been there through thick and thin, and my sister, *Sara Averick-Rosenfeld*, who generously offered her professional advice and input. If you look in the encyclopedia under "Loyalty and Friendship above and beyond the call of duty", you will see the pictures of *Michael and Mahra Hart*. I am grateful to *Rabbi Elisha Prero*, for nearly four decades of friendship and his valuable input and feedback during the writing of this book. His wife *Miriam Prero* also deserves mention for her warm hospitality and for tolerating me at her Shabbat table during my many discussions with her husband. A special expression of gratitude must go out to "Coach" *Mirjam Orbach* without whose invaluable guidance, it is highly doubtful that this project would have come to fruition. I must thank *Dr. Diane Medved* for her warm and enthusiastic encouragement while the manuscript was in its early stages and to her husband *Michael Medved* who gave her the manuscript to read in the first place. *Dr. Edward Peltzer*, an accomplished ocean chemist, who graciously took valuable time out of his busy schedule to review and critique the sections on Origin of Life and answer many of my questions, and *Dr. Joseph Walder*, CEO of Integrated DNA Technologies, Inc., who also was kind enough to clarify for me some of the finer points of organic chemistry. It was a unique privilege and experience to engage in mortal intellectual combat, via a series of e-mails, with *Dr. David Berlinski*. His frank and incisive comments forced me to carefully evaluate anything I wrote on the subject of Origin of Life. Luckily for me, *Dr. Paul Nelson*, a fellow of the Discovery Institute, lives here in the Chicago area only a short distance from my home, and I was able to meet with him a number of times and discuss different aspects of the manuscript. It was also through Dr. Nelson that I met *Professor Richard Weickart* of California State University-Stanislaus, who generously took time out of a very busy academic schedule to review the manuscript. *Rabbi Dr. Akiva Tatz*, renowned lecturer on Jewish philosophy and mysticism, of the Jewish Learning Exchange in London, England reviewed some of the early drafts and offered helpful advice. *Rabbi Dov Fischer,* a distinguished Orthodox rabbi and professor of law in California, and my dear friends *Rabbi Yosef Kauffman, Sam Veffer, and Drew Steinberg* all took the time and effort to give me their valuable feedback and suggestions. The same goes for *Dr. Gary Schreiber. Aharon Ungar* also imparted important feedback in the early stages of the project. *Dr. Jerry Sherman,* an old grade school buddy with whom I reconnected, via Facebook, provided unique, challenging ideas and input. Although I only met with her briefly, *Suri Goldstein* also furnished me with some very useful ideas. Early on, I was fortunate enough to have met *Mark and Carrie Burns* of Good News Radio based in Champagne-Urbana, Illinois. Mark was kind enough to not only review the manuscript but offered valuable advice based on his years of experience in broadcasting. I am very grateful to *Mary Burt*, of Mesa, Arizona, for her expert and professional editing. The same goes to *Lisa Neiberg* for her crucial editorial input into the early chapters of the book. It was a pleasure to work with an immensely talented graphic designer such as *Devorah Haggar. Alexander Gendler,* a veteran journalist and publisher, not only encouraged and inspired me, but offered his expert advice on the world of publishing.

This book was made possible in part with the assistance of NISHMA, based in Toronto, Ontario. NISHMA is an international organization dedicated to Torah research and education, under the direction of the distinguished rabbinic scholar, *Rabbi Benjamin Hecht* and his wife *Naomi Hecht.* (See www.Nishma.org)

Most important of all: Praise and endless gratitude to the One who "graciously endows man with wisdom and teaches insight to a frail mortal,"* the One "without beginning and without end,"* who is "my Rock and my Redeemer,"* *The One, Almighty Creator of the universe; the Infinite, Eternal, God of all mankind.*

*From the
traditional Jewish
morning prayer service

Part I

Fundamentals

— Chapter 1 —

*Introduction to
Modern Atheism 101*

— Chapter 2 —

*The Ground Rules:
Guidelines for Discussing the
Existence of God*

Chapter 1

Introduction to Modern Atheism 101

BORDERS Book Store – N. Lincoln Avenue, Chicago, Illinois

In June 2007, I had just returned to the United States after having resided in Jerusalem for the previous fourteen years. Standing in a BORDERS book store was a brand new experience, as this particular icon of corporate America had not yet reached Israel. As I looked around the store for the first time, something rather peculiar began to happen. Despite being an Orthodox Rabbi, I found myself gripped by an irresistible fascination with the seemingly endless parade of atheist manifestos displayed in strategic locations throughout: Books with titles such as *The God Delusion, God is Not Great: How Religion Poisons Everything, The End of Faith, and God: The Failed Hypothesis.* I confess! When I saw these titles for the first time I experienced an anticipatory thrill.

The thrill that I felt was similar to the sensation that I imagine a World War I pilot (an era when there still was a sense of chivalry between warring opponents) in his Sopwith Camel biplane might have felt as he engaged a worthy opponent in a dogfight; relishing the opportunity to do battle with a skillful foe, yet brimming with confidence that he would emerge victorious. There are few things I enjoy more than a vigorous and honest battle of intellect versus intellect, worldview versus worldview, idea versus idea. I soon became acclimated to my new surroundings and thoroughly enjoyed the simple pleasure of sitting in a comfortable chair, drinking coffee, and reading and reading.

I have taught Jewish theology and philosophy for nearly 30 years and I lost track long ago of the countless hours I have spent with thousands of students of all ages; teaching, discussing, arguing, debating the existence (or non-existence) of God, spirituality, the ultimate purpose of our lives… From that day in

June 2007, until mid-August of the same year, I spent day after day, hour after hour, wading through the combined onslaught of the 21st century's most popular atheistic ideologues. However, my initial excitement quickly dissipated and finally faded away. To paraphrase the great blues singer B.B. King, "the thrill was gone."

Was a little bit of intellectual honesty too much to hope for?

I had hoped to find in these manifestos at least a little bit of cutting-edge intellectual searching and honesty. I was sorely disappointed. While Richard Dawkins' pronouncement in *The God Delusion,* that "the God of the Old Testament is...petty, unjust, vindictive, bloodthirsty, misogynistic, homophobic, racist, infanticidal, genocidal, *etc.,*" [1] may, for some, have an irreverently bold and strident ring, it is more the proclamation of a stance than it is the outcome of intellectual inquiry. Can an intellectually honest and open minded person ignore the fact that this same deity commands the Israelites not to take revenge or bear a grudge, to view the use of inaccurate weights in business as an abomination, to view all human beings as created in the image of God, to open our hands wide to those in poverty, not to oppress the stranger who lives among us, to leave a portion of every field unharvested for the poor, never go to war against an enemy without first offering peace, that "justice, justice shall your pursue", to "love your neighbor as yourself"?

Jewish Scripture is the single most influential piece of literature in the history of mankind. Is Dawkins *obligated* to agree with distinguished historian Paul Johnson who writes in his monumental historical treatise, *A History of the Jews,* "to them [the Jews and their Scripture], we owe the idea of equality before the law, both divine and human; of the sanctity of life and the dignity of the human person; of the individual conscience and so of personal redemption...of peace as an abstract ideal and love as the foundation of justice, and many other items which constitute the moral furniture of the human mind?" [2] Perhaps not; but even if Dawkins has decided to completely reject the biblical worldview, it stands to reason that a *slightly* more nuanced evaluation would have been in order.

It's clear to me that the chain of venomous one-dimensional invective cited above, offers us much more insight into the inner workings of the soul of Richard Dawkins than it offers us any meaningful insight into understanding the biblical narrative or the concept of the One God who is at the center of it all.

While I have never been particularly impressed by the intellectual firepower brought to bear by skeptics, atheists, and freethinkers in their attacks on belief in God, I have striven to respond seriously to their expressed views. I wish the same could be said for our new breed of militant skeptics. Bombastic titles like *God is Not Great: How Religion Poisons Everything**, (Everything?!), ranting about people who profess religious faith, ("When their beliefs are...common we call them "religious;" otherwise they are...called "mad," "psychotic," or "delusional." [3]), and the rehashing of philosophical parlor tricks like, "Can God create a stone that is too heavy for him to lift?," [4] do not, in my opinion, contribute to the expansion of our intellectual or spiritual horizons. Perhaps GREENPEACE activists could have been galvanized to stage one of their publicity-stunt protests; after all, *entire forests* were cut down to print these atheist books. Wouldn't it have been simpler to reprint Bertrand Russell's succinct essay, "Why I Am Not Theist," ** and have been done with it?

It was clear to me that the gauntlet had been thrown down. I resolved on the spot to write a book in response; a book whose essential purpose would be to demonstrate the abject intellectual poverty of atheism and of its modern proponents.

About the title...

When I first mentioned to people the title I had chosen for this book, most were immediately curious from where I had picked the phrase "Nonsense of a High Order" and what was its specific connection to the ideology of atheism. It was a phrase coined by the late Sir Fred Hoyle, distinguished British mathematician, physicist, and astronomer. In an article that appeared in *New Scientist*, Nov. 1981, Hoyle writes:

---

*An atheist manifesto by Christopher Hitchens published in 2007.
** This was printed as an excerpt from Russell's book, *Why I Am Not a Christian*.

Imagine 10^{50} blind persons each with a scrambled Rubik's cube, and try to conceive of the chance of them all simultaneously arriving at the solved form. You then have the chance of arriving by random shuffling, of just one of the many biopolymers on which life depends. The notion that not only the biopolymers but the operating program of a living cell could be arrived at by chance in a primordial organic soup here on the Earth is evidently *nonsense of a high order.* *

It was crystal clear to Hoyle – a world renowned scientist – that for life to emerge from non-life billions of years ago by means of some undirected process in a pre-biotic soup was a scientifically absurd proposition. I will show throughout this book that Hoyle's pointed characterization of a random, undirected emergence of life as being "nonsense of a high order" applies equally to the rest of atheistic thought.

As a fitting introduction to our subject matter, consider making the acquaintance of one of the high clergy in the modern atheist hierarchy, a British gentleman by the name of Christopher Hitchens.

An Atheist "Sees the light"

Born in 1949 and educated at Baliol College, Oxford – Hitchens is a highly accomplished author and journalist. He has written books on Thomas Jefferson, Thomas Paine, Henry Kissinger, and Bill Clinton, among others. His columns and articles have appeared in prestigious publications around the world and he is regularly interviewed on radio and television. In 2007 his atheistic magnum opus was published under the title, *God is Not Great: How Religion Poisons Everything.* This work was followed swiftly by a compilation entitled, *The Portable Atheist: Essential Readings for the Non-Believer.*

In a debate with the Rev. Al Sharpton shortly after the publication of *God is Not Great,* Hitchens recounted to the audience how even as a young boy he "saw the light" of atheism:

> I was nine when I thought I saw through it, when my biology teacher told me that God was so good as to have made vegetation green because it was the color most restful to our eyes. And I thought, Mrs. Watts, this is nonsense...I just knew she'd got everything all wrong. [5]

---

*All emphasis in quoted citations is mine unless otherwise indicated.

As Hitchens grew older he received a fine education and acquired an admirable command of the English language. Nevertheless, I suspect that a careful analysis of his views on such weighty issues as racism, morality, and democracy – considered through the prism of his staunch atheistic worldview – might in fact leave an honest thinker wondering if his intellectual progress in this particular area didn't stall at the level of a nine year old boy daydreaming during Mrs. Watts' science class.

On Racism, Morality, & Democracy:
The Godless World of Christopher Hitchens

In a September 2007 lecture at Sewanee University in Tennessee peculiarly entitled, "The Moral Necessity of Atheism", Hitchens expressed his loathing of the "primitive" concept of racism. He resolutely advanced the argument that atheism, with its implicit notion that human beings merely represent another evolutionary branch of the animal kingdom, deals a fatal intellectual blow to racism as a concept:

> Through the DNA we find that in some sense, some of Genesis is vindicated. We are in a way part of an animal creation and we share part of their material in our own make up. I as a mammal never kind of doubted that I had this relationship with ground worms and other creatures. It does make short work of racism. It means racism is no longer something we have to argue with...we may be some distance from being able to completely pronounce its utter defeat, but it's over as an argument...racism is a primitive, stupid construct made out of literally nothing. [6]

In other words, if we accept the premise that our existence on the earth is only possible via the magic of Darwinian evolution; if we would remind ourselves, as non-believing paleontologist Stephen J. Gould has put it, that "we are here because one odd group of fishes had a peculiar fin anatomy that could transform into legs,"[7] if we would just reflect on our shared relationship to ground worms, our response would be to join hands and triumphantly break into a chorus of *We Shall Overcome*.

To be fair, if the atheist/Darwinian view is accurate, we *are* all brothers in the sense that we are equally related to ground worms. Astonishingly though, Hitchens – blinded by the brilliance of his third grade epiphany – has failed to realize the ultimate emptiness of such a statement.

All men are equal...equal to what?

Through the eyes of the atheist, being related to ground worms does not make all of mankind brothers in the sense that we are all equally *valuable*. It makes us brothers in the sense that we are equally *void of all significance*. A ground worm is insignificant. There nothing ennobling or inspiring in one's being related or equated to a ground worm. Thus, the species *Homo sapiens* is also insignificant. In the atheistic worldview both are nothing more than infinitesimally small specks of "dust in the wind;" random, meaningless collections of molecules and chemicals spinning in space. But why should I bore the reader with my rendition of the atheist view of reality? Let's let the atheists speak for themselves. Dr. Peter Walker, a space physicist at Rice University informs us that:

> [humans] are carbon based bags of mostly water on a speck of iron-silicate dust revolving around a boring dwarf star in a minor galaxy in an underpopulated local group of galaxies in an unfashionable suburb of a supercluster. [8]

Similarly, the eminent astrophysicist Sir Arthur Eddington proclaims, "We are bits of stellar matter that got cold by accident, bits of a star gone wrong." [9] The late astronomer, Carl Sagan, leaves very little to the imagination as far as his viewpoint of mankind's place in the grand scheme of things, "The very scale of the universe...speaks to us of the inconsequentiality of human events in the cosmic context." [10] In the world of the atheist, all life on earth drowns in an ocean of insignificance in relation to the countless billions of galaxies in our universe.

I fervently agree that racism is "stupid." Other than that, Hitchens and I have nothing in common regarding our views on racism. For the believer, racism is "stupid" because all human beings are created in the image of God; all stand equal before their infinitely powerful Creator. The intrinsic value of a human being derives from his relationship to God and is not predicated on his physical and mental abilities and certainly not the color of his skin. For the atheist, however, racism is "stupid" not because of some noble notion of the brotherhood of all men, but because of the absolute *insignificance* of all men, no matter what their race or color. The distinguished evolutionary biologist George Gaylord Simpson has informed us that "Man is the result of a purposeless [evolutionary]...process." [11] H.L. Mencken put it a little more bluntly: Man is a "sick fly" spinning around in space on a "dizzy ride" to nowhere. [12]

In the atheistic universe of Hitchens and his cohorts, man's life is insignificant and his death is insignificant. His words and thoughts are insignificant and his endless collection of ideologies is insignificant. Not only is the skin color and racial type of a "sick fly" purposelessly "revolving around a boring dwarf star" not worth a moment's thought, *nothing* about his existence is worth a moment's thought.

The world according to Hitchens: Racism = "stupid," American Democracy = "stupider"

Despite the undeniable non-value of human existence in the atheistic view of reality, Hitchens stubbornly persists in his puffed-up role as a noble man of reason by expressing not only his distaste for racism, but his enthusiastic support of democratic principles. In the same lecture at Sewanee University, Hitchens proclaimed his admiration for American democracy:

> The American Revolution is the only one still standing...the only one that has any merit or virtue left in it, and I think this confers upon us a certain responsibility...[It] should be a great deal better appreciated than it is, and a great deal more cherished, and a great deal more firmly upheld at home as well. [13]

Not surprisingly, he ignores a very *inconvenient* truth. If racism is "stupid" for the reasons that he advances, then the ideology of democracy must be even "stupider." American Democracy is built on the premise (as stated in the Declaration of Independence) that "We hold these truths to be self evident, that all men are created equal, that all men are endowed by their Creator with certain unalienable rights, that among these are life, liberty, and the pursuit of happiness." This makes perfect sense to me because I believe that all men are created in the image of God, and all men stand equal before their infinite Creator.

What would be the intellectually honest reaction of an atheist to this statement in the Declaration of Independence? Not only are men not created equal, they are not created at all. We are only here because, "one odd group of fishes had a peculiar fin anatomy that could transform into legs." Not only are men not endowed with unalienable rights, there is no creator to endow them with any inherent rights whatsoever. In Darwinian terms, as described above, we are a kind of glorified tuna fish. What inherent rights does a tuna have? (The right to be picked by Star Kist?)

In his introduction to *The Portable Atheist*, Hitchens declares, "I am writing these words on July 4, 2007, the anniversary of the proclamation of the world's first secular republic." It is unmistakably clear from the Declaration of Independence itself that this statement is an outright lie. No one has ever stated the obvious truth about American Democracy with more crystal clear and penetrating incisiveness than the great writer and thinker, G.K. Chesterton:

> The Declaration of Independence dogmatically bases all rights on the fact that God created all men equal; and it is right, for if they were not created equal, **they were certainly evolved unequal.** There is no basis for democracy except in a dogma about the Divine origin of man. (Chapter 19, *What I Saw in America*, 1922) [14]

To the atheist, the idea that all men are equal is clearly nonsense of a high order. In what way are they equal? Some are brilliantly intelligent and some are amazingly stupid. Some are highly competent and talented, some are completely inept. Some are robust and powerful, some are sickly and weak. Some are clearly born to lead and some seem born to follow. Most significantly, some are "fit to survive" and some are not so "fit to survive." Thus, a perfectly sensible atheistic ideology would be the one that was advocated by such atheists as George Bernard Shaw, H.G. Wells, and Havelock Ellis; that the sickly, the mentally ill, and deformed babies should be put to death so they don't contaminate society with their inferior genes. (It is worth noting that they advocated murdering human misfits regardless of race and skin color, conclusive evidence for Hitchens' assertion that atheism "makes short work of racism.") To be fair, G.B. Shaw did say that they must be put to death "in a decent human way." [15] This will be discussed at length in a later chapter.

Prominent atheists proclaim: Life has no value and no meaning

One of the more egregious intellectual blunders of atheists like Hitchens is to espouse noble ideals (like democracy and equality) that only make sense if a transcendent God/Creator exists, and when no one is looking simply drop him out of the picture. They then hope nobody notices (including themselves) that removing God from the equation effectively destroys any possible rational foundation for the very ideal they are promoting. If Christopher Hitchens wants to assign a higher value to the upright walking primate called *homo sapiens* or to some particular dreamed-up ideology, he should at least display some intellectual courage and integrity (the reader is urged not to hold his or her breath while waiting for this to happen) and admit that from the viewpoint of the atheist it is an artificial construct "made out of literally nothing" that has no objective reality. In a letter to Marie Bonaparte in 1937, Sigmund Freud wrote,

> The moment a man questions the meaning and value of life, he is sick, since objectively neither has any existence. [16]

Freud's conclusions are echoed by another atheist, the Nobel Prize winning physicist Dr. Steven Weinberg: "The more we know of the cosmos, the more meaningless it appears." [17] Professor Will Provine of Cornell University explains that atheism inescapably leads to the conclusion that, "There is no hope whatsoever of there being any deep meaning in human life...you're here today and you're gone tomorrow and that's all there is to it." [18] If Freud, Weinberg, and Provine can state this simple, obvious truth that is part of the atheistic world view, why can't Hitchens? As a matter of fact, *he does*. Later on in the same lecture Hitchens responds to a question from someone in the audience as follows:

The question for me would rather be, this being the case, [that there is no purposeful creation], then why care, why do I bother? That's a very good question. It also doesn't have a conclusive answer. [19]

REALITY CHECK PLEASE

A successful and ostensibly intelligent author is lecturing to a group of students at a respected liberal arts university:

A) He informs the audience that implicit in his worldview is the fact that in objective reality life has no meaning, purpose, or value. He has no answer to the questions: Why care? Why bother? (confirmed by Freud, Weinberg, and Provine).

B) He finds inspiration for humanity in the fact that we are all related to ground worms.

C) An inescapable implication of his atheistic worldview is that the two diametrically opposed ideologies of racism and democracy (and everything in between), are equally insignificant, "stupid", and "made out of literally nothing" artificial constructs.

D) The title of the lecture is "The Moral Necessity of Atheism"

E) *What's wrong with this picture?* Funny, the last time I looked, a meaningless existence, life having no objective value, being on the same qualitative level as an insect*, and conjuring up ideologies from my imagination, were not on *my* list of things that created "The Moral Necessity" of anything at all.

The Real Deal of Atheism

If Hitchens had presented an honest and candid articulation of his world outlook as an atheist, it would have gone something like this:

MY FELLOW GROUND WORMS:

It is important for you to know that religion poisons everything! Imagine how beautiful life would be if only we would stop trying to treat our fellow man like he was created in the image of God, stop

---

* Technically of course, a ground worm is not an *insect*. Please excuse my exercise of poetic license.

treating him as if the Creator endowed him with unalienable rights, stop pretending that all men stand equal before their Creator, and start treating him like a purposeless carbon based bag of water revolving around a boring dwarf star, like bits of stellar matter gone wrong, like a sick fly, like the ground worm that he is, like a tuna fish that sprouted legs...

Remember, it is religion that poisons everything! The only thing religious people do is to go around killing each other in the name of God. I ask you honestly, does any rational, logical, skeptical, atheistic, scientific minded person really think it's necessary to believe in God if you want to go around killing people? Of course not! Don't let those fanatics brainwash you. Stalin** and Pol-Pot murdered **millions** and I am proud to remind you that they were fellow atheists. Anything those religious people do, we can do much, much better.

Let's be totally honest. As an atheist I assert that Adolf Hitler's racist notion that the Aryan race is superior to all other races is a "stupid" construct "made out of literally nothing." By the same token, Thomas Paine's idea that all men are **created equal** is also a "stupid" construct "made out of literally nothing." There is, however, an important difference between the two...Thomas Paine did not have that silly moustache.

On second thought, since as a result of Darwinian evolution species evolve to higher and higher levels of sophistication and intelligence, it actually is quite possible that one particular race, say for example the Aryan race, through the process of natural selection actually did evolve to a superior level and some of the other races actually are inferior. In other words, just like some types of monkeys and primates are smarter than others.....oops, better not go there, that line of reasoning could really get me in trouble...

In the final analysis I really don't know what difference it makes anyway, since I have no conclusive reason to care one way or the other. However, please keep in mind that all of us atheists, including myself, Dr. Sigmund Freud, Dr. Steven Weinberg, Dr. Will Provine, etc., assert that there is no objective purpose or value to human life, and the universe is meaningless and pointless. This of course means there is no real point in me speaking to you, or for you

---

**Joseph Stalin, tyrannical dictator of the Soviet Union from 1924-1953
  Pol-Pot, Prime Minister of Kampuchea (Communist Cambodia) from 1976-1979

to listen to me for that matter...which makes me wonder...why exactly do I keep speaking anyhow?...But even more important, why do you keep listening? The main thing to remember is this: Although I haven't the faintest idea why, all these things are necessary for morality!

What causes atheists to advance ideas that are senseless?

The issue is certainly not lack of intelligence. Steven Weinberg and Will Provine are, to say the least, quite intelligent. When Christopher Hitchens discusses world politics, history, or literature he might very well make some astute observations (I hope that does not go to his head).

What then *does* lead the atheist to say things that can only be described as "nonsense of a high order?" As I will point out, the doctrine of atheism is so devoid of reason and logical consistency that in order to remain a non-believer the atheist must consistently disconnect from and ignore or distort certain obvious truths and realities. I call this phenomenon the "atheistic disconnect," and I will point out numerous examples of it throughout this book. I admit that atheists are not the only ones who disconnect from certain truths and realities in order to maintain a belief in a particular world view; in all fairness they would most certainly accuse me of doing the same thing. In the final analysis though, I leave it to the reader to carefully weigh the evidence and make his or her own decision about this most crucial and fundamental of issues. However, before we go any further, it is imperative when dealing with a subject matter such as ours to set out some basic philosophical underpinnings and conceptual paradigms for our discussion. I call these...*The Ground Rules*.

Chapter 2

The Ground Rules:
Guidelines for Discussing the
Existence of God

<u>Ground Rule #1</u>: *Seeking the Truth*

There is a trial going on, one that is crucial and earth shaking. Newspaper editors wanting to sensationalize a trial will bill it as the "Trial of the Century." What I am referring to is not the "Trial of the Century;" it is *The* Trial, period. It is the decision a human being makes about the existence of the Creator, of God. It is without a doubt the single most important decision we ever make. The entire meaning, purpose, and direction of our own lives; the way we relate to our families, loved ones, and the entirety of humanity, hangs on this decision.

It is my opinion that the reality of the Creator, or the existence of God, is really quite apparent. None of the ideas that I have presented or that I am going to present on this subject are particularly complicated or difficult. Most of them can be understood by a reasonably intelligent teenager and quite possibly even children of a younger age if they have above average comprehension. Based on my experience it is clear to me that the truly significant issue is not the evidence for the existence of God, the evidence is relatively straightforward and clear. The real issues, as I see them, are twofold.

The first issue is that not everybody has been trained to think. What I mean is that in the same way that some people are not handy with a screwdriver, jig-saw, or monkey wrench, many people are not "handy" with that amazing tool, computer, analyzer, evaluator of data, in short, the thinking machine that is the human brain. This is not a reflection on the individual's native intelligence; proper analysis of an abstract or philosophical concept is a skill he or she may never have acquired. I might add that

I consistently found this to be a problem even among those who have been educated at top notch universities. Regarding this, I hope I have presented my ideas in a clear enough fashion that even newcomers to this topic will be able to follow.

"A man hears what he wants to hear, and disregards the rest" [1]

    The second issue is much more serious, and cuts to the core of the essential nature of a human being. Quite simply, it is the *desire for truth*. If people have not assigned "truth" a top slot on their list of priorities, it does not matter what is said to them and what evidence is presented. In fact, and I say this without a trace of facetiousness, even if God himself would tell them something, they would simply shrug it off and continue on their merry way. If this is unclear, the following example will help illustrate this behavioral tendency that human beings exhibit when confronted with uncomfortable facts or ideas.

    On March 13, 1964 a young woman named Kitty Genovese was stabbed to death in front of her apartment building in the Kew Gardens section of Queens, NYC. What made this crime so notorious and famous was that thirty eight witnesses watched from the large apartment complex as she was murdered and not one of them called the police. The murderer, Winston Moseley, was eventually caught, tried, and put in prison. I watched a documentary film made about this case which included an interview of Moseley in prison. During the interview he spoke freely about the fact that he stabbed this young woman to death, how much he regrets what he did, and how much he had changed during his years in prison. A few moments later Moseley's mother is interviewed and she emphatically declares that she "knows" that her son never killed anyone. She repeats this several times. The juxtaposition of these two scenes – of watching Moseley himself describe how he stabbed a woman to death and then watching his mother declare that she "knows" that her son never killed anyone – was jarring to say the least. If I had not seen the interview with Moseley and had only watched the interview with his mother, I think she would have planted seeds of doubt in my mind about the guilt of her son. That's how unequivocal and convincing she was.

Either we find the truth, or we live with a lie

The conclusion is obvious. If a person does not want to believe even the most obvious fact, if there is an agenda that is more important than the truth, there is absolutely nothing that will convince that person. This woman's psychological and emotional need to believe her son to be innocent was much greater than her desire for the truth (my purpose is obviously not to pass judgment on her). Consequently, she "knows" that her son did not commit murder.

Although it is easy for most people to understand why this woman was prepared to deny reality to fit her own agenda, the point is that we are all perfectly capable of doing the same thing. Actually, to say we are *capable* of doing it is very misleading. I would suggest to the reader that *the struggle to seek the truth and let the truth determine our agenda, rather than use our personal agenda to determine what we will accept as truth, is the essential battle we must be prepared to fight if we wish to be fully human.* The alternative to finding the truth and living with the truth is living with lies, falsehood, and hallucination.

The late Rabbi Noah Weinberg, founder and Dean of the Aish Hatorah Rabbinical Seminary in Jerusalem, once noted that, "Every human being exhibits a Nobel Prize level of genius and creativity when it comes to one particular area: *rationalization.*"[2] The most dangerous enemy of truth is not a lie. The real enemy of truth is when we ourselves *choose* a comfortable lie of our own creation over the truth.

The siren song of "The Matrix"

A striking dramatization of this basic human struggle was presented in the film *The Matrix*. At some future time, machines have taken over the world. Human beings are kept in a sleep state where their brains are hooked up to a massively complex computer program called "The Matrix." The computer program gives these comatose people the illusion that they are actually living a real life as we know it. A few humans have escaped and are fighting the machines. One of these escapees makes a deal with the machines: In return for betraying the rest of his group, he will be reconnected to "The Matrix" and in this *illusory dream state* will be someone "very important."

We all face the same dilemma: Am I prepared to make the sacrifices necessary to live with reality or like the traitor in that film, will I choose a comfortable fantasy and illusion instead? All of us must ask ourselves the following questions: How badly do I want the truth? Would I be prepared to live in poverty for the truth? Would I be prepared to take a *10% cut in income* for the truth? Would I be prepared to give up watching the Super Bowl (when my home team is playing) for the truth?

That last question in particular may sound silly, but if you find that even thinking about lowering your income or missing the Super Bowl scares you, then you could very well end up like Winston Moseley's mother, denying an obvious reality because you feel it threatens your comfortable way of life. I urge everyone reading this book to meditate on this idea and start mustering the necessary determination and fortitude to seek the truth at all costs.

Ground Rule #2: *Defining Fanaticism*

Whenever religion, God, or the concept of truth is being discussed, invariably someone is going to start throwing around the f-word: *fanatic*. My experience has been that most people have never bothered to think about what this word really means and will stare dumbfounded if asked to actually give a meaningful definition of a fanatic. Usually they will offer something like, "religious people who believe they have the truth are fanatics," or "people who think they are right and everyone else is wrong are fanatics," or "people who will kill for what they believe in are fanatics." A moments thought will reveal that not only are these answers not definitions, but followed to their logical ends, they all lead to quite foolish conclusions.

"Religious people who think they have the truth are fanatics"

According to this understanding of the concept what makes them fanatics? Is it *A)* because they think they have the truth, or *B)* because the assumption is that their beliefs are false? If it is *A)* that would mean *anyone* who thinks they know the truth is a fanatic. That would include people who believe the earth is round, biologists who believe in Darwinian evolution, and atheists like Sam Harris. If it is *B)*, then it has nothing to do with the fact that they are religious per se, it's because anyone who believes falsities is a fanatic. This is quite unsatisfying because you have now begged the question: What is the truth? It goes even further; is this to say that every time someone holds a mistaken idea they are considered to be in the category of a fanatic? Scholars constantly revise theories. Does this mean that if one of their theories turns out to be mistaken (*i.e.,* false) they were, until now, fanatics?

"People who think they are right and everyone else who disagrees is wrong"

This is completely ridiculous. It would mean that anyone who is convinced they are right about a particular subject should be labeled as a fanatic. There is no escaping from the fact that if a person thinks they are clearly right on a particular subject, there is an implicit declaration that anyone who disagrees is wrong.

"People who kill for what they believe in are fanatics"

That of course would mean that all the soldiers who fought the Germans and Japanese in World War II were fanatics. It would mean that all policemen who shoot at armed robbers are fanatics. They were, and are, ready to kill and die for what they believe in.

We clearly have to do much better than this if we are going to understand what fanaticism really is and the significance of the concept in our discussion. The clearest and most meaningful definition of a fanatic I ever heard was the one proposed by Rabbi Noah Weinberg:

> Fanaticism has nothing to do with what you believe or how passionately you believe it. The definition of a fanatic is someone who believes in a particular idea or doctrine, <u>no matter what it may be</u>, and says, "This is what

I believe, it's the truth, and don't disturb my comfortable beliefs and ideas with your questions, observations, and certainly not with facts. I'm right, I'm comfortable, and I am determined not to think about it anymore." [3]

What distinguishes the passionate believer in a cause or ideology from the fanatic is not what they believe, but whether or not they are open to questions, to considering another point of view, or being theoretically ready to reconsider their position. The fanatic "discusses" or "argues" only to justify his beliefs and agenda, never to discover truth. In short, fanaticism is not a function of *what* one believes; it is a function of how – on an internal level – one emotionally and intellectually *relates* to those beliefs. The fanatic is someone who has *shut off his or her mind* and is unwilling to consider anything that presents a challenge to their dearly held belief system.

A Litmus Test for fanaticism

We now have a meaningful definition of a fanatic. It becomes clear that there is *no ideology* that is free from fanatics. The fact that a person advocates his or her position with great passion and self sacrifice has nothing to do with fanaticism. A person can present his position very calmly, quietly, politely, and still be a total fanatic. Winston Moseley's mother is a fanatic when she denies her son is a murderer; there is nothing anyone could say, no matter how reasonably stated, that would change her mind. If someone were to show her the interview of her son admitting to murder, she would simply claim that he was coerced or threatened with torture.

This means that determining who is really guilty of fanaticism is not always such an easy task. However, I can give you at least one almost sure-fire *indicator* that someone is a fanatic: When an individual expresses indignation at the suggestion that there are adherents of his or her *own* ideology who might be fanatics, or denies the possibility of such, it is almost always an indication of the fanatical nature of that particular individual. For example, if you meet a feminist ideologue who denies that there could be such thing as a fanatical feminist, or who bristles at the suggestion that such a thing is possible, she herself is undoubtedly a fanatical feminist. Only someone who has shut off their *own* mind could be so blind as to deny the possibility of fanaticism in their own particular ideological community. I think this strikes an intuitive chord with most people but even if it's unclear trust me on this one. The same applies to Jews, Christians, Moslems, Mormons, freethinkers, homosexual activists, global warming activists, pro-abortion activists, scientists, conservatives, liberals, socialists, capitalists, and most definitely, atheists.

Ground Rule #3: *It is critical to clarify how we know and decide that something is true*

The philosophical term for Ground Rule #3 is *epistemology*. How do we know what we know? What does it mean to "prove" something? What does it really mean when we say we "know" something is true? In light of the fact that we are talking about knowledge of the existence of God, it is quite important to spend a little bit of time on this subject.

The first decision a human being must make is whether or not it is possible to bridge the gap between oneself and reality. In other words, can we actually know and discern the world around us? I mention this right at the beginning, because I cannot tell you how many times I have been involved in discussions about the existence of God when suddenly the person I am talking with says, "Well, maybe we don't really know anything. Maybe we are just dreaming this reality" (or some variation on that theme).

How we know the world around us is real, or how we are sure of our own reality can be a fascinating subject to discuss. However, there is no escaping the fact that ultimately it boils down to how you choose to answer the following question: Do you trust your senses, your mind, and your brain, to give you accurate data with which to interface with reality? Please answer yes or no. There are no other options. If your answer is "no, I do not trust that my mind and senses can convey accurate information with which I can form a coherent picture of reality," discovering the truth about *anything* is going to be a rather difficult task. On the other hand, if you answered "yes" please continue reading and it will not be necessary to bring up the subject again.

Once the decision is made that we can make sense of the world around us, it becomes relatively easy to formulate a working definition of what it means to "know" and/or to "prove" something (including "knowing", and "proving" God's existence). *"Knowing" means to know beyond a reasonable doubt and "proving something" means evidence that proves it beyond a reasonable doubt.* It is not possible to know anything or to prove anything to a higher level of clarity than "beyond a reasonable doubt." There are of course many different lower levels of clarity where the odds might be in your favor but there still is reasonable doubt.

I would suggest to you that both what we call "mathematical" proof and "scientific" proof fall into the same category. It is crucial to understand why even in science and math, the highest level of clarity achievable is "beyond a reasonable doubt."

There is always room for unreasonable doubt

We have all seen the typical courtroom drama where the defense attorney in a criminal trial approaches the witness, and says, "Mr. Jones, we have heard your testimony earlier in this trial…isn't it *possible* you made a mistake? Mr. Jones, please answer the question, isn't it *possible* you made a mistake?" Mr. Jones hesitates and mumbles, "well it's *possible*, but…", and the defense attorney immediately interrupts and says, "That will be all Mr. Jones, you may step down." Then, while the witness sits there sputtering, the judge ends it by turning to Mr. Jones and saying, "The witness is excused." The defense attorney slyly smirks, the district attorney grimaces, and the witness is left gaping foolishly.

In fact, there is an easy remedy for the district attorney. Since what is required in a criminal trial is proof beyond a *reasonable* doubt, he simply has to ask the witness the following: "Mr. Jones, you said it's *possible* you made a mistake, however, do you have any *reasonable doubt* that you made a mistake? Is there any *reasonable doubt* that your testimony is not accurate?" Of course, the answer to that question would be an emphatic "no!"

My point is very simple. No matter what propositions you are dealing with, whether theories in the fields of statistics, math, or science, guilt or innocence in criminal trials, or the issue of the existence of God, there is always *unreasonable doubt*. I repeat, no matter what issue we are discussing you can *always raise unreasonable doubt*. Ask yourself, isn't it *possible* the roof will cave in within the next 30 seconds? If it's *possible* then why don't we run out immediately? The answer is simple; it may be possible, but it is not reasonable.

The exact same principle applies to scientific experiments. Let's propose a hypothetical experimental trial of a new medication with two groups of 1000 cancer patients. In Group 1, the group which receives the new medication, 999 are cured. In Group 2, which does not receive the new medication, nobody is cured. I go to another hospital and repeat the experiment with the same results. Isn't it *possible* there is some explanation other than the medicine to explain why the patients are healthier? Yes, it's *possible,* but at some point in the experiment it ceases to be *reasonable.*

There is no such thing as a proof that does not have unreasonable doubt

Even 2+2=4, can be doubted (*unreasonably,* of course). Many people are incredulous when they hear that statement and ask, "How can anyone doubt that 2+2=4, isn't it mathematically inescapable?" In response to this I have presented my students with the following scenario: We all know that that Einstein's Theory of Relativity is scientifically accepted across the board. We all know that part of that theory is that time is relative. As we move at a faster velocity or in the presence of a large gravitational field, time actually slows down relative to people who are moving slower, or relative to people who are in the presence of a smaller gravitational field. This scientifically proven fact is perhaps one of the most counter-intuitive realities that we simply have to accept as being true. Before Einstein published the theory and it was proven conclusively, you would have thought that the idea of time being relative was totally insane. So now I ask you: Isn't it possible that there is a mathematician or physicist somewhere right now who is coming up with a new scientific theory that will show us that in the same way we were all mistaken about the true nature of time, we have all been mistaken about the true nature of 2+2 =4? Isn't it *possible*? I have now been succeeded in raising unreasonable doubt in my students' minds; of course, they have no choice but to answer "yes."

We see then that it is *possible*, but *totally unreasonable* to doubt that 2+2=4. It is crucial to realize that when considering any type of scientific or philosophical issue, I do not have to consider unreasonable doubt. I do not have to consider *every* possibility, only *reasonable* possibilities.

A culprit from Outer Space is the guilty party

Two men go into a sealed bank vault with only one door. Suddenly, a shot rings out. One man is found holding a smoking gun and the other is dead on the floor of a gunshot wound. At the trial the defense attorney says to the jury, "Isn't it *possible* that a crew member from the Starship Enterprise beamed down into the bank vault, shot the man, stuck the gun in my client's hand, and beamed back up? Isn't it *possible*?!" The answer of course is that we don't care one bit if it's *possible*. We only care if it's *reasonable*. I cannot begin to tell you how many outrageous and absurd unreasonable doubts and arguments I have heard people raise when it comes to the issue of existence of God. Ridiculous possibilities and permutations of possibilities that they wouldn't dream of bringing up for anything else all of a sudden become standard fare for this issue

We do not need to demonstrate or know "mathematically" or "scientifically" that God exists. We just need to demonstrate it or know it *reasonably*. Lest anyone doubt the power and significance of knowing something reasonably, I would like to point out that every day we stake our lives on reasonable propositions.

When you cross the street you calculate how much time you have until the truck coming in your direction reaches you. How do you know for sure that your brain is calculating the distance and speed properly? Maybe the truck is in reality much closer. After all, philosopher David Hume demonstrated that just because your eyes and brain worked properly yesterday, it doesn't mean they are going to work properly today. Actually, some professors of philosophy have been known to stand frozen on the curb for hours because of this problem. The rest of us however, say HO-HUM to David Hume, cross the street, and continue on our way.

Every single day millions of people enter aircraft and fly all over the world. To get into an airplane with a pilot who does not know how to fly is to risk almost certain death. How many people have "proof" that the pilot actually is qualified? How many people have gone up to the cockpit and investigated who the pilots are and if they are certified? It simply is a highly reasonable proposition that the uniformed men in the cockpit are really pilots. Conversely, it is a highly unreasonable proposition that anyone could get into the cockpit of the airplane who was not a qualified pilot.

If you are ready to risk your life without a moment's hesitation on a very reasonable proposition (remember this the next time you step into an elevator), please don't engage in sophistry by pulling Hume and Kant* out of your hat when it comes to the existence of God. There are any number of philosophical ideas that seem startling and fascinating inside the university lecture hall, but once outside have little or no connection to our everyday reality. David Hume demonstrated that just because the sun rose yesterday and the day before, this in no way proves that the sun will rise tomorrow. He is correct, we really don't know with absolute certainty that the sun will rise tomorrow (or that the elevator cable won't snap). So what?

Just because an event is not <u>impossible</u> does not mean that it is <u>reasonable</u>

I would like to close the section on epistemology with a classic example of, *A)* exactly the type of "unreasonable doubt" argument that I have been talking about, *B)* exactly the type of highly unskilled thinking and analysis that I mentioned earlier, and *C)* truth being shamelessly subordinated to agenda. All three of these are miraculously rolled into only one statement by atheist

---

* David Hume and Immanuel Kant; two highly influential 18th century philosophers who wrote seminal works on epistemology and metaphysics.

Mark Isaak.

In his book, *The Counter Creationism Handbook,* Isaak makes the following remark regarding the serious challenges scientists face as they attempt to formulate a plausible, *naturalistic* explanation for the origin of life (*i.e.,* an explanation of the origin of the first living bacterium that would not require a willful act of creation by an intelligent designer):

> Nobody denies that the origin of life is an extremely difficult problem; that it has not been solved though, does not mean it is impossible. [4]

What does he mean when he says it is not "impossible?" **Translation:** It is an extremely difficult problem that has not been solved, but it is *possible* we will find a naturalistic solution. Of course it would have been just as meaningful and true if Isaak had stated the following: "The origin of life is an extremely difficult problem that has not been solved and it's not impossible that we *won't* find a solution." In other words, it is *possible* there is no naturalistic scientific solution. To sum up: Isaak has effectively informed us that it is *possible* there is a naturalistic solution, and that it is *possible* there is not a naturalistic solution. This of course is about as meaningful as telling us that it is possible that a pregnant woman will give birth to a boy and it is possible that she will give birth to a girl. Isaak, for some bizarre reason feels he is enlightening us with vital, significant information. What he has completely avoided and ignored (most likely on purpose), is analyzing the only issue that has any relevance and significance at all: namely, what is the most *reasonable* possibility regarding the origin of life.

Isaak toes the party line

An honest and truthful way for Isaak to state his point would have been: *Everyone agrees that finding a purely scientific and naturalistic explanation for the origin of life is an extremely difficult problem. In fact, despite the enormous efforts of scientists all over the world, no plausible naturalistic solution has yet been demonstrated.*

The problem, of course, is that such a statement might

indicate that the notion of an intelligent designer is a very reasonable proposition. If Mr. Isaak had written such a statement, it also would have indicated that his motivation for writing his book was discovering and presenting the truth and not simply toeing the atheist party line. Please remember Mr. Isaak, proving that Elvis is still alive is *also* an extremely difficult problem, but it is not *impossible* that we will find an answer.

To add insult to injury, after Isaak lists six of the *purely* speculative theories about the naturalistic origin of life, he lists as possibility #7 (I'm not kidding): "Something that no one has thought of yet." [5] Yes Mr. Isaak, you are absolutely correct, "something that no one has thought of yet" is always a possibility...*Ladies and gentleman of the jury, the prosecution has presented eyewitness evidence against my client, fingerprint evidence against my client, and DNA evidence against my client...I would like to present you with a reason to find my client innocent...Uh, Umm...SOMETHING THAT NO ONE HAS THOUGHT OF YET...*

In fact I would like to present the reader with a *possible* reason to believe that the earth is flat, that 2+2=5, and that Elvis *is* still alive: SOMETHING THAT NO ONE HAS THOUGHT OF YET!

Ground Rule #4: *There is a difference between belief in God and belief in a particular religion*

In November 2006 there was an "e-mail debate" about the existence of God between conservative radio talk show host and author, Dennis Prager, and atheist author Sam Harris. I found it on a website entitled jewcy.com, and the debate was entitled "Why Are Atheists So Angry?" In Sam Harris' opening email, he writes the following:

> Incompatible beliefs about this God, [i.e. the God of monotheism], long ago shattered our world into separate moral communities — Christians, Muslims, Jews, etc. — and these divisions remain a continuous source of human violence. [6]

Leaving aside the issue of religion being a source of strife and violence, (it will be dealt with elsewhere in the book), Sam Harris presents a subtly, but significantly inaccurate description of what separates Jews, Muslims, and Christians. It is not "incompatible beliefs about this *God*" which creates the separation; it is incompatible beliefs of what this God *has revealed to mankind,* or perhaps more specifically, incompatible beliefs as to *how this God wants us to relate to those outside of the particular faith community.* The beliefs about God himself however are quite compatible.

It is important to understand that the basic description if you will, or the basic theological understanding of "The One God" conceptually, is quite similar in any religion that is in the general category of monotheism. Without trying to oversimplify the issue, even when examining the pure monotheism of Judaism and Islam, and the Christian concept of the Trinity, the difference in many ways is really more technical and academic (albeit still theologically significant), than anything else.

It is quite safe and accurate to say that when the concept of God himself is isolated from the particular details of the "holy scripture" in each of these religions, we will find that Jews, Moslems, and Christians are pretty much in agreement about the nature of God. (For Jews, the Holy Scripture consists of *The Five Books of Moses* plus the *Prophets,* and *Writings;* for Moslems it is the *Koran;* for Christians, the entire Jewish Bible plus the *New Testament* – these clearly *are* sources of separation.) God is the all-powerful, all knowing, eternal, transcendent Creator of the Universe, the source of all being, who for motives beyond our comprehension has created the universe and all that it contains, and "desires" to have a relationship with mankind.

Creator and Scripture: Two distinct, separate issues

What emerges from this is that "Creator," and "Scripture," are two completely separate issues. It is quite possible to have a clear knowledge or belief in the existence of God the Creator, whom I described above, while still having doubts about, or even rejecting, all Holy Scripture. I have met many such people in my years of experience as a teacher.

This book is not about scripture or a particular religious dogma. It is about the existence of God, the Creator. It is also about the proposition that God has created human beings with certain innate "hard wiring" that makes it clear to us that the purpose of our existence revolves around a relationship with this God. It may very well be true that without divine revelation we are pretty much in the dark about what he may want from us or how we should relate to him. That however, does not change the fact that he created us and we are seeking him. If this book brings the reader to conclude that there is a Creator or strengthens his belief in the Creator, while at the same time having no particular effect on his opinion regarding a specific scripture or religious dogma, this book will have achieved it's purpose. Within the parameters of this book I am a "missionary" for belief in God, not a particular religion.

<u>Ground Rule #5</u>: Even though I am a Rabbi, this book is not about "defending the faith" of Judaism

Harris, Hitchens, Dawkins and other atheist propagandists lambaste many different religions and their scriptures in their writings and speeches. As I made quite clear, this book is not about scripture or a particular religion. Therefore, excepting the few remarks I will make here and perhaps some tangential remarks scattered throughout, I do not even intend to put forth a comprehensive defense of Judaism against these vituperative railings. Suffice it to say the following...

Generally, these atheist writers display spectacular ignorance about what Judaism is, and most crucial of all, how Jews have understood and related to the *Torah* (Bible) for the past several thousand years.

A pilot's manual for an F-15 fighter-bomber is not written to enable the average person to pick it up, read it and attempt to fly an F-15. The manual is written with certain assumptions about the knowledge, background and training of the person who is reading. Without this knowledge, background, and training there is no possible way for the uninitiated reader to have a proper understanding of what the manual is and what it is supposed to accomplish. The Jewish *Torah* is no different. Speaking as an ordained Orthodox Rabbi who has been a Jewish educator for three decades, I can categorically state the following: It is not possible to have a coherent or accurate understanding of either the mission and nature of the Jewish people, Jewish law and

Jewish religious obligations, nor the *weltanschauung* of the Jew, by reading an English adaptation, of an English translation, of a Latin translation, of a Greek translation of a Hebrew Bible. The *Torah* as a *Jewish* Scripture does not mean whatever any particular reader thinks it means any more than the manual for the F-15 means whatever any particular reader thinks it means. Judaism has *its own* guidelines, parameters, and traditions, regarding the study, interpretation, and applications of, the *Torah*. Any explication of the *Torah* that is made in ignorance of, or outside of these guidelines (no matter how fascinating, creative, or novel it may be), has nothing to do with Judaism. Judaism and its *Torah* are not beholden to, nor defined by the personal musings or speculative theories of a group of new age atheists. If an individual wants to criticize the *Torah* worldview he should first and foremost take the trouble to find out what it actually is. As I pointed out above, a superficial reading of an English translation of the text is at best, a scratching of the surface of a real understanding of Judaism. (To put it colloquially: The devil *can and does* quote Scripture for his own purpose)

As long as we are on the subject of the devil quoting scripture, if awards were given out for grotesque distortions of Judaism by atheistic authors, Christopher Hitchens would be in a class by himself (ironically enough, he is Jewish). His obscene depiction of a Jewish circumcision ceremony [7] could have been plagiarized from the pages of *Der Sturmer,* the rabidly anti-Jewish, quasi-pornographic tabloid published by Julius Streicher, a Nazi war criminal who was executed by the Allies in 1946. The way in which Hitchens portrays the ceremony is so vulgar and divorced from reality that one could justifiably wonder whether it might not be a projection of his own unresolved issues involving the genitals of young boys. At the very least, it indicates some sort of pathology, be it emotional, spiritual, or intellectual. If that weren't sick enough, he also informs us (obviously after months of painstaking research on the subject) that Orthodox Jewish couples have intercourse through a "hole in the sheet."[8] It would have been closer to reality if he had informed us that the earth was flat. After all, at least from our limited perspective the earth *looks* flat. Where did he dig up this disgusting lie? It is obvious that he simply made it up. In light of the above, we can safely assume that unless presented with con-clusive evidence to the contrary, anything Christopher Hitchens writes about Judaism is either a distortion, an outright fabrica-tion, or presented so out of context that it is the equivalent of an outright fabrication. Having said that, I will resist the tempta-tion to speculate about other unresolved issues that are afflict-ing his soul.

In any case, if Hitchens, Dawkins, or Stenger (*God: The Failed Hypothesis*) want to read the *Torah* and understand it in their own distorted way, they should at least display some basic integrity (again I caution the reader against holding his or her breath while waiting for this to happen), and call it Stengerism, Hitchensism, Dawkinsism, or any other name that suits them. Just don't call it Judaism. My assumption is – and I believe it is a quite reasonable assumption – that they have grossly distorted facts about other faiths as well.

Ground Rule #6: *Regarding the "Leap of Faith"*

After careful analysis I've concluded there is only one valid point that is raised in the atheist assault on religion. However, before I elaborate on that point, I want the reader to take note that I specifically wrote assault on religion, not assault on belief in God or a Creator. Perhaps it is best to let a Nobel Prize win-ning atheist philosopher, Bertrand Russell, express the idea that I was alluding to:

> Many orthodox people speak as though it were the business of skeptics to disprove received dogmas rather than of dogmatists to prove them. If I were to suggest that between the Earth and Mars there is a china teapot revolving about the sun in an elliptical orbit, nobody would be able to disprove my assertion provided I were careful to add that the teapot is too small to be revealed even by our most powerful telescopes. But if I were to go on to say that, since my assertion cannot be dis-proved, it is intolerable presumption on the part of human reason to doubt it, I should rightly be thought to be talking nonsense. [9]

Russell's statement, which addresses itself to specific ideologi-cal dogmas, is clearly and self-evidently true. (However, by the end of this book it will be clear why it does not apply to belief in God).

If someone has chosen to believe in a specific religious *or* non-religious system of values or any other items which fall in the category of "dogma", then it is perfectly valid to ask: How do you know it is true? To say something is true because it can't be *disproven* is intellectually unacceptable. Does Sam Harris want me to accept his atheistic system of "morality" as valid? If so, he must *prove* to me how his system could possibly be anything other than his totally subjective feelings on the subject which are essentially meaningless to those who don't share his subjective attachments. On the other hand, if I want someone to accept the Ten Commandments as the word of God, that person is perfectly justified in asking for a rational reason to believe that they actually *are* the word of God.

There are those who say that you must take a "leap of faith" and believe that certain things are true. If a fitting metaphor for discovering the truth about our existence is the slow, methodical, doggedly determined climb to the top of a tall mountain peak; then a leap of faith, in my opinion, is like jumping off the side of the mountain and expecting to miraculously end up at the summit. One of my mentors, Rabbi Yaakov Weinberg* (of blessed memory) noted, "If you close your eyes and take a leap of faith, you can land *anywhere you want to.*" [10] With a leap of faith not only can you accept any type of ideological or religious dogma no matter how absurd, but it is even possible to believe that the first bacterium – which is more functionally complex and sophisticated than any machinery ever produced by human technology – could actually spontaneously assemble itself without an intelligent designer! To put it simply, with a leap of faith it is possible to believe the highest nonsense of the highest order.

Ground Rule #7: *Evolution – A fundamental premise of this book is that the topic of Darwinian Evolution is irrelevant to our discussion about the existence of God*

This book is not concerned with the following: Darwinian Evolution and Natural Selection. As far as I'm concerned,

---

*Rabbi Yaakov Weinberg (1923-1999), formerly Dean of the Ner Israel Rabbinical Seminary in Baltimore, Maryland, was considered to have been among the foremost Talmudic scholars and theologians in the Orthodox Jewish world.

getting into that fracas as a non-biologist/scientist is getting involved in the ideological equivalent of the Battle of Stalingrad. We shall demonstrate in the coming chapters, that contrary to popular belief, Darwinian Evolution is irrelevant to our question. None of this, of course, has anything at all to do with the topic of the origin of life. As Professor Richard Dawkins, a zealous proponent of atheism, writes in *The God Delusion,* "Darwinian evolution proceeds merrily once life has originated. But how does life get started?" [11]

Yes, Professor Dawkins, how *does* life get started? This book is most definitely concerned with the origin of life.

Part II

Origin of Life and The Scientific Distortions of the Non-Believer

————————————

— Chapter 3 —

*Yes, Professor Dawkins, How **Does** Life Get Started?*

— Chapter 4 —

Objections To A Supernatural Creator

— Chapter 5 —

Actually, The Watchmaker Has 20/20 Vision

Chapter 3

Yes, Professor Dawkins,
*How **Does** Life Get Started?*

A running battle that is at least 2000 years old

The conflict between skeptic and believer regarding the existence of God has been going on for much longer than many people realize. In Talmudic literature there are records of encounters between Jewish Rabbinic sages and Greek and Roman skeptics that took place over 2000 years ago. One of the central questions in this ongoing struggle is how did life come to be on the Earth? The Book of Genesis clearly states that "in the beginning" life on Earth was the result of a divine act of creation. The atheist counters that there is no need to invoke mythological fairy tales about a supernatural creator, and that the enormous complexity and variety of life on our planet can all be explained through scientific/naturalistic means. In fact, over the next several chapters we will discover that a divine act of creation is the only explanation for life on Earth that is *not* a fairy tale.

Much more crucial than Darwinian Evolution; How did life begin?

In modern times, when believers and skeptics argue about science and religion, invariably the first subject that comes up is Darwinian evolution and natural selection. In my years of teaching I have heard the word *Archaeopteryx* (which Darwinians claim is the transitional fossil between reptiles and birds), so many times that the sound of it has the same effect on me as screeching chalk on a blackboard. Despite this, if I felt it was crucial and fundamental in our search for the truth about the existence of God, I would do battle with Charles Darwin and his loyal followers. However, in my opinion, the theory of evolution is beside the point and is a non-issue. In fact, if it will make the skeptics and non-believers happy, for arguments sake I am even prepared to accept the fact of evolution of the species as explained by the Neo-Darwinian theory of your choice. Those non-scientists like myself who sincerely seek the truth would do well to simply bypass evolution. Darwinian evolution is the Maginot Line of atheism. The critical issue that needs to be addressed is: *How did life begin?*

Interestingly enough, after coming to this conclusion myself I actually found someone on the other side who agrees with me wholeheartedly:

> If I were a creationist, I would cease attacking the theory of evolution...and focus instead on the origin of life. This is by far the weakest strut of the chassis of modern biology. The origin of life is a science writer's dream. It abounds with exotic scientists and exotic theories, which are never entirely abandoned or accepted, but merely go in and out of fashion. [1]
>
> (John Horgan, Senior Writer, Scientific American)

"In The Beginning" — Origin of Life and Darwinian evolution are two completely separate and unrelated issues

Many people are under the impression that Darwinian Evolution is a neat scientific package that explains *everything* about life on this planet; including the beginning of life from the primeval "organic soup," the development of apes and human beings, and even why the Chicago Cubs have not won a World Series in 100 years. This simply is not true. *Origin of Life and Evolution of the Species* are totally separate issues and must be investigated and understood in different ways. (*Nobody* could explain the Cubs*) It is important to note that this assertion is not a matter of scientific controversy.

Dr. Eugenie Scott, Executive Director of the fiercely pro-evolution National Center for Science Education (NCSE), writes in her book *Evolution vs. Creationism: An Introduction:*

---

* I confess, I am a hopeless Cubs fan.

Although some people confuse the origin of life with evolution the two are conceptually separate. Biological evolution is defined as the descent of living things from ancestors from which they differ. Life had to precede evolution! ...We know much more about evolution than the origin of life. [2]

Here is how an article appearing on the NCSE website describes the difference between the two:

The origin of life and evolution are two separate notions. The fact that there is much to learn about how the first living creatures originated has little to do with the truth or falsity of evolution. Thus an intelligent designer could have made the first forms and then they evolved... [3]

Evolution of the "species" has nothing to do with the origin of life itself

In other words, the theory of evolution of the "species" is based on random mutations in the replication of the DNA of a living organism. Sometimes by pure luck these random mutations confer a survival advantage to the particular organism, which in turn makes it more likely that these traits will be passed along to surviving offspring. Eventually all these little changes add up and starting from the original microscopic bacteria, here we are! However, even going on the assumption that the theory is true, it is all based on an existing self-replicating organism with a fully functioning genetic code; Darwinian evolution and natural selection are only operative and relevant from that point forward – *Darwinian evolution in no way at all accounts for the existence of the first self-replicating bacterium.*

In truth, no scientist alive today would claim that evolution started with what is the "simplest" known living organism, *i.e.,* some form of bacteria. As we shall see, there is really nothing simple at all about a bacterium and all agree that the notion of a fully functioning DNA-based bacterium popping out of a pre-biotic soup somewhere on the ancient earth is preposterous. Most scientists offer as a *point of conjecture and speculation* that a purely naturalistic origin of life must begin with some form of simple self-replicating molecule. No one has ever seen such a self-replicating molecule existing in a natural state, and whether or not they have ever existed is a purely speculative proposition. They have only recently been ingeniously *designed,*

constructed, and manufactured by the worlds leading chemists
and microbiologists who follow scrupulously controlled manufacturing processes, under the most rigorous of laboratory conditions; in other words, under conditions that bear a striking
resemblance to an automobile assembly line, but no resemblance
at all to nature. These self-replicating molecules are themselves
fantastically complex pieces of molecular machinery. In a later
section we will discuss the implications that these products of
human scientific genius have on our question about the existence
of a creator.

Introducing Richard Dawkins

Professor Richard Dawkins, born in Kenya (then a British
colony), in March of 1946, is the "Grand Old Man" of contem-
porary atheism. He is held in papal-like awe by ideologically
committed atheists all over the world. Educated at Oxford in
England, he has held prestigious academic positions in both the
United States and Great Britain. He studied under Nobel Prize
winning ethologist Nikolaas Tinbergen in Balliol College,
Oxford and the University of Oxford. Two of his most well
known atheistic classics are *The Blind Watchmaker: Why the
Evidence of Evolution Reveals a Universe without Design* (1986),
and *The God Delusion* (2006) which has sold over 1.5 million
copies and has been translated into 31 languages. Dawkins confirms the clear distinction between *Evolution of the Species and
Origin of Life:*

> But how did the whole process start?...nobody knows how it happened,
> but somehow...a molecule arose that just happened to have the property
> of self-copying. [4]

> Life still has to originate in the water, and the origin of life may have been
> a highly improbable occurrence. Darwinian evolution proceeds merrily
> once life has originated. But how does life get started?...Once the vital
> ingredient – some kind of genetic molecule – is in place, true Darwinian
> natural selection can follow. [5]

But interestingly enough, though Dawkins throughout his
books is adamant about the clarity of science on the mechanism

of evolution of the species, he presents a very different evaluation regarding scientific clarity on origin of the first life:

> But the spontaneous arising by chance of the first hereditary molecule strikes many as improbable. Maybe it is – very, very improbable...The origin of life is a flourishing, if speculative, subject for research. The expertise required for it is chemistry and it is not mine. I watch from the sidelines with engaged curiosity, and I shall not be surprised if, within the next few years, chemists report that they have successfully midwifed a new origin of life in the laboratory. Nevertheless, it hasn't happened yet. [6]

Professor Dawkins will need a comfortable seat while watching from the sidelines

In fact, Dawkins will be sitting on the sidelines watching curiously for a *very long time*. What we will actually discover is that even scientists who have the required expertise are essentially clueless when it comes to understanding how life began. It is not the lack of knowledge about the chemistry of the "simplest" life that stands in their way; it is exactly the opposite. The more scientists understand, the more vexing the puzzle becomes. In order to illustrate just how difficult a time scientists are having in their attempts to discover how life began, consider the following theory which was proposed by two of the 20th century's most brilliant scientific minds, Francis Crick and Leslie Orgel.

A strange theory for the Origin of Life: It was sent here by men from outer space

The following obituary appeared in *Astrobiology Magazine* (Aug. 2, 2004) on the passing of Nobel Laureate Dr. Francis Crick, who together with James Watson discovered the structure of DNA:

> FRANCIS CRICK REMEMBERED — The British molec⁀ ⁀gist Francis Harry Crick died on Wednesday at the age of 88... In 197_ ⁀ⁱck] and chemist Leslie Orgel published a paper in the journal Icarus suggesting that life may have arrived on Earth through a process called "Directed Panspermia..."Directed Panspermia" suggests that life may be distributed by an advanced extraterrestrial civilization.[7]

Crick and Orgel are not the only prominent scientists to seriously suggest that life may have come from "men from Mars" or from organic molecules that arrived from outer space. Dr. Robert Shapiro, Carl Sagan, J. Craig Venter, Richard Dawkins, and E.O. Wilson are also part of the impressive, all-star line-up of scientists who strongly feel that we will find life on other planets. Nobel Prize winner Dr. Christian DeDuve suggests that "the universe is awash with life." [8] Even the NCSE, whose stated mission is "to keep evolution in the science classroom and scientific creationism out" officially informs us of the following:

> Scientists today propose two general explanations [for the origin of life]:
> 1. The natural origin of life on earth from non-living matter according to chemical laws
> 2. **Origin of life in outer space and subsequent colonization of earth.** [9]

Does it strike anyone as odd that associates of the NCSE and the aforementioned scientists – who are* world class physicists, mathematicians, chemists, biologists and microbiologists – could actually sit around their lab tables and seriously discuss the idea of an alien civilization "seeding" our world with life? Did they also make the pilgrimage to Roswell, New Mexico where UFO enthusiasts are certain that the U.S. government has secretly imprisoned men from outer space for decades? Did these "Men in White" (lab coats) peruse the *National Enquirer* for alien abduction stories like the "Men in Black?" How many times *did* Francis Crick watch *Invasion of the Body Snatchers?*

Hopefully, by the end of this chapter we will understand not only what compelling scientific realities were behind the formation of this seemingly bizarre theory, but how it also leads us to the unmistakable conclusion that life on earth is the result of a divine act of creation. In the meantime, however, let's start from the *very beginning*, which is always a very good place to start.

Important note for the reader: Over the next several pages we will examine some of the various *speculative* hypotheses that expert scientists have proposed to explain a naturalistic origin of life. I caution readers, particularly those without a scientific

---

*As the above article noted, Francis Crick died in 2004. Dr. Leslie Orgel passed away in 2007, and Carl Sagan in 1996.

background, not to get confused or overwhelmed by the specific scientific details of the different proposals. The particulars of each of these hypotheses are for our purposes irrelevant. Our focus is on **A)** the glaring lack of any conclusive supporting evidence for these theories, and **B)** the forcefulness with which these scientists attack and ridicule each other's ideas.

What do experts in Chemistry have to say about the Origin of Life?

Richard Dawkins admitted that he does not possess the required expertise in chemistry for origin of life research, but the late Dr. Leslie Orgel, a world renowned chemist and a leader in *Origin of Life* research certainly did. Orgel was a proponent of the "RNA first" theory, which hypothesizes that in the step-by-step series of chemical processes that eventually led to life, RNA (ribonucleic acid) preceded DNA (deoxyribonucleic acid).* In his conclusion to an article entitled "The Origin of Life on Earth" Orgel describes the status of the "RNA first" theory:

> The precise events giving rise to the RNA world remain unclear. As we have seen, investigators have proposed many hypotheses, but evidence in favor of each of them is fragmentary at best. The full details of how the RNA world, and life, emerged may not be revealed in the near future. Nevertheless, as chemists, biochemists and molecular biologists cooperate on ever more ingenious experiments, they are sure to fill in many missing parts of the puzzle.[10]

In other words, Dr. Orgel does not know how life, or RNA, originated; but despite his own assertion that the details may not be discovered in "the near future," he is certain that scientists will continue progressing and "are sure to fill in many missing parts of the puzzle."

Two chances to "fill in missing parts of the puzzle:" 1) SLIM and 2) NONE

---

*DNA contains the actual genetic material of the organism. RNA is a "simpler" macromolecule that plays a crucial role in the replication of DNA and the synthesis of proteins by the living cell.

Dr. Robert Shapiro, a self proclaimed agnostic who is Professor Emeritus of Chemistry and Senior Research Scientist at New York University, and another leading chemist in the *Origin of Life* field, is a little more skeptical about finding "parts of the puzzle" in the "RNA first" theory of Orgel. The essential problem is that nucleotides, the complex molecules which are the building blocks of RNA, have never been shown to form by any naturalistic process. They must be manufactured in the laboratory in a sequence of carefully controlled reactions via a discipline that scientists call "prebiotic synthesis." In an article entitled "A Simpler Origin of Life," Dr. Shapiro points out the obvious: **"Unfortunately, neither chemists nor laboratories were pres   on the early Earth to produce RNA."** [11] He then discus   probability of these nucleotides being produced by a r   .om process on the early Earth:

> Picture a gorilla at an immense keyboard connected to a word processor. The keyboard contains not only the symbols used in English and European languages but also a huge excess drawn from every other known language and all of the symbol sets stored in a typical computer. The chances...can be compared to those of the gorilla composing, in English, a coherent recipe for the preparation of chili con carne. With similar considerations in mind Gerald F. Joyce of the Scripps Research Institute and Leslie Orgel of the Salk Institute concluded that the spontaneous appearance of RNA chains on the lifeless Earth "would have been a near miracle." [11]

Dr. Orgel Counter-Punches

Dr. Shapiro, after concluding that the "RNA-first" theory is clearly nonsense, suggests another "more likely" scenario for the origin of life; he calls it "Metabolism First." In an article entitled "The Implausibility of Metabolic Cycles on the Prebiotic Earth," Dr. Orgel has this to say about Shapiro's hypothetical solution for what happened "in the beginning:"

> Theories of the origin of life based on metabolic cycles [*i.e.* "Metabolism First"], cannot be justified by the inadequacy of competing theories: they must stand on their own...solutions offered by supporters of geneticist or metabolist scenarios that are dependent on **"if pigs could fly"** hypothetical chemistry are unlikely to help. [12]

Oh my! It seems that staying up late in the lab trying to figure out how life started can cause even a scientist to get a little testy. Never fear, *Origin of Life* scientists are not *always* nasty when rejecting other theories. These scientists do not *always* use harsh language such as "if pigs could fly hypothetical chemistry." They are also capable of politely dismissing someone else's theory in the manner of true gentlemen. Read how gracefully and diplomatically Dr. Leslie Orgel tells Dr. Graham Cairns-Smith that his "clay crystal" *Origin of Life* theory belongs in the trash with yesterday's newspaper:

> Graham Cairns-Smith of the University of Glasgow…proposed that the very first replicating system was inorganic. He envisaged irregularities in the structure of a clay…On theoretical grounds, however, it seems *implausible*. Structural irregularities in clay that were complicated enough to set the stage for the emergence of RNA probably would not be amenable to accurate self replication.[13] (Rogets II Thesaurus – Synonyms for "Implausible:" *flimsy, improbable, inconceivable*. Wordnet 3.0, Princeton University: *having a quality that provokes disbelief*)

Someone else (Physicist and Information Theorist, H.P. Yockey) also does not like the Cairns-Smith clay crystal theory:

> G. Cairns-Smith, a biochemist at the University of Glasgow…hypothesizes that clays may have formed the first self-replicating structures…Crystals are not a viable explanation for the origin of a mechanism which would generate sufficient information content into inert matter to produce the genome necessary for life. Although crystals are ordered…they carry very little information…they are similar to the old story of a law student who had too little sleep and too much caffeine and wrote the same sentence over and over again on every line of his examination book. His examination essay was very ordered and very redundant. Redundancy is the main characteristic of crystal structure, but complex sequences and information are characteristics of life forms…a crystal has a highly ordered structure but low intelligence or information content…Cairns-Smith is **grossly mistaken** in his hypothesis that the information density in a crystallite is at all similar to the information content in DNA. [14]

Dr. Michael Denton, an Australian microbiologist, also points out the vast gulf between the "orderliness" of a crystal and the simplest living organism:

Between a living cell and the most highly ordered non-biological system such as a crystal or a snowflake there is a chasm as vast and as absolute as it is possible to conceive. [15]

Dr. Graham Cairns-Smith fights back and fires a broadside at the "RNA first" theory:

Dr. Cairns-Smith, in his book, *Seven Clues to the Origin of Life,* also points out the implausibility of naturally forming nucleotides. He explains that there are 14 major chemical/molecular "hurdles"[16] that must be overcome for nucleotides to form naturally in a primitive earth scenario. The only way that scientists know of to overcome these 14 serious hurdles is by "organic synthesis" or "prebiotic synthesis," a precise manufacturing process that takes place in the *laboratory*. Each of these 14 processes themselves consists of many separate laboratory operations involving "lifting, pouring, mixing, stirring, *etc.*" [17] Cairns-Smith points out that while each separate operation by itself may not be that complicated; they must be carried out in a rigorously specific and exact sequence. When this manufacturing procedure is at all prolonged "it becomes absurd to imagine"[18] that such a process could have happened by chance on the primitive earth. Thus, Cairns-Smith concludes, "simple amino acids are plausible prebiotic products, primed nucleotides are not." [19] He then goes on to calculate the probability of nucleotides forming through a random process:

But you may say, with all the time in the world, and so much world, the right combinations of circumstances would happen some time?...The answer is no: there was not enough time, and there was not enough world...It would be a safe oversimplification...to say that on average the 14 hurdles that I referred to in the making of primed nucleotides would each take 10 unit operations – that at least 140 little events would have to be appropriately sequenced. (If you doubt this, go and watch an organic chemist at work; look at all the things he actually does in bringing about what he would describe as "one step" in an organic synthesis.)...

We can say that the odds against a successful unguided synthesis of a batch of primed nucleotides on the primitive Earth are similar to the odds against a six coming up every time with 140 throws of the dice...This is a huge number, represented approximately by a 1 followed by 109 zeroes. This is the sort of number of trials that you would have to make to have a reasonable chance of hitting on the one outcome that represents success. Throwing one dice once a second for the period of the Earth's history would only let you get through about 10^{15} trials, so you would need about 10^{94} dice. That is far more than the number of electrons in the observed Universe. [20] *

It's Miller Time!

Dr. Stanley Miller was another of the leading researchers in the Origin of Life field (he passed away in 2007). He first burst onto the scene as a graduate student at the University of Chicago. His famous experiment in 1953 – which consisted of sending electric current through a chamber containing chemicals assumed to be present in Earth's early atmosphere – sent shockwaves through the scientific world. The experiment yielded amino acids which are the "building blocks" of proteins, and therefore of life. It seemed that if a simple electric current combined with young earth chemicals could produce amino acids, the secret to the origin of life was right around the corner. Unfortunately for Dr. Miller that's about as far as it went. Physicist and science author, Dr. Paul Davies, explains:

> Making amino acids is what a physicist would call "thermodynamically downhill," which means it is a natural process that occurs automatically, like crystallization. But hooking the amino acids together into long chains to make proteins goes the other way. That is an "uphill" – a statistically more difficult or unlikely – process. Let me give you an analogy. It's a little bit like going for a walk in the countryside, coming across a pile of bricks and assuming that there will be a house around the corner. There is a big difference between a pile of bricks and a house. [21]

Graham Cairns-Smith, whose clay-crystals theory was so effortlessly declared implausible by Orgel, also offers his viewpoint on the Miller experiment:

> It is true that some of the simpler amino acids have been found in complex mixtures generated under conditions simulating those that might have been present on the primitive Earth...but all such "molecules of life" are always minority products and usually no more than trace products. Their detection often owes more to the skill of the experimenter than to any powerful tendency for the "molecules of life" to form...In sum, the ease of synthesis of the "molecules of life" has been greatly exaggerated. [22]

* This is roughly equivalent to a snowball's chance in hell.

Sir Fred Hoyle also hammers away:

> To press the matter further, if there were a basic principle of matter which somehow drove organic systems toward life, its existence should easily be demonstrable in the laboratory. One could, for instance, take a swimming bath to represent the primordial soup. Fill it with any chemicals of a non-biological nature you please. Pump any gases over it, or through it, you please, and shine any kind of radiation on it that takes your fancy. Let the experiment proceed for a year and see how many of those 2000 enzymes [needed for life] have appeared in the bath. I will give the answer, and so save the time and trouble and expense of actually doing the experiment. You would find nothing at all, except possibly for a tarry sludge composed of amino acids and other simple organic chemicals. How can I be so confident of this statement? Well if it were otherwise, the experiment would long since have been done and would be well know and famous throughout the world. The cost of it would be trivial compared to the cost of landing a man on the Moon...In short there is not a shred of evidence that life began in an organic soup here on earth. [23]

Dr. Robert Shapiro delivers the coup de grace:

> Let us sum up. The experiment formed by Miller yielded **tar** as its most abundant product...The very best Miller-Urey chemistry...does not take us very far along the path to a living organism. A mixture of simple chemicals, even one enriched in a few amino acids, no more resembles a bacterium than a small pile of real and nonsense words, each written on an individual scrap of paper, resembles the complete works of Shakespeare. [24]

An interview with Dr. Stanley Miller, where he matter-of-factly rejects several Origin of Life theories

Although in the following interview, Miller does not directly respond to the harsh criticisms cited above, he does make short shrift of other *Origin of Life* theories. He is also quoted in a *New York Times* article (May 23, 2007) as describing the "metal catalyst" *Origin of Life* theory proposed by Dr. Gunter Wachtershauser (who had called Miller's theory a "blind alley"), as "overblown" and that it failed to show how copious amounts of amino acids could be produced, as his own work had done.

> **Question:** Doesn't the Panspermia theory look at the question of ultimate origins of life in a slightly different way?

Miller: It may be that life came to Earth from another planet...but that still doesn't answer the question of where life started. You only transfer the problem to the other solar system....Along these lines, there is a consensus that life would have had a hard time making it here from another solar system, because of the destructive effects of cosmic rays over long periods of time. [**So much for Panspermia**]

Question: What about submarine vents [under the ocean, another theory about the beginning of life], as a source of prebiotic compounds?

Miller: Submarine vents don't make organic compounds, they decompose them...At the present time, the entire ocean goes through those vents in ten million years. So all the compounds get zapped every ten million years. (In an article in *DISCOVERY* (1992) Miller was a little more blunt; he called the submarine vent theory "a real loser", and complained to the reporter, "I don't understand why we even have to discuss it.") [**So much for submarine vents.**]

Question: Tell us about your recent work and the lagoon idea.

Miller: The primitive Earth had...lagoons, and beaches. Our hypothesis is that the conditions may have been ideal on these beaches or drying lagoons for prebiotic reactions...for the simple reason that the chemicals were more concentrated in these sites...Our most recent research tackled the problem of making...**cytosine** in prebiotic conditions. For some reason it just doesn't work very well under dilute conditions. We showed that it works like a charm once you get things concentrated and dry it out a bit. This changed my outlook on where to start looking for prebiotic reactions. [25]

Dr. Miller, meet Dr. Shapiro – this is what he thinks of your "lagoon idea":

Dr. Robert Shapiro had this to say about Miller's experiment and the plausibility of cytosine forming naturally on the primitive earth:

The exceptionally high urea concentration [needed to produce the cytosine] was rationalized in the NATURE paper by invoking a vision of drying lagoons on the early Earth. In a published rebuttal, I calculated that a large lagoon would have to be evaporated to the size of a puddle, without loss of its contents to achieve that concentration...The analogy that comes to mind is that of a golfer, who having played a golf ball through an 18 hole course, then assumed that the ball could also play itself around the course in his absence. He had demonstrated the possibility of the event, it was only necessary to presume that some combination of natural forces (earthquakes, winds, tornadoes, and floods, for example) could produce the same result, given enough time. No physical law need be broken for spontaneous RNA formation to happen, but the chances against it are…immense. [26]

A brief review of current Origin of Life theories

So far, the greatest scientific minds in the world involved in naturalistic *Origin of Life* research have produced the "gorilla typing recipes for chili con carne" theory, the "if pigs could fly" theory, the "implausible, and grossly mistaken" theory, the "it becomes absurd to imagine such a thing" theory, the "theory that would need more throws of the dice than there are electrons in the universe" theory, the "not a shred of evidence, and words on scraps of paper resembling the works of Shakespeare" theory, the "men from mars seeded the universe" theory, the "it still doesn't answer where life started" theory, the "submarine vents don't create organic compounds, they destroy them" theory (also known as "the real loser, and I don't understand why we even have to discuss it" theory), the "blind alley" theory, the "overblown" theory, and my personal favorite: the "golf ball playing 18 holes by itself" theory.

In a statement cited above from the *The God Delusion,* Dawkins wrote, "I watch from the sidelines with engaged curiosity, and I shall not be surprised if within the next few years, chemists report that they have successfully midwifed a new origin of life in the laboratory." [27] From what we have seen so far, it would be more appropriate to say that Dawkins is watching not from "the sidelines" but from a "ringside seat" as *Origin of Life* scientists duke it out and rip one another's theories to pieces. Where do things really stand with scientists and the origin of life?

Are Scientists guilty of "Faith" in Origin of Life theories?

Yes, according to Dr. Gerald Kerkut, Professor Emeritus of Neuroscience at the University of Southampton, who wrote the following in 1960, when he filled posts as Professor of both Physiology and Biochemistry:

> The first assumption was that non-living things gave rise to living material. This is still just an assumption...There is, however, little evidence in favor of abiogenesis [life from non-life] and as yet we have no indication that it can be performed...It is therefore a matter of **faith** on the part of the biologist that abiogenesis did occur and he can choose whatever method...happens to suit him personally; the evidence for what did happen is not available. [28]

Dr. Andrew Scott, a veteran science writer who holds a PhD. in Chemistry from Cambridge University, raises similar doubts about scientific attitudes towards *Origin of Life:*

> But what if the vast majority of scientists all have faith in the one unverified idea? The modern "standard" scientific version of the origin of life on earth is one such idea...Has the cold blade of reason been applied with sufficient vigor in this case? Most scientists want to believe that life could have emerged spontaneously from the primeval waters, because it would confirm their belief in the explicability of Nature...They also want to believe because their arch opponents – religious fundamentalists such as creationists – do not believe in life's spontaneous origin. It is this combative atmosphere which sometimes encourages scientists writing and speaking about the origin of life to become as dogmatic and bigoted as the creationist opponents they so despise. [29]

Scott, in an article entitled "Update on Genesis", offers more of his candid observations on *Origin of Life* research:

> Take some matter, heat while stirring, and wait... That is the modern version of Genesis. The fundamental forces of [physics] are presumed to have done the rest. They made the elements form... nucleic acids... proteins... they became surrounded by membranes and evolved into complex cells and eventually into us...But how much of this neat tale is firmly established, and how much remains hopeful speculation? In truth, the mechanism of almost every major step, from chemical precursors up to the first recognizable cells, is the subject of either controversy or complete bewilderment. [30]

Lest anyone think that Scott is a fanatically religious creationist with an axe to grind:

> Personally, I consider fundamentalist creationism to be a far sillier idea than the craziest of all the crazy notions which scientists have ever proposed, but

> as scientists gloat over the deficiencies of non-scientific accounts of our origin...they should not ignore the considerable deficiencies in their own account. At the moment scientists certainly do not know how, or even if, life originated on earth from lifeless atoms. They do have a few plausible ideas on the subject, but many more rather implausible ones. [31]

Point of Information: <u>None</u> (*i.e. Zero*) of the scientists mentioned or quoted in this chapter are creationists or identify themselves with the Intelligent Design movement.

I have some good news and some bad news about Origin of Life theories...

The good news is that despite what Dr. Andrew Scott said above, there are no crazy scientific theories about the *Origin of Life*. The bad news is: the reason why there are no crazy scientific theories about the *Origin of Life* is because none of them are in the category of Science. Allow me to explain. The true state of *Origin of Life* research is best summed up in this statement by Dr. Christian DeDuve, cytologist and biochemist, who was awarded the Nobel Prize for Medicine in 1974:

> Even if life came from elsewhere, we would still have to account for its first development...How this momentous event happened is still **highly conjectural, though no longer purely speculative.** [32]

I must admit, I was confused in trying to understand exactly what Dr. DeDuve meant by "highly *conjectural,* though no longer purely *speculative*," so I decided to research it a little:

> **Wordnet Online Dictionary:** Conjecture: **A.**) <u>*noun*</u> – a hypothesis that has been formed by *speculating*...usually with little hard evidence. (synonym: **speculation**) **B.**) <u>*verb*</u> – to believe on uncertain or tentative grounds. (synonym: **speculate**)

Now I understand. He didn't mean that it's *highly **conjectural,** though no longer purely **speculative;*** he really meant that it's *highly **speculative,** though no longer purely **conjectural**...*or maybe he meant to say *we're shooting in the dark*. All joking aside, it is clear that DeDuve is telling us that "how this momentous event happened" is both highly speculative *and* highly conjectural (in other words, *we're shooting in the dark*). DeDuve wrote this in 1995. In 2006, Dawkins candidly informed us that "the origin of life is a flourishing, if *speculative* subject for research." [33] Interestingly enough, Francis Crick wrote the following in his book *Life Itself,* in 1981, "Every time I write a paper on the origin of life, I determine I will never write another one, because there is too much speculation running after too few facts." [34]

I guess in the 25 years between 1981 and 2006 not much was going on (besides a lot of speculating). The wry comment on this subject by the late Dr. Michael Crichton (author of *Jurassic Park*) is worthwhile noting at this point, "Most areas of intellectual life have discovered the virtues of speculation, and have embraced them wildly. In academia, speculation is usually dignified as theory." [35] In short, the present scenarios hypothetically describing the origin of life are not in the category of Science: they are in the category of speculation and conjecture which is exactly what Science is not. Just because the person speculating and conjecturing happens to be a scientist, that does not magically turn his words and thoughts into *Science.*

A Riddle: When does Science Fiction become a plausible Scientific Theory?

At least now we understand why a brilliant scientist like Francis Crick could seriously entertain the possibility of life coming from an alien civilization (of which there exists not a scrap of evidence) and not be afraid of being laughed out of his Nobel Prize or being considered even crazier than a creationist. After all, as Sherlock Holmes informed us in *The Hound of the Baskervilles,* when you have eliminated the impossible, then whatever option remains, no matter how improbable – even little green men – must be the truth. As Crick himself writes, "An honest man, armed with all the knowledge available to us now, could only state that in some sense, the origin of life appears at the moment to be almost a miracle." [36]

Let's follow this drama as it unfolds step by step. **1)** Life arising on Earth by itself is almost impossible (or "almost a miracle" which means the same thing) **2)** Crick was an avowed atheist, and therefore, a transcendent act of creation is excluded *a priori, i.e.* it is impossible. **3)** Where then did life come from? It seems to be a mystery. But instead of publishing an article humbly stating: *"We don't have the faintest idea how life started; we are so far from an answer that one Nobel Prize winning scientist jokingly suggested we start talking about life coming from men from outer space."* – **We actually get a Nobel Prize winning scientist suggesting that life came from men from outer space!** What is even more amazing is that he did not become a laughingstock. This fact alone should indicate to the dispassionate observer that something is not quite right in *Origin of Life* research. We will return to the Directed Panspermia theory – affectionately referred to in scientific circles as the "ET phone home" theory – a little later in this chapter. For now, however, let's get to the bottom of where things really stand regarding *Origin of Life* research.

The Emperor finally removes his clothes

In the words of eminent physicist and information theorist H.P. Yockey:

> One must conclude that, contrary to the established and current wisdom, a scenario describing the genesis of life on earth by chance and natural causes which can be accepted on the basis of fact and not faith has not yet been written. [37] **The entire effort in the primeval soup paradigm is self-deception.**[38] [This was written in 1992. On Feb. 3, 2010 an article appeared on the *Science Daily* website with the headline, "New Research Rejects 80–Year theory of Primordial Soup as the Origin of Life"]

Dr. Stuart Kauffman, a highly distinguished scientist at the University of Vermont's Complex Systems Center (also a self-proclaimed atheist), virtuously acknowledges both his own ignorance and the ignorance of his colleagues:

> We do not, in fact, know how or where life started...there are several alternative views about how life emerged on Earth, none established... clearly none of the theories [are] adequate. [39]

Dr. Paul Davies, in his book *The Fifth Miracle: The Search for the Origin and Meaning of Life,* puts it this way:

Many investigators feel uneasy about stating in public that the origin of life is a mystery, even though behind closed doors they freely admit they are baffled. [40] The problem of how and where life began is one of the great outstanding mysteries of science. [41]

Even Richard Dawkins admits his ignorance on this one, "But how did the whole process start...nobody knows how it happened." [42] The exquisite, unvarnished, and unadorned truth is that science and scientists simply do not know how life began. Plumbers don't know, electricians don't know, housewives don't know, Republicans don't know, Democrats don't know, and scientists also don't know. The only advantage scientists have over the rest of us on this subject is that after having explored all these different avenues in the laboratory and coming up empty handed, they really know that they don't know.

Why are scientists having such a hard time figuring out this problem?

Up until this point we have been discussing and illustrating the factual reality that not only do scientists not know how life began, but that competing theories are ridiculed and dismissed in the strongest of language. However, we have not discussed directly *why* this subject is so difficult, and the enormous challenges that scientists face as they try to discover what really happened "in the beginning."

In truth, all the difficulties and challenges in this area of research could be summed up in one succinct statement by Ilya Prigogine, who was awarded the Nobel Prize for Chemistry in 1977, "But let us have no illusions...[we are still] quite unable to grasp the extreme complexity of the simplest of organisms." [43] Again, Dr. Davies:

What stands out as the central unsolved puzzle in the scientific account of life, is how the first microbe came to exist...The living cell is the most complex system of its size known to mankind. Its host of specialized molecules...executes a dance of exquisite fidelity, orchestrated with breathtaking precision...How did something so immensely complicated, so finessed, so exquisitely clever, come into being all on its own? How can mindless molecules... cooperate to form something as ingenious as a living organism? [44]

Scientists have fabricated invisible cogwheels, motors the size of a pin-head, and electrical switches as tiny as individual molecules...the burgeoning field of nanotechnology – building structures and devices measured on a scale of billionths of a meter promises to revolutionize our lives...but...nature got there first. The world is already full of nanomachines: they are called living cells. Each cell is packed with tiny structures that might have come straight from an engineer's manual. Miniscule tweezers, scissors, pumps, motors, levers, valves, pipes, chains, and even vehicles abound. The various components fit together to form a smoothly functioning whole, like an elaborate factory production line. The miracle of life is not that it is made of nanotools, but that these tiny diverse parts are integrated in a highly organized way...with a fine tuning and complexity as yet unmatched by any human engineering...how do all these mindless atoms know what to do?...somehow, collectively, these unthinking atoms get it together and perform the dance of life with exquisite precision. [45]

Dr. Robert Shapiro puts a slightly different spin on the same idea, "The difference between a mixture of simple chemicals and a bacterium is much more profound than the gulf between a bacterium and an elephant." [46] Dr. Robert Hazen, in his book *Genesis: The Scientific Quest for Life's Origin*, writes the following:

We [know] that the simplest living cell is intricate beyond imagining, because every cell relies on the interplay of millions of molecules engaged in hundreds of interdependent chemical reactions. Human brains seem ill suited to grasp such multi-dimensional complexity. [47]

Dr. Michael Denton elaborates:

Although the tiniest living things known to science, bacterial cells, are incredibly small, each is a veritable micro-miniaturized factory containing thousands of elegantly designed pieces of intricate molecular machinery, made up altogether of one hundred thousand million atoms, far more complicated than any machine built by man and without parallel in the non-living world...we would see that nearly every feature of our own advanced machines had its analogue in the cell: artificial languages and their decoding systems, memory banks for information storage and retrieval, elegant control systems regulating the automated assembly of parts and components, error fail-safe and proof reading devices utilized for quality control...What we would be witnessing would be an object resembling an immense automated factory, a factory larger than a city and carrying out almost as many unique functions as all the manufacturing activities of man on earth. **However, it would be a factory which** would have one capacity not equaled in any of our own most advanced machines, for it would be capable of replicating its entire structure within a matter of hours. [48]

Dr. Graham Cairns-Smith also touches on Denton's last point about the cell's amazing ability to self-replicate:

It may seem hardly surprising that no one has ever actually made a self-reproducing machine, even though Von Neumann laid down the design principles more than 40 years ago. You can imagine a clanking robot moving around a stock-room of raw components choosing the pieces to make another robot like itself...There is nothing clanking about E. coli [a bacteria found in the human stomach], yet it is such a robot, and it can operate in a stock room that is furnished with only the simplest raw components...Is it any wonder that Von Neumann himself, and many others, have found the origin of life to be utterly perplexing? [49] [In other words, "self replication" does not mean a Xerox machine making a copy of what's written on a piece of paper, it would mean a Xerox machine making another Xerox machine!]

Far from there being a million ways in detail in which [life] could have got under way, there seems now to have been no obvious way at all. The singular feature is in the gap between the simplest conceivable versions of organisms as we know them, and components that the Earth might reasonably have been able to generate. This gap can be seen more clearly now. It is enormous. [50]

The staggering level of functional complexity of the simplest living organisms can be viewed from a slightly different angle, in the following description of an IBM project to build a supercomputer:

It takes an IBM supercomputer an entire year to accomplish what the cell does in one minute

In October of 1999, IBM announced that it was launching a $100 million research initiative to build a computer that could perform a quadrillion computations per second [a quadrillion is 1 followed by 15 zeros or a thousand trillion]. The project was dubbed Blue Gene. The purpose of the computer was "to help researchers understand how proteins are created, knowledge that could lead to a better understanding of diseases and uncover possible cures." An article on *CNET News* went on to describe in more detail what tasks the computer would perform:

> Blue Gene will take on the problem of protein folding, the biochemical process by which complex molecules are constructed by instructions carried in the DNA. As proteins are assembled from components called amino acids, the long strand of molecules twists and folds in a three dimensional bundle, leaving some active sites protruding from the protein to react with the environment.
>
> How exactly the protein will fold up is governed by basic rules of how atoms attract and repel each other, Horn said. [Paul Horn, Senior Vice-President of IBM research] But the size of proteins, often with thousands of atoms, makes predicting that arrangement a very difficult task. Hemoglobin – also known as the red blood cells that carry oxygen throughout the body – is made of 600 amino acids, for example.
>
> Blue Gene's final product, due in four or five years, will be able to "fold" a protein made of 300 amino acids, Horn said. **But that job will take an entire year of full time computing.** [51]

Once the molecular machinery of a cell assembles a particular protein, it takes about one minute for it to fold into its precise three-dimensional shape without which the protein will not function. This means that the microscopic cellular protein factory enables the precision folding process of proteins to function approximately 500,000 times faster than a computer making a thousand trillion computations per second. (It is also worth noting that most proteins are significantly larger than 300 amino acids.) Nobel Laureate Dr. Francis Crick describes protein folding as a "miracle of molecular construction." [52] The problem is obvious to any thinking person: How does the "simplest" bacteria – each being a "micro miniaturized factory...far more complicated than any machinery built by man," accomplishing "ingenious marvels of construction and control, with a fine tuning and complexity as yet unmatched by any human engineering," and performing tasks with ease that strain the capabilities of a super-computer – assemble itself "naturally" with no intelligent designer to help things along? It strains human credulity well beyond the breaking point to believe that it could happen by chance.

Richard Dawkins (with no expertise in chemistry), has solved the problem of the Origin of Life!

In his book, The God Delusion, Dawkins tells us:

> It has been estimated that there are between 1 billion and 30 billion planets in our galaxy, and about a hundred billion galaxies in the universe...now suppose the origin of life, the spontaneous arising of something equivalent to DNA really was a quite staggeringly improbable event. Suppose it was so improbable as to occur on only one in a billion planets...and yet even with such absurdly long odds, life will still have arisen on a billion planets. [53]

There you have it, "life on a billion planets." Why didn't I think of that? DNA all over the cosmos if we just knew where to look for it. Despite the fact that earlier in the same chapter Dawkins admitted that "the expertise required for it [*Origin of Life* research] is chemistry and it is not mine", he still neatly manages to tie the whole package together, wrap it in beautifully colored ribbon, and even add a personal greeting card. In the universe according to Dawkins, the odds are that there is life on a billion planets. Let's see what the chemists have to say on the subject.

Dr. Robert Shapiro — Chemist:

Dr. Robert Shapiro, in his classic work, *Origins: A Skeptics Guide to the Creation of Life on Earth,* calculates the odds for the spontaneous self-assembly of the simplest living organism known to have ever existed: a bacterium. In order to illustrate the patent absurdity of such a notion, he sets up an impossibly favorable scenario in order to maximize the possibility of the random occurrence of such an event. The hypothetical set up is as follows: **A)** the time allowed for each attempt at spontaneously assembling a bacterium from simple chemicals is one minute (even though an actual bacterium takes 20 minutes to self replicate). **B)** One billion years is allowed for these one minute trials to take place. This is several times more than the actual maximum amount of time available for life to form on earth. **C)** The available space is *the entire earth covered by an* *ocean 10 kilometers deep!* **D)** That entire space is divided into tiny reaction chambers of bacterial size: 1 square micrometer apiece (a micrometer is one millionth of a meter.) **E)** Every minute for one billion years a new attempt is made to spontaneously assemble a bacterium in each of these chambers. Even given such an unrealistically favorable set of circumstances Dr. Shapiro comes to the following conclusion:

> Harold Morowitz, a Yale University physicist...has calculated the odds [against success in a single trial]...1 chance in 10 to the 100 billionth power...The improbability involved in generating even one bacterium is so large that it reduces all considerations of time and space to nothingness...we would truly be waiting for a miracle. [54]

DNA *is out of the question, what about a "simple" RNA replicator?*

Perhaps we are being too ambitious when we talk about the probabilities of a bacterium emerging spontaneously. As we saw earlier, even the simplest bacteria are so complex as to boggle the mind. What about a simple replicator molecule being generated randomly, which is obviously far less complex than a bacterium? Richard Dawkins (a biologist, not a chemist) informs us that:

> A molecule which makes copies of itself is not as difficult to imagine as it seems...the small building blocks were abundantly available in the soup surrounding the replicator. (from *The Selfish Gene*, (Dawkins), as quoted by Dr. Robert Shapiro in *Origins: A Skeptics Guide to the Origin of Life*, p. 167)

Dr. Robert Shapiro, commenting on the above cited passage, nonchalantly, condescendingly, and summarily dismisses Dawkins. After explaining that the simplest self-replicating RNA molecule would consist of about 20 nucleotides, or about 600 atoms bonded together in a strictly precise arrangement, he goes on to calculate the odds of such an event occurring:

> **We badly need the point of view of the Skeptic once again...**[Let's use the example of] the monkey at the typewriter. Let's call him Charlie the Chimp. Charlie...types out one line per second; completely at random...

we want our monkey to type out "to be or not to be, that is the question", which has 40 characters...The chances then become 45^{40} or about 10^{66} to 1. This number is 10 million times greater than the number of trials maximally available for the random generation of a replicator on the early earth. There we have it. If the chances for getting the replicator at random from a prebiotic soup are less than that of striking "to be or not to be, that is the question", by chance on a typewriter, we had best forget it. The replicator would have about 600 atoms. The chances of Charlie typing a 600-letter message correctly are 1 in 10^{992}. [55]

At a conference of some of the world's leading scientists sponsored by *Edge*, held in August 2007, Shapiro was a little more candid about how he viewed Dawkins' understanding of the origin of life:

> Richard Dawkins wrote a wonderful book but the place where he absolutely blew it was in a section on the origin of life...he has no other recourse – he's not a chemist – than to invoke some improbable event...so his schoolboy howler is the section on origin of life. [56]

Dr. Francis Crick — Nobel Prize Winning Microbiologist explores the fascinating world of Polypeptides:

> To produce this miracle of molecular construction all the cell need do is to string together the amino acids...in the correct order. This is a complicated biochemical process, [accomplished by] a molecular assembly line, using instructions in the form of nucleic acid tape (the so called messenger RNA)...Here we need only ask, how many possible proteins are there? If a particular amino acid sequence was selected by chance, how rare of an event would that be? This is an easy exercise in combinatorials. Suppose the chain is about hundred amino acids long; this is, if anything, rather less than average length of proteins of all types. Since we have just twenty possibilities at each place, the number of possibilities is twenty multiplied by itself some two hundred times. This is...approximately 10^{260}, that is a one followed by 260 zeroes! The number is quite beyond our everyday comprehension...the number of fundamental particles (atoms, speaking loosely) in the entire visible universe...is estimated to be 10^{80}... [it is] quite paltry by comparison to 10^{260}. Moreover we have only considered a polypeptide chain of a rather modest length. Had we considered longer ones as well, the figure would have been even more immense. [57]

I don't want to bore the reader with endless citations of probability calculations, I think I have made my point; but just to close the circle, I will cite one more. Here is the full statement from Sir Fred Hoyle, from whence the title of this book was taken:

> At all events, anyone with even a nodding acquaintance with the Rubik cube will concede the near impossibility of a solution being obtained by a blind person moving the cube faces at random. Now imagine 10^{50} blind persons each with a scrambled Rubik cube, and try to conceive of the chance of them all simultaneously arriving at the solved form. You then have the chance of arriving by random shuffling, of just one of the many biopolymers on which life depends. The notion that not only the biopolymers, but the operating program of a living cell could be arrived at by chance in a primordial organic soup is evidently nonsense of a high order.

The simplest living bacterium came from somewhere; what are the options?

For the dispassionate, truth seeking, intellectually honest individual, there are clearly only two possible answers or solutions to the question: *How did life begin?*

I. A Naturalistic Origin (which includes two sub-categories)
A) Pure chance, blind luck
B) An explanation that showed how the known laws of physics and chemistry could account for the beginning of life. (Or a combination of **A** and **B**)

II. A Conscious, Deliberate Act of Creation
That is, a willful, conscious act of design and creation, by an intelligent, conscious creator.

How does one go about deciding how to answer this most crucial of questions? To start off, let's analyze how Francis Crick and Leslie Orgel approached this issue in 1973 when they proposed Directed Panspermia as a solution.

Francis Crick and Leslie Orgel — "ET Phone Home"

When Francis Crick and Leslie Orgel first suggested that

life on Earth had been seeded by an alien civilization, what were the underlying assumptions they were making in order to reach that conclusion? The first obvious assumption is that they felt that blind luck had nothing to do with the origin of the first living organism on our planet. Crick's earlier cited probability calculations regarding the formation of polypeptides should make that quite clear. The second assumption was that they could not think of a natural law or combination of physical laws that would cause inanimate matter to organize into living things (at least not on Earth). If they knew of such a law or of such a process, why would they place the origin of life somewhere else in the universe but not on Earth? The third assumption was that only highly sophisticated and technologically advanced beings could have ensured that life would survive interstellar travel. That is why they hypothesized an advanced alien civilization that seeded our planet with life.

What "directed panspermia" does not address, of course, is how life came to exist in the first place. It is also a mystery why Crick and Orgel felt that the challenges posed by interstellar travel could only be overcome by the "intelligent design" of advanced aliens, while the challenges involved in life itself coming into existence – challenges which are exponentially more problematic – could be overcome with no intelligent help at all. In fact, my own approach is similar, in a number of ways, to that of Crick and Orgel.

How did Rabbi Averick decide on (II), a willful conscious act of creation by a creator?

The steps I took to arrive at this conclusion are quite easy to follow.

<u>Chance:</u> Despite the protestations of Richard Dawkins that there should be life on a billion planets by pure luck (there is of course, no meaningful evidence of life on any planet other than our own), the probability calculations made by <u>*experts* in the field</u> (Shapiro, Cairns-Smith, Hoyle, Morowitz, Crick, etc.) make it clear that chance and blind luck are the choices for those who have abandoned all reason and rationality.

<u>*Natural Law or Laws:*</u> Dr. Stuart Kaufman, Dr. Christian DeDuve, Dr. Leslie Orgel, Dr. Francis Crick, and other *Origin of Life* researchers have made it exceedingly clear that they have no naturalistic, scientific explanation of how life began. We have cited several prominent scientists who have even accused *Origin of Life* researchers of being guilty of "faith" and wishful thinking. (I again remind the reader that none of the scientists cited in this chapter are creationists or identify with the Intelligent Design movement) Sir Fred Hoyle went so far as to say that if there was some "natural law" that drove matter towards life, it should be incredibly easy to prove it in the laboratory and it has not been proven. There is a lot of *speculating and conjecturing,* but speculation and conjecture are as irrelevant in the process of deciding how life began as they are in deciding the guilt or innocence of a defendant in a criminal trial.

<u>*Creator:*</u> As we have already discussed, no scientist has been able to explain how something as astoundingly complex and sophisticated as a living cell (or a "simple" self-replicating molecule), could be assembled naturally, using the known physical laws of our universe. What are we to conclude?

Picture a man shipwrecked on a small island in the Pacific Ocean. His name is Joe. He has searched the island from top to bottom and is absolutely certain that he is the sole inhabitant. Day after day goes by. Slowly and painfully he resigns himself to the possibility that this is where he may spend the rest of his life. One morning after waking, he discovers a previously unexplored stretch of beach on the island and is stunned to see a circle in the sand made out of a series of small pebbles, with a bunch of larger pebbles inside that form a smiley face. Next to the smiley face are the words, "Good Morning Joe" (also formed by pebbles). Unless this rock sculpture was created by Joe himself while he was sleepwalking, it is obvious that someone else who knows Joe visited the island. Theoretically, of course, the face and the words could have already been there in the sand when he arrived. After all, if we use the logic of Richard Dawkins, in the endless billions upon billions of worlds and galaxies in our universe, such a phenomenon could have happened by chance at least once, right? Despite this theoretical possibility, if someone actually asserted that there was a "naturalistic" explanation for the message in the sand, they would rightly be declared a lunatic or a madman...unless they could prove it beyond a reasonable doubt (good luck). In other words, I do not need to *prove* that the smiley face and words are created; that is the obvious, undeniable, self-apparent truth. The burden of proof is on the one who claims that there is a naturalistic explanation.

It's obvious that the simplest living organism we know of today – a bacterium – is more functionally complex and sophisticated than a smiley face in the sand. In fact the machinery of the living cell is more sophisticated than anything that can be produced by human technology. I do not need to *prove* that it was created, any more than I need to *prove* that a smiley face in the sand with the words "Good morning, Joe" is created. It is the simple obvious truth. (Remember, we are not talking about various life forms evolving from a pre-existing DNA-based organism, we are discussing the very first such organism and its origin.) It is this simple obvious truth that is overlooked by Dr. Frank Sonleitner of the NCSE who writes, "What scientific evidence exists to support intelligent design? The only direct evidence for intelligent design, spontaneous generation, has been disproved!" [58]

There is nothing "simple" about a simple self-replicating molecule

The exact same thing holds true for a "simple" self-replicating molecule, whose existence in nature is at *best* a weak and purely speculative hypothesis, and at worst an absurdly implausible notion born of wishful thinking. The fact that the world's leading scientific geniuses can produce such a molecule has little, if any, bearing on our issue. Nobody doubts that a GM plant in Detroit can produce a Chevy Impala. However, nobody would therefore conclude that naturalistic processes could also produce a Chevy Impala. Nobody doubts that highly intelligent scientists, building on the knowledge of other highly intelligent scientists, with millions of dollars of research money and cutting edge technology at their disposal, can achieve remarkable things.

Dr. Robert Shapiro wrote the following in 1999, in anticipation of the creation in the laboratory of "self sustained RNA evolving systems," *i.e.*, the self replicating molecules we have been mentioning. (The extraordinary achievement of designing and manufacturing such systems – albeit that their ability to self-replicate is only in the most highly limited sense – was recently announced by Dr. Gerald Joyce and Dr. Tracey Lincoln of the Scripps Research Institute in La Jolla, California [59]):

> The media probably will announce it as the demonstration of a crucial step in the origin of life...The concept that the scientists are [actually] illustrating is one of Intelligent Design. No better term can be applied to a quest in which chemists...prepare a living system in the laboratory, using all the ingenuity and technical resources at their disposal... [60]

Shapiro goes on to say that watching top-level scientists manufacture these amazing pieces of molecular machinery in the laboratory evokes in him the same kind of awe as when he watches a skilled golfer play a difficult course at well under par. He wryly concludes, "To imagine that related events could take place on their own appears as likely as the idea that the golf ball could play its own way around the course without the golfer." [61] At a lecture sponsored by the Harvard Origins of Life Initiative in October of 2008, Shapiro had this to say about connecting prebiotic synthesis conducted in the laboratory with the theory that life evolved on Earth from naturally occurring RNA. ["RNA first" theory]:

> While chemists have succeeded in making the molecules of life – or their components – in the lab out of simpler molecules...the tightly controlled processes in a chemistry lab can't be mistaken for what would have happened on the early Earth. **Any abiotically prepared replicator before the start of life is a fantasy**. [62]

At this point in our discussion it is probably worth noting what Nobel Prize winning microbiologist, Dr. Francois Jacob, had to say on our subject, "It goes without saying that the emergence of this RNA and the transition to a DNA world implies an impressive number of stages, **each more improbable than the previous one**." [63] Dr. Gerald Joyce himself, although writing in a more subdued tone, essentially agrees with Shapiro that nobody understands how the "RNA World" scenario could have developed under natural conditions:

> After contemplating the possibility of self-replicating ribozymes emerging from pools of random polynucleotides and recognizing the difficulties that must have been overcome for RNA replication to occur in a **realistic** prebiotic soup, the challenge must now be faced of constructing a **realistic** picture of the origin of the RNA World...it must be said that the details of this process remain obscure and are not likely to be known in the near future. [64]

In fact, in an article entitled "The Origins of the RNA World," Dr. Joyce explicitly points out that while the RNA World concept has helped guide scientific thinking and has focused experimental efforts, "this concept does not explain how life originated." [65]

Atheist Novelist Rebecca Goldstein advances a very poor argument against the existence of God

After hearing world class scientists in the *Origin of Life* field describe the possibility of a naturally forming replicator as "absurd," "utterly perplexing," a "fantasy," "self-deception," a "near miracle," that a plausible explanation "remains unknown," that it's as likely to occur as a golf ball playing its way around an 18 hole course by itself, that as yet we have no "realistic" scenario for such an occurrence, that each of the many steps involved in such a process is "more improbable than the previous one," and that in any case, the entire area of research "does not explain how life originated," one can only marvel at the chimerical approach of Rebecca Goldstein to this issue in her novel, *36 Arguments for the Existence of God – A Work of Fiction:*

> But the mathematician John Von Neumann proved in the 1950's that it is theoretically possible for a simple physical system to make exact copies of itself from surrounding materials. Since then, biologists and chemists have identified a number of naturally occurring molecules and crystals that can replicate in ways that can lead to natural selection...eventually leading to precursors of the replication system used by living organisms today. [66]

Since she is not a scientist, I think we can give her the benefit of the doubt and assume she was not engaging in a deliberate attempt to deceive readers with her gross misrepresentation of the facts; she is just disturbingly ill informed.

The Skeptic bears the burden of proof

The burden of proof is not on me to prove an intelligent creator; that is blindingly obvious; the burden of proof is on those who claim that there is a naturalistic explanation. How appropriate are the previously cited words of the atheist philosopher Bertrand Russell in this instance:

> Many orthodox people speak as though it were the business of skeptics to disprove received dogmas rather than of dogmatists to prove them. If I were to suggest that between the Earth and Mars is a china teapot revolving about the sun in an elliptical orbit, nobody would be able to disprove my assertion provided I were careful to add that the teapot is too small to be revealed even by our most powerful telescopes. But if I were to go on to say that since my assertion cannot be disproved, it is intolerable presumption on the part of human reason to doubt it, I should rightly be thought to be talking nonsense.

The irony of course, is that in this case it is the believer's position that is the obvious truth, and the skeptic's "dogma" that must be proven. In simple terms: If you want me to believe that the awe-inspiring level of functional complexity that is found in a living bacterium is the result of an undirected natural process starting from raw, inorganic chemicals (*i.e.,* life from non-life)...then prove it! The fact that I am unable to *disprove the possibility* of a naturalistic explanation is completely irrelevant; that very point is the major thrust of Russell's observation. It is clear that this obvious point *also* escapes Dr. Frank Sonleitner when he writes on the NCSE website:

> Modern ideas about the [emergence] of living things from non-living components...may not yet have come anywhere near answering all our questions about the process, but... **none of this research has indicated that biopoesis** [life from non-life] **is impossible.** [67] [emphasis added]

Please note: Nothing could be more revealing about the blank wall scientists face in trying to understand the origin of life, than the fact that the best news that an NCSE zealot like Sonleitner can offer is that a naturalistic explanation is not "impossible."

It seems that Sonleitner copied his approach from Mark Isaak in his *Counter Creationism Handbook* (or maybe Isaak copied from Sonleitner), "Nobody denies that origin of life is an extremely difficult problem, that it has not been solved though, does not mean that it is **impossible**." [68] (Isaak) Maybe they both received this particular mantra of Scientific Naturalism from Dr. Paul Davies, "Just because scientists are still uncertain how life began does not mean life **cannot** have had a natural origin." [69] In other words, just because they are uncertain does not mean that it's **impossible!** Actually, it seems that all of these men received their scientific faith tradition from the great master himself, Dr. Francis Crick, who wrote the following in his book, *Life Itself*, in 1981:

> An honest man, armed with all the knowledge available to us now, could only state that in some sense, the origin of life appears at the moment to be almost a miracle, so many are the conditions which would have had to have been satisfied to get it going. But this should not be taken to imply that...it **could not** have started on the earth by a perfectly reasonable sequence of fairly ordinary chemical reactions. [70]

This is a positively sterling example of the "atheistic disconnect." The origin of life is *miraculous,* but don't worry, that doesn't in any way imply that it's *impossible* that it could have happened by itself. Imagine pleading with the pit boss of a Las Vegas casino as his goons unceremoniously toss you into the street: *I know it seems **miraculous** that I could have won 100 hands of black jack in a row by pure natural luck, but it's not **impossible!!!!*** (With a steamroller of an argument like that you'll be back at the black jack tables in no time, right?) In Chapter Two I pointed out (as does Bertrand Russell above) the foolishness of arguing that a proposition should be given credence because it cannot be *disproved* or because it is not *impossible.* Imagine the ludicrousness of a District Attorney presenting the following argument to a jury: *I may not have presented any evidence that the defendant is guilty, but nobody has proved that it's **impossible** for him to be guilty.*

I haven't the slightest idea how anyone would go about

proving that the step by step assembly of the first bacterium by a naturalistic process is *impossible*, any more than I have the slightest idea how Sonleitner would go about proving that the existence of a china teapot revolving around the sun in an elliptical orbit in between the Earth and Mars is *impossible;* but no rational person is going to take either of these propositions seriously without conclusive evidence. I would also like to point out that if we are accepting "it's not impossible" as a valid argument, then how about this one: "it's not *impossible* that God created he world in seven days, 6000 years ago, and made it look like it's billions of years old?"

The Scientific concept called "Emergence" has nothing to do with the Origin of Life

Scientific observation and experimentation have shown that certain types of seemingly "designed" patterns emerge naturally, like crystallization and snowflakes. The famous experiment of Dr. Stanley Miller showed that certain types of amino acids also form naturally (It is a "thermodynamically downhill" process, to use Dr. Paul Davies' term). Some scientists call these patterns *Emergence*. Another fascinating naturally emerging pattern is described by Mineralogist Robert Hazen:

> When moving water (or wind for that matter) flows across a flat layer of sand, new patterns arise. Periodic sand ripples appear, as sand grains are sorted by size, shape, and density...I've seen this classic rippled surface cover hundreds of square meters of shallow water in patterns so hypnotically regular that I hesitated to disturb the symmetry by walking on it. [71]

Despite the phenomena of these "hypnotically regular" patterns, the observations have also shown clearly that there are limits to what can emerge. If someone would attempt to explain the formation of a smiley face and the words "Good morning Joe," as naturally emerging patterns caused by "moving water [flowing] across a flat layer of sand," Dr. Hazen would be the first to declare that such a person had completely lost touch with reality. Imagine claiming (with no conclusive evidence to support it) that not only were the words "Good morning Joe" and the smiley face formed by the same forces that create "ripple patterns" in the sand, but that they also created a living bacterium "containing …intricate molecular machinery, made up altogether of one hundred thousand million atoms, far more complicated than any machine built by man."

In summation: The idea that something as functionally complex as a DNA based bacterium (or "self-sustained evolving RNA systems") could emerge through an undirected, naturalistic process is an absurd proposition that can be rejected out of hand, *unless it can be demonstrated to be true; and not only has it not been demonstrated, no evidence exists that could even be remotely considered as even a partial demonstration of such an assertion.*

Atheistic objections to a Creator as the obvious solution for the origin of life generally fall into one of four categories:

1. **Non-Scientific** – A supernatural creator (*i.e.,* who is outside of the material universe) is not in the category of science
2. **Atheistic Nonsense of a High Order** – when we get to these, they will speak for themselves
3. **Science will find an answer** – (in other words: be patient, we're working on it)
4. **Philosophical** – These types of objections attack the internal logic of the "Argument from Design," or attack the argument on other philosophical grounds.

In the following two chapters we will deal with each of these objections, one at a time.

Chapter 4

Objections to A Supernatural Creator

Objection #1: Non-Scientific — A Supernatural Creator is not in the category of Science

"Back Off, I'm a Scientist!" (*Bill Murray – in the film* **Ghostbusters**)

Many lay people have somehow been brainwashed into thinking that scientists are qualitatively different than the rest of humanity. The impression is that the scientist, through some bizarre mutation, has leapfrogged to the top of the evolutionary ladder, *Homo scientistus,* one step above the rest of us lowly *Homo sapiens.* In his book, *The Monkey Business,* renowned evolutionary paleontologist Niles Eldredge, addresses this fanciful view of the scientific world:

> Many scientists really do seem to believe they have a special access to the truth. They call press conferences to trumpet marvelous new discoveries. They compete hard for awards and prizes. And they expect to be believed- by their peers and, especially, by the public at large. Throwing down scientific thunderbolts from Olympian heights, scientists come across as authoritarian truth givers whose word must be taken unquestioned. That all the evidence shows the behavior of scientists clearly to be no different from the ways in which other people behave is somehow overlooked in all this. [1]

Eldredge writes elsewhere:

> ...in the competitive fray that is science, data forging, plagiarism, and all manner of base but utterly human failings make a mockery of the counter image of detached objectivity... [2]

Dr. Stephen J. Gould seconds Eldredge; in his view, the notion that scientists are detached robots operating on pure logic is simply hokum:

> Our ways of learning about the world are strongly influenced by the social preconceptions and biased modes of thinking that each scientist must apply to any problem. The stereotype of a fully rational and objective "scientific method" with individual scientists as logical (and interchangeable) robots is self serving mythology. [3]

Scientists as a whole are no better or worse than the practitioners of any other trade or profession. There are scientists who are scrupulously honest and of impeccable integrity, and there are some who are petty, vindictive, and underhanded. It may be true that there is a system in place to keep scientists on the straight and narrow: for example, for a scientist to publish an article in a respected journal it must be reviewed by his peers. However, there is also a regulatory system in place to oversee the activities of bank executives; that doesn't mean that there aren't bankers who will cook the books when they find an opportunity, will find other ways to fudge data to their own advantage, and will even engage in outright thievery if they think they can get away with it. Scientists want honor, recognition, and job security just like everyone else. Scientists have exhibited neither a higher nor lower moral caliber than any other group of people. In Nazi Germany, Imperial Japan, and the former Soviet Union, as well as other places in the world, scientists have been responsible for mind numbing atrocities and the production of horrific weapons of destruction. Scientists are tempted by greed, jealousy, lust, pride, and envy, no more and no less than any other group. Some scientists act on their prejudices, and look to promote their agenda whenever they have the opportunity.

> I sometimes think scientists really don't notice their colleagues have flaws. But in my experience scientists are very human people; which means that some are troubled, deceitful, petty, or vain. [4]
> (Dr. Michael Crichton)

Scientific expertise is not transferable to other intellectual disciplines

Most important of all: Their scientific expertise is not in any way transferable to other disciplines. A Noble Prize winning chemist may have no more expertise in World History than an average high school student; in fact he may have less. A Nobel Prize winning physicist does not necessarily have any more insight into the wisdom of living a happy life and success in marriage and raising children than the plumber who comes to fix his sink. It goes further than that. He may have no more expertise in philosophy, metaphysics, psychology, and theology than any particular orthodox rabbi. I defer to the physicist exclusively on the subject of *Physics*. When a brilliant and highly accomplished scientist expresses opinions or draws conclusions in areas that are outside of his expertise; or when it is clear that he is being motivated by pre-conceived notions or a personal agenda, it would be a flagrant assault on the entire concept of intellectual integrity to grant him special dispensation due to his standing in the scientific world. In this chapter, I will bring example after example to demonstrate that *Origin of Life* researchers routinely draw conclusions in areas outside of their expertise and are consistently motivated by pre-conceived notions and/or personal agenda. In fact, it is my contention that among these scientists it has become standard operating procedure.

Origin of Life research is based on pre-conceived assumptions; however, the job of the scientist is not to <u>make</u> assumptions, but rather to <u>test</u> assumptions!

Imagine the following scenario: You are told you have a terrible disease. There are only two medical researchers, Dr. A and Dr. B, who might have a cure. Both are reputed to be encyclopedic in their knowledge and brilliant researchers. Dr. A tells you he has been working on finding a cure for this disease for years and has an experimental therapy prepared if you are willing to try it. Dr. B says he is also working on a cure but explains to you that he started his research with certain *assumptions,* and he ignores any approach or evidence that contradicts those *assumptions*. Which Doctor will you choose? Is there really any question? Could anyone possibly trust a man who tells you that he is locked into one way of thinking? Isn't it glaringly obvious that the essential purpose of any type of research is not to *make* assumptions, but to *test* assumptions? Isn't it clear that medical research (or any type of research) that is not based on an absolute commitment to seeking the truth wherever it leads, is not only worthless but potentially very dangerous? Keeping this in mind, let's carefully examine the following statement by a Nobel Prize winning scientist who is also a prominent researcher in the *Origin of Life* field:

> This leaves a window of perhaps 200-300 million years for the appear-
> ance of life on earth. This duration was once considered too short for the
> emergence of something as complex as a living cell. Hence suggestions
> were made that germs of life may have come to earth from outer
> space...[perhaps, as suggested by Crick] on a spaceship sent out by some
> distant civilization. No evidence of these proposals has yet been
> obtained...**It is now generally agreed that if life arose spontaneously**
> **by natural processes – a necessary assumption if we wish to remain**
> **within the realm of science** – it must have arisen fairly quickly, more in
> a matter of millennia or centuries, perhaps even less...[5] (Dr. Christian
> DeDuve, Nobel Laureate in Medicine, 1974)

In my opinion, any honest truth-seeking individual should scream in outrage after reading what Dr. DeDuve wrote: "A *necessary assumption* if we wish to remain within the realm of science"– If he had written that it was a *theoretical* assumption that scientists wanted to test, I would have no objection. However, what possible reason would a scientist have for making an *assumption* in order to "remain within the realm of science"? In order to block out ideas that make him uncomfortable or even frighten him? In order not to have to admit that there is a limit to his ability to scientifically explain the world? In order to avoid confronting a reality that he hopes does not exist? Is Science a servant of Truth, or is Truth the servant of Science? Isn't the purpose of all intellectual inquiry to discover the truth? Isn't the goal of a human being supposed to be to "remain within the realm of *truth*?" Dr. Paul Davies, seemingly oblivious to the inherent intellectual corruption contained in such an approach, concurs with Dr. DeDuve:

> I should like to say that the scientific attempt to explain the origin of life proceeds from the **assumption** that whatever it was that happened was a natural process…no supernatural intervention. Scientists have to start with that assumption. [6] [Please note: It is not to test the assumption which drives the scientific investigation; it is simply assumed to be true.]

From which Mt. Sinai was issued the proclamation that all inquiry must be based on *assumptions* that keep us within the "realm of science?" What if the truth is not to be found within purely naturalistic processes? What if reason, logic, and the results of our inquiries point to an answer that is not within "the realm of science?" Should we ignore those logical conclusions and/or results? If what I am seeking is the *truth*, what possible reason would I have for caring if it was within the "realm of science" or not? How can a man as brilliant as DeDuve make such an intellectually obscene statement? All of DeDuve's conclusions are based on this unproven assumption. How is it possible to trust any of those conclusions? Regarding Crick's proposal that life originated from aliens in outer space DeDuve writes above, "No evidence for these proposals has yet been obtained." Neither has any evidence been obtained that life arose on earth from a natural process! It is amazing how such an intelligent man can be oblivious to reason and logic when it suits his agenda.

The Truth-Seeker's Approach to Origin of Life is radically different

If DeDuve had been approaching the issue as a truth-seeker, the passage in question would have been written something like this:

"If life arose spontaneously by natural processes" – this is an assumption for which I have no conclusive evidence (if any at all), and it can only be approached as one of the possibilities in our search for the origin of life. Another possibility is that life arose by a completely supernatural process. For example, we know that beyond a certain point in the Earth's past, life as we know it could not survive due to the intense heat of the Earth's surface. At one point, it cooled down enough for life to begin. Sometime in between that point and approximately 3.6 billion years ago life began on Earth. Due to the effects of the intense heat on rock formations, we have no way of knowing if life started a million years after that point or within 15 minutes after that point. If we could theoretically go back in time and found that bacteria formed within 30 seconds after the Earth was cool enough to support life, we would have to conclude that a supernatural creator was at work. Alternatively, if in our research we ever reach the conclusion – based on our scientific knowledge and our reasoned judgment – that we are unable to find any plausible natural process which could have resulted in life, we would also have to conclude that in all likelihood a supernatural creator was responsible. Anyone who rules out the possibility of a supernatural creator just because it is "not within the realm of science" or "naturalistic processes" has perverted and twisted human reason. A man who sincerely seeks the truth, will never lock himself into any pre-conceived assumptions or notions.

The Articles of Faith of the Religion of Scientific Naturalism (i.e. the religion whose central dogma is that <u>everything</u> must have a scientific, naturalistic explanation)

DeDuve is by no means alone in this fatally flawed approach to *Origin of Life*. Dr. Robert Shapiro also joins in this assault on open-minded rational inquiry:

> One favorite analogy [of believers] involves the discovery of a watch... It would function only if its components had been put together...by a watchmaker...Similarly, the existence of bacteria and other living beings, all of which are much more complex than a watch, implies the existence of a creator...We will not take this escape route in our book, for we are committed to seeking an answer within the realm of science...A being with the capacity to create a watchmaker would be the most complex of the lot. By following this line of reasoning, we have made our problem more difficult rather than simpler, and we can resolve it only by introducing supernatural forces. We must look for another solution if we wish to remain within science. [7]

In other words, by definition you make a problem "more difficult" if your logic and reason lead you to conclude that there is a supernatural creator. Shapiro brazenly throws the quest for truth under the bus. He will make whatever sacrifices are necessary to "remain within science," after all he is "committed" to finding a scientific answer. It is just as foolish and mistaken for a scientist to believe that his "commitment" to finding a scientific answer magically creates a scientific reality, as it is for a theologian to believe that his "commitment" to finding a religious answer magically creates a spiritual/metaphysical reality. The only "commitment" worth making is to finding the truth. Shapiro does not say that he is committed to finding the true answer. In fact, in order to "remain within science," Shapiro is prepared to abandon and ignore a perfectly good "line of reasoning" (his very own words). In Dr. Shapiro's mind truth and science have become interchangeable. This is intellectually unacceptable!

Dr. Paul Davies loyally repeats the catechism:

> In the coming chapters I shall argue that it is not enough to know how life's immense structural complexity arose; we must also acc for the origin of biological information. As we shall see, scientists are still very far from solving this fundamental conceptual puzzle...**However it is the job of scientists to solve mysteries without recourse to divine intervention.**[8]

Note: It is not the job of scientists to seek the *truth*, it is their job to "avoid recourse to divine intervention," and defend the faith of Scientific Naturalism to the bitter end.

Another example of intellectual blindness on the part of Origin of Life researchers

Imagine an east-west interstate highway with a rest stop standing in the median between the two roads. There is an exit ramp from the eastbound highway leading to the rest stop, and an identical ramp from the westbound highway. Inasmuch as there is no other access to the rest stop, there are only two possible ways for a vehicle to enter: from the east or from the west. Two men standing in the rest stop notice a car pull up without either having seen from which direction it came. The following dialogue ensues:

Man #1: Which direction do you think that car came from?

Man #2: Well, **barring the possibility** that it came from the west, it must have come from the east.

Man #1: What kind of ridiculous answer is that? There are only two possibilities to begin with. All you have told me is that if we only consider one possibility, then there is only one possibility. That is like saying 1 equals 1. That type of statement is known as a tautology. It is pointless, meaningless and gives me no new information.

Man #2: Well, what did you want from me when you asked the question?

Man #1: I wanted to know if you had any observations or empirical evidence that would indicate which direction it came from. In other words do you have any evidence that would indicate which of the two possibilities is true?

There are only two possibilities to explain the origin of life. **1)** Natural Processes (*i.e.,* which includes luck or chance, or a plausible explanation using the laws of physics and chemistry), or **2)** Divine Intervention, *i.e.,* a supernatural creator. Keeping this in mind, let's see what insights Dr. Robert Hazen has to offer into the origin of life:

> How did life arise?...The Biblical account...hardly puts the origin question to rest. **Barring divine intervention,** life must have emerged by a natural process – one fully consistent with the laws of chemistry and physics. [9] (Dr. Robert Hazen)

What point is Dr. Hazen making when he informs us that the Biblical account, *i.e.,* a supernatural creator, "hardly puts the origin question to rest?" Is he simply trying to tell us that he does not believe in a supernatural creator? Is he attempting to show us why the idea of a supernatural creator is irrational or unacceptable? In fact, all he gives us is a meaningless tautology: "Barring divine intervention, life must have emerged by a natural process." In other words, if no other force is at work in the universe with regards to the origin of life except natural processes ("barring divine intervention"), then the only force at work in the universe with regards to origin of life is natural processes.

Simply stated, if we arbitrarily decide to only consider one of the possibilities, then there is only one possibility.

Hazen's statement is as about as meaningful, informative, and scientific as the following: "Barring naturalistic processes, life must have emerged by divine intervention." Any scientist (or any clear thinking individual for that matter), including Hazen, Dawkins, DeDuve, etc, would have screamed in outrage that the above statement is nothing more than narrow-minded, dogmatic Creationism. Hazen's declaration, in fact, is nothing more than narrow-minded, dogmatic Scientific Naturalism.

I have some important news for Dr. Hazen and his colleagues. Divine intervention in the origin of life is either true or it is not true. Divine intervention does not magically appear just because I or anyone else believes in it, but neither does it magically disappear just because it does not fit someone's scientific faith agenda. It does not cease to be an issue or a possibility because it is dismissed with a pointless and meaningless offhand remark. The relevant question is: *why* are you barring divine intervention?

Doctor Hazen implicitly tells us that his position is based on a leap of faith, not evidence

In fact, Hazen does offer an explanation as to why he has chosen to ignore the possibility of a supernatural creator:

> Scientists believe [how very scientific] in a universe ordered by natural laws; they resort to the power of observations, experiments, and theoretical reasoning to discover those laws...Scientists surmise [even more scientific!] that life arose on the blasted, primitive Earth from the most basic of raw materials: air, water, rock. Life emerged nearly 4 billion years ago by natural processes completely in accord with the laws of chemistry and physics... [10]

Dr. Hazen has done nothing other than tell us his first article of faith. How did scientists "surmise" that life emerged by "natural processes completely in accord with the laws of chemistry and physics?" Because "scientists *believe* in a universe ordered [only] by natural laws." The first dogma and belief of *Origin of Life* research is to completely ignore the possibility of a supernatural creation. There is no question that this statement is based on a leap of faith, for in the very next sentence (and any number of other places in the book) he informs us that it is not based on evidence:

> ...yet details of that transforming origin even pose mysteries as deep as any facing Science. How did non-living chemicals become alive?...the epic history of life's chemical origins is woefully incomplete [11]...what we know about the origin of life is dwarfed by what we don't know. It's as if we were trying to assemble a giant jigsaw puzzle. A few pieces clump together here and there, but most of the pieces are missing and we don't even have the box to see what the complete picture is supposed to look like. [12]

He even cites a rather scathing and caustic remark by prominent *Origin of Life* researcher, Dr. Stuart Kauffman, "Anyone who tells you that he or she knows how life started on the sere Earth some 3.45 billion years ago is a fool or knave." [13] Dr. Hazen is even prepared to consider the possibility of blind luck – despite the probability calculations that have relegated to the realm of complete and utter irrationality the idea that the first living organisms arose by pure chance:

> It is possible, of course, that life arose through an improbable sequence of many chemical reactions. If so then living worlds will be rare in the universe and laboratory attempts to understand the origin process will be doomed to frustration. An unlikely sequence of unknown steps cannot be reproduced in any plausible experimental program. [14]

The only possibility which is FORBIDDEN by Hazen's Scientific Naturalism Faith Principles is a *Creator*.

More brilliant Scientists declare their "faith" in Science...

In an article entitled, "The Origin of Life on Earth", Dr. Leslie Orgel tells us:

> When the earth formed some 4.6 billion years ago, it was a lifeless, inhospitable place. A billion years later it was teeming with organisms resembling blue-green algae. How did they get there? How, in short, did life begin?...Before the mid-17th century, most people believed that

God had created humankind and other...organisms...Darwin, bending somewhat to the religious biases of his time, posited in the final paragraph of The Origin of the Species that the "Creator" originally breathed life "into a few forms or into one." Then evolution took over...In private correspondence...he suggested life could have arisen through chemistry, "in some warm little pond, with all sorts of ammonia and phosphoric salts." For much of the 20th century, origin of life research has aimed to flesh out Darwin's private hypothesis – to elucidate how, **without supernatural intervention** spontaneous interaction of the relatively simple molecules dissolved in the lakes or oceans of the prebiotic world could have yielded life's last common ancestor. [15]

Please note that Orgel does not say that *Origin of Life* research has aimed to discover if Darwin's private hypothesis has any validity, or if it can empirically be shown to be true. He makes it clear that *Origin of Life* researchers have declared their allegiance of faith to this proposition and are simply trying to figure out how it happened. What I also find disturbing is that Orgel is less than candid with his readers. He fails to mention, that although "for much of the 20th century" (and at this point well into the 21st century) *Origin of Life* research has "aimed to flesh out Darwin's private hypothesis," that particular endeavor has until now, met with absolute and utter failure.

Dr. Orgel, however, has added another dimension to the faith of Scientific Naturalism by invoking the name of Darwin. I guess by tracing the theory of life emerging from non-life back to Darwin, it somehow gives it more......holiness? Amazingly enough, at one time in his career Orgel was prepared to accept the possibility of "men from Mars" as the answer to our question. If you will recall, he co-authored the paper on Directed Panspermia with Francis Crick. I honestly have a hard time understanding why a rational person would consider aliens from space but not even bother to consider a supernatural creator. (Maybe he spent too much time watching *Star Wars*)

Orgel was a true believer in Darwin's "private hypothesis" for at least 40 years (any allusion to Biblical events purely coincidental). As of yet, the Darwinian *Origin of Life* messiah has failed to arrive. How many more years are the true believers prepared to wait before *considering* another answer?

Dr. Stephen J. Gould declares his faith:

> The earth is 4.6 billion years old, but the oldest rocks date to about 3.9 billion years because the earth's surface became molten early in its history...The oldest rocks...to retain cellular fossils [date] to 3.55 billion years...Thus, life on the earth evolved quickly and is as old as it could be. **This fact alone seems to indicate inevitability, or at least predictability, for life's origin from the original chemical constituents of atmosphere and ocean.** [16]

How do we know that life originated from the original chemical constituents of atmosphere and ocean in a purely naturalistic process? Because, as Gould tautologically informs us, life is as old as it could be, therefore it obviously originated *inevitably or predictably* from the atmosphere and ocean...Is that a fact? Why did Gould overlook the simple reality that when he wrote his article (and it still holds true today), scientists had nothing more substantive than highly speculative ideas about how life could have originated "naturally," that *Origin of Life* researchers are "baffled" and "perplexed" as to how life started? Maybe the reason that life is "as old as it could be" is because it was created. Maybe life is not "inevitable" or "predictable" at all. After all, nobody was there to see what happened and there is no scientist alive today who would claim, even in his wildest imagination, that he could predict how life would inevitably arise under *any* particular set of naturalistic circumstances. However, Gould is forbidden by his faith in Scientific Naturalism from considering such a possibility. Gould may very well have been a great scientist, but it is clear that his dearly held preconceived notions distorted his objectivity on this issue.

For Pure Entertainment Value, We interrupt this presentation of Objection #1 (to be continued), with <u>Objection #2: Atheistic Nonsense of a High Order</u>, from Dr. Frank Sonleitner of the NCSE

Dr. Sonleitner is a professor of zoology at the University of Oklahoma. I guess because he writes for the NCSE, he takes a more aggressive approach – the best defense is a good offense. The following is from his article on the NCSE website. I have underlined the passages on which I will comment:

Origin by an intelligent designer (creator) is tenaciously held by certain religious groups who, for political reasons, pretend that it is a scientific explanation...Everything about the creation is claimed to be supernatural...<u>Hence this idea is not an explanation (let alone a scientific one), but a reaffirmation of a religious miracle</u>...All scientists that espouse this idea do it for religious reasons (i.e. the Bible says so), and not because of any scientific evidence for it...They have admitted this in court proceedings...<u>In fact, creationists have stated that it is impossible to know anything scientific about the origin of life.</u> [17]

Let's analyze some of the assertions Sonleitner makes in the above paragraph:

1.) "In fact, creationists have stated that it is impossible to know anything scientific about the origin of life" – I don't really know if what Dr. Sonleitner has stated here is true or not. However, it might be instructive to review what *Scientists* know about the origin of life. I remind the reader that none of the distinguished scientists and academics cited below, (including several Nobel Laureates), are creationists or active proponents of Intelligent Design theory:

<u>Dr. Stuart Kauffman</u>: *We do not, in fact, know how or where life started...clearly none of the theories above is adequate...* [18]

<u>Dr. Richard Dawkins</u>: *...but how did the whole process start?...nobody knows how it happened...* [19]

<u>Dr. Chris Wills</u>: *The biggest gap in evolutionary theory remains the origin of life itself.* [20]

<u>Dr. Kenneth Miller</u>: *However, the most profound unsolved problem in biology is the origin of life itself.* [21]

<u>Dr. Andrew Knoll</u>: *We don't know how life started on this planet. We don't know exactly when it started, we don't know under what circumstances...I don't know if [we will ever solve the problem]...I imagine my grandchildren will still be sitting around saying it's a great mystery.* [22]

<u>Dr. Jack Szostak and Dr. Alonso Ricard</u>: *Every living cell, even the simplest bacterium, teems with molecular contraptions that would be the envy of any nanotechnologist...It is virtually impossible to imagine how a cell's machines...could have formed spontaneously from non-living matter...The actual nature of the first organisms and the exact circumstances of the origin of life may be forever lost to science...One of the most difficult and interesting mysteries surrounding the origin of life is exactly how the genetic material could have formed...* [23]

<u>Dr. Jack Szostak</u>: *Understanding how life emerged on Earth is one of the greatest challenges facing modern chemistry.* [24]

<u>Dr. Darrell Falk and the Biologos Website</u>: *From all that we know about the state of Earth 3 to 4 billion years ago and what we know about the complexity of the building blocks of life – DNA, RNA, amino acids, sugars – no entirely plausible hypothesis for the spontaneous origin of life has been found...the origin of life is simply a particularly compelling example of an unsolved mystery we would like to understand.* [25]

<u>Dr. H.P. Yockey</u>: *One must conclude that...a scenario describing the genesis of life on earth by chance and natural causes which can be accepted on the basis of fact and not faith has not yet been written.* [26]

<u>Dr. J. Craig Venter</u>: *(in a remark to Dr. Robert Shapiro about the absence of any plausible naturalistic theory of the origin of life) ...the theory behind theory is that you come up with truly testable ideas. Otherwise it's no different than faith. It might as well be a religion if there's no evidence for it.* [27]

<u>Dr. Freeman Dyson</u>: *First of all I wanted to talk a bit about origin of life...That has been a hobby of mine. We're all equally ignorant as far as I can see. That's why somebody like me can pretend to be an expert.* [28]

<u>Dr. Milton Wainwright</u>: *So much has been written about the Origin of Life that it might seem that little else needs to be said. Despite the lack of conclusive or convincing evidence it is generally*

accepted that life originated on Earth from simple chemicals...Are we getting any closer to an understanding of the origin of life?...The reality is that, despite the egos of some, the existence of life remains a mystery. It is not merely that biology is scratching the surface of this enigma; the reality is that we have yet to see the surface! [29]

<u>Dr. Gerald Kerkut</u>: *...the first assumption was that non-living things gave rise to living material. This is still an assumption...there is however, little evidence in favor of abiogenesis [life from non-life], and as yet we have no indication that it can be performed...it is therefore a matter of faith on the part of the biologist that abiogenesis did occur...* [30]

<u>Dr. Andrew Scott</u>: *In truth the mechanism of almost every major step, from chemical precursors up to the first recognizable cells, is the subject of either controversy or complete bewilderment. At the moment scientists certainly do not know how, or even if, life originated on earth from lifeless atoms.* [31]

<u>Dr. Christian DeDuve</u>: *How this momentous event occurred is still highly conjectural...* [32]

According to most experts, life arose naturally by way of processes entirely explainable by the laws of physics and chemistry. However, there is no definitive proof of this statement since the origin of life is not known. [33]

<u>Dr. Francois Jacob</u>: *It goes without saying that the emergence of this RNA and the transition to a DNA world implies an impressive number of stages, each more improbable than the previous one.* [34]

<u>Dr. Stanley Miller and Dr. Leslie Orgel</u>: *It must be admitted from the beginning that we do not know how life began.* [35]

<u>Dr. Lynn Margulis</u>: *How matter in a bath of energy (or how energy in a brew of matter) first accomplished the feat of life is not known...how did the first bacterium originate? Again, no one knows.* [36]
To go from bacterium to people is less of a step than to go from a

mixture of amino acids to a bacterium. [37]

Dr. Francis Crick: *Every time I write a paper on the origin of life, I determine I will never write another one, because there is too much speculation running after too few facts.* [38]

Dr. Ken Nealson: *Nobody understands the origin of life, if they say they do they are probably trying to fool you.* [39]

Dr. Graham Cairns-Smith: *The singular feature is in the gap between the simplest conceivable version of organisms as we know them, and components that the Earth might reasonably have been able to generate. This gap can be seen clearly now. It is enormous...Is it any wonder that [scientists] have found the origin of life to be utterly perplexing?* [40]

Dr. George Whitesides: *The Origin of Life. This problem is one of the big ones in science. It begins to place life, and us, in the universe. Most chemists believe as I do, that life emerged spontaneously from mixtures of molecules in the prebiotic Earth. How? I have no idea...On the basis of all chemistry I know, it seems to me astonishingly improbable.* [41]

Dr. Robert Hazen: *The epic history of life's chemical origins is woefully incomplete. Daunting gaps exist in our knowledge, and much of what we have learned is hotly debated and subject to conflicting interpretations.* [42]

...what we know about the origin of life is dwarfed by what we do not know...most of the pieces are missing...and we don't [even know] what the complete picture is supposed to look like. [43]

The Origin of Life Gordon Research Conference (Jan. 10-15, 2010, Galveston, Texas): *The origin and early development of life whether specifically on earth, or possibly elsewhere in the universe, remains one of the great unsolved scientific problems.* [44] (from the description of the conference on the Gordon Research Conferences website)

Nature.com blogs (Nature Publishing Group) – Anna Kushnir 3/9/2009: *The Origins of Life Initiative and the Harvard Alumni Association hosted a day long symposium at Harvard's Science Center entitled "The Future of Life" focused on discussing...what is life, and how did it begin? [Among the speakers were] J. Craig Venter...Jack Szostak...George Whitesides...George Church...It may be difficult to believe, but there was a common theme to this seeming cacophony of scientific expertise and discovery. The theme was "we just don't know." No one knows how life began – or even how to define "life" if you want to get all philosophical about it...Underneath it all, it was refreshing to hear a bunch of really smart folks say "we don't know." It was humbling and put things in a grandiose perspective. No one knows how we all got to be here, but the researchers in the Origins of Life Initiative and beyond are trying to find out.* [45]

Dr. Eugenie Scott: *Whether the proponents of [conflicting origin of life theories] finally convince their rivals as to the most plausible origin of the first replicating structures, it is clear that the origin of life is not a simple issue...If life itself is difficult to define, you can see why explaining its origin is also going to be difficult...there is not yet consensus on the sequence of events that led to living things.* (Talk about understatements!) [46]

Dr. Robert Shapiro: *The difference between a mixture of simple chemicals and a bacterium is much more profound than the gulf between a bacterium and an elephant.* [47]

The weakest point...is our lack of understanding of the origin of life. No evidence remains that we know of to explain the steps that started life here, billions of years ago. [48]

I'm always running out of metaphors to try and explain what the difficulty is. But suppose you took Scrabble sets, or any word game sets, blocks with letters containing every language on earth and you heap them together, and then you took a scoop and you scooped into that heap, and you flung it out on the lawn there and the letters fell into a line which contained the words, "to be or not to be that is the question," that is roughly the odds of an RNA molecule appearing on the earth. [49]

<u>Dr. Paul Davies</u>: *...what stands out as the central unsolved puzzle in the scientific account of life, is how the first microbe came to exist. Peering into life's innermost workings serves only to deepen the mystery. The living cell is the most complex system of its size known to mankind...How did something so immensely complicated, so finessed, so exquisitely clever, come into being all on its own? How can mindless molecules, capable of only pushing and pulling their immediate neighbors cooperate to form something as ingenious as a living organism?...the problem of how and where life began is one of the great outstanding mysteries of science...many investigators feel uneasy about stating in public that the origin of life is a mystery, even though behind closed doors they freely admit they are baffled...*[50]

<u>The Scripps Research Institute (Press Release) – "Top Scientists Explore the Origin of Life in Annual Lasker Lecture at Scripps Research Institute Florida Campus" (3/16/2010)</u>: *[Dr. Brian] Paegel, an assistant chemistry professor at Scripps Research Institute's Florida Campus, described...his research, "Both Jack [Szostak] and I are working on how life* **might** *have begun on our planet because figuring that out would begin to answer most of the questions we have about ourselves and our universe...it would explain whether or not we are unique in the universe, or if this really is the natural consequence of oxygen, carbon, and other organic material coming together.*[51]

<u>Dr's Stochel, Brindel, Macyk, Stasicka, Szacilowski</u>: *Most of the biochemical processes found within all the living organisms are well understood at the molecular level, whereas the origin of life remains one of the most vexing issues in chemistry, biology, and philosophy...Numerous theories tackle the origin of life, but there is no direct evidence supporting any of them.*[52]

<u>Dr. Christopher McKay</u>: *The origin of life remains a scientific mystery...we do not know how life originated on the Earth.*[53]

<u>Dr. Gerald Joyce and Dr. Michael Robertson</u>: *...the concept of an RNA World has been a milestone in the scientific study of life's origins. While this concept does not explain how life originated, it has helped to guide scientific thinking and has served*

to focus experimental efforts. [54]

Dr. Klaus Dose: *More than 30 years of experimentation on the origin of life in the fields of chemical and molecular evolution have led to a better perception of the immensity of the problem of the origin of life on earth rather than to its solution. At present, all discussion on principal theories and experiments in the field either end in a stalemate or in a confession of ignorance.* [55]

Dr. Werner Arber: *Although a biologist, I must confess that I do not understand how life came about...The most primitive cell may require at least several hundred different specific biological macromolecules. How such already quite complex structures may have come together, remains a mystery to me.* [56]

Dr.'s E. Ben Jacob, Y. Aharonov, Y. Shapira: *Bacteria, being the first form of life on earth, had to devise ways to synthesize the complex organic molecules required for life...3.5 billion years have passed and the existence of higher organisms depends on this unique bacterial know-how. Even for us, with all our scientific knowledge and technological advances, the ways in which bacteria solved this fundamental requirement for life are still a mystery.* [57]

Dr. Harold P. Klein: *The simplest bacterium is so damn complicated from the point of view of a chemist that it is almost impossible to imagine how it happened.* [58]

Dr. Frank Sonleitner: **Modern ideas about the [emergence] of living things from non-living components...[have] not yet come anywhere near answering all our questions about the process...**[59] **(NCSE Website)**

Dr. Andrew Scott: *It is this combative atmosphere which sometimes encourages scientists writing and speaking about the origin of life to become as dogmatic and bigoted as the creationist opponents they so despise.* [60] [I hope Dr. Sonleitner is listening]

Dr. Stuart Kauffman: *Anyone who tells you that he or she knows how life started on the sere Earth some 3.45 billion years ago is **a fool*** *or a knave.* [61] [I *really* hope Dr. Sonleitner is listening]

I don't know if it is *impossible* to know anything scientific about the origin of life, but it's rather obvious that at the present time *Scientists* (including Sonleitner himself) don't know anything scientific about the origin of life.

Intelligent Design is not an "explanation"

Sonleitner goes beyond other scientists who state matter of factly that life started naturalistically and then simply ignore the issue of a creator. Sonleitner is not afraid to directly confront the issue and he takes the bull by the horns. He boldly informs us that the proposition of a supernatural creator is invalid because "it's not an explanation."

2.) "*Everything about the creation is claimed to be supernatural... hence this idea is not an explanation (let alone a scientific one.)*" – I understand what he means when he says it is not a *scientific* explanation, we have already discussed that. What does he mean when he says that the concept of a supernatural creator (*i.e.,* a creator outside of the physical universe) of life on earth it is "not an explanation?" Why is it not an explanation?

Websters Third New International Dictionary: "explain": *To give reason for or cause of – account for (he was unable to "explain" his strange conduct)*
American Heritage Dictionary: *To offer reasons for or a cause of*

It seems clear to me that a supernatural creator fits the definition of an "explanation" very precisely. It is proposed as "the cause of, the reason for, and accounts for," the first living organism. Sonleitner can say that he *disagrees* with the explanation or that in his opinion it is the *wrong* explanation, but what could he possibly mean when he says "it is not an explanation?" He makes this strange assertion more than once. Later in the same article, when explaining the difference between *Origin of Life* and Darwinian evolution, he writes:

The fact that there is much to learn about how the first living creatures originated has little to do with the truth or falsity of evolution. Thus an intelligent designer could have made the first forms and then they evolved. **But, as I have previously discussed, that doesn't explain anything.**

Sonleitner conveys the same idea several paragraphs later using slightly different language, "[the source of life's origin] can't be intelligent design! We have already mentioned that this supernatural belief denies the possibility of understanding life's origin."

What is he talking about? If I reasonably conclude that *chance* and *natural physical laws* cannot explain the origin of life – and that leads me to conclude that the most reasonable explanation for the existence of the first living organism is a supernatural creator – that means I *understand* that life's origin is caused by a creative act of a supernatural creator.

In vain will we search Sonleitner's words for an underlying rational principle that clarifies his strange usage of the terms, "understanding" and "explanation." However, once we accept that he is issuing two faith- based proclamations, everything falls into place. If as an article of faith you have declared "a supernatural creator" to be arbitrarily excluded from the category of "explanation" (and who gives a damn what those blasphemous dictionaries say), then it can't possibly "explain anything." If as an article of faith, "understanding" only applies to those things considered to be in "the realm of science" (as DeDuve phrased it), then obviously a supernatural creator "denies the possibility of *understanding* life's origin." Of course, how silly of me.

Does Dr. Sonleitner believe in miracles?

3.) "Hence this idea...is [just] a reaffirmation of a religious miracle"

How would Sonleitner feel about a non-religious miracle?

Dr. Francis Crick: An honest man, armed with all the knowledge available to us now, could only state that in some sense, the origin of life appears at the moment to be **almost a miracle.** [62]

...to produce this **miracle** of molecular construction, all the cell need do is to string together the amino acids...in the correct order. This is a complicated biochemical process, [accomplished by] a molecular assembly line, using instructions in the form of nucleic acid tape... [63]

Dr. Graham Cairns-Smith: Now I cannot deny all these possibilities: **that life on the Earth may be a miracle,** or a freak, or an alien infection. And I agree that the confidence was misplaced that supposed in the fifties that the answer to the origin of life would appear in some footnote to the answer to the question of how organisms work... [64]

It is not just the sheer size of even the smallest libraries [of the simplest organisms], it is not just that nucleotide units are rather complex...and difficult to join together...it is not just the need for enzymes...it is not just that ribosomes are so very sophisticated...There seems to be a more fundamental difficulty. Any conceivable kind of organism would have to contain messages of some sort and equipment for reading and reprinting the messages; any conceivable organism would thus have seem to have to be packed with machinery and as such **need a miracle (or something)** for the first of its kind to have appeared. [65]

Dr. Robert Shapiro: ...With similar considerations in mind, Gerald F. Joyce of the Scripps Research Institute and Leslie Orgel of the Salk Institute concluded that the spontaneous appearance of RNA chains on the lifeless Earth "would have been a **near miracle.**" I would extend this conclusion to all of the proposed RNA substitutes that I mentioned above [that their appearance would have also been a **near miracle**]... [66]

The improbability involved in generating even one bacterium is so large that it reduces all considerations of time and space to nothingness. Given such odds, the time until the black holes evaporate and the space to the ends of the universe would make no difference at all...we would truly be waiting for a **miracle.** [67]

Dr. Euan Nisbet: Life is improbable, and it may be unique to this planet, but nevertheless it did begin, and it is thus our task to discover how the **miracle** happened. [68] (Professor of Geology, University of London)

Dr. Paul Davies: ...the various components fit together to form a smoothly functioning whole, like an elaborate factory production line – the **miracle** of life is not that it is made of nanotools, but that these tiny diverse parts are integrated in a highly organized way. [69]

...abiogenesis [life from non-life] strikes many as virtually **miraculous**...It is even conceivable that scientists will one day create life of some sort in the laboratory, and thus...demonstrate convincingly that a **miracle** isn't needed. [66]

You might get the impression from what I have written not only that the origin of life is virtually impossible, but that life itself is impossible...fortunately for us, our cells contain sophisticated chemical-repair-and-construction mechanisms, handy sources of chemical energy to drive processes uphill, and enzymes with special properties that can smoothly assemble complex molecules from fragments...But the primordial soup lacked these convenient cohorts of cooperating chemicals...So what is the answer? Is life a **miracle** after all? [71]

Gee, forget about creationists! Nobel Prize winner Francis Crick, organic chemist and molecular biologist Dr. G. Cairns-Smith, Dr. Robert Shapiro, Professor Emeritus of Chemistry at N.Y. University, Dr. Euan Nisbet, Professor of Geology, and Dr. Paul Davies, physicist (whose book is titled *The Fifth Miracle: The Search for the Origin and Meaning of Life*), don't seem to be embarrassed to mention *Origin of Life* theories and *miracle* in the same breath.

I'm quite aware that none of these scientists believe life came about by a divine act of creation. In fact, all of them still believe that one day a scientific solution will be found. (It would be interesting to find out how long they are prepared to wait.) However, when they are confronted with their own paucity of real knowledge of how life started and the lack of clear direction to scientifically find a solution, they find that the word "miracle" becomes a very handy, descriptively accurate, and a highly appropriate noun to use when describing the dizzying complexity of the simplest living organisms. It seems to me that in light of all of the above, Sonleitner should lighten up a little and perhaps be prepared to open up his *extremely* narrow mind a bit.

<u>We now continue with Objection #1 — A Supernatural Creator is Non-Scientific</u>

Dr. Robert Shapiro — Skeptic about conventional Origin of Life Theories — A True Believer in the Faith of Scientific Naturalism

Dr. Robert Shapiro (among many other accomplishments) is the author of *Origins: A Skeptics Guide to the Creation of Life on Earth*. In it he argues quite forcefully that some of the commonly held theories (RNA World and related theories) among *Origin of Life* researchers are highly inadequate and can be considered to be in the category of wishful thinking. Despite his skepticism about these theories, when it comes to dealing with the possibility of a creator, Dr. Shapiro toes the party line:

> Dear Mr. Evans,
> ...I agree with him [Professor Michael Behe, proponent of Intelligent Design] that conventional origin-of-life theory is deeply flawed. I disagreed with him about the idea that one needed to invoke an intelligent designer or a supernatural cause to find an answer. I do not support intelligent design theories. **I believe that better science will provide the needed answers.** Sincerely Yours, Robert Shapiro [from an email to "Skip" Evans of the NCSE on the Pandas Thumb website] [72]

Dr. Shapiro is not afraid to challenge his scientific colleagues. In a separate email on the same site, he admits that those who agree with his own particular theory about the origin of life ["metabolism first"] are "a minority in the field." Despite this professional courage he will not allow himself to be guilty of heresy by considering the possibility of a creator. He proudly proclaims his "belief" [how scientific!] that science will answer all our questions. Is there any good reason why Dr. Shapiro could not have stated something along the following lines?

> At the present there is no scientific theory that adequately describes how life originated. There are highly competent scientists like Professor Behe who claim that the only reasonable explanation is an intelligent designer; *i.e.*, a living cell is simply too complex and sophisticated to have originated through any naturalistic process. While this is a distinct possibility, I do not believe we have

exhausted all the naturalistic possibilities for the origin of life. Until it is clear to me that we have reached that point I am not prepared to support intelligent design theories.

Even if he *had* written those exact words, I would still have disagreed with him, but at least it would be clear that we are not dealing with a man who has shut off his mind to ideas just because they are "politically incorrect" among his colleagues.

What is so attractive about outer space that causes a rational, logical scientist to prefer the "Star Trek" approach to Origin of life, while refusing to even consider a Creator?

In the following passages from Shapiro's book, *Planetary Dreams*, I have underlined those parts upon which I will comment:

The discovery of a second separate origin of life within a single Solar System would strongly suggest that the laws of nature include some principle (I shall call it the Life Principle) which favors the generation of life...The entire history of the Universe can then be interpreted in terms of a process called Cosmic Evolution. A new vision can be built around this concept that provides a sense of purpose for our own future.

The weakest point in this belief structure is our lack of understanding of the origin of life. No evidence remains that we know of to explain the steps that started life here...If a broadly based Life Principle exists...then some signs of its handiwork should be detectable on the other worlds of our system... [73]

Is there such thing as a "Life Principle"?

1.) "The discovery of a second separate origin of life within a single Solar System would strongly suggest that the laws of nature include some principle (I shall call it the Life Principle) which favors the generation of life."

Let's review the simple facts: No scientist has any real idea how life started on the planet Earth. Dr. Stuart Kauffman went so far as to label one who claims to know *a fool or a knave*. If life were found on another planet, it would not change anything at all. Scientists would still be completely baffled as to how life started; the only difference would be that now, life on *two* planets would be inexplicable. Until scientists have demonstrated empirically that the laws of physics and chemistry can account for the natural formation of a fully functioning bacterium (or at the very least, a naturally emergent self-replicating molecule capable of evolving) the only reasonable conclusion would be that the creator also created life on a second planet. Or alternatively, it would be at least as reasonable a possibility as the one presented by Shapiro.

I have another question for Dr. Shapiro: Why would you propose an unproven, non-scientific, mystical theory like "The Life Principle," and present it as if it were science? If you are speaking as a mystic, or if you want to present your own personal stream of consciousness, please go ahead; but don't misuse your impressive credentials in chemistry by trying to palm this off as scientific theory. One could suggest this is an example of what Niles Eldredge was referring to when he stated that some scientists think they have "special access to the truth...throwing down scientific thunderbolts from Olympian heights."

2.) "The weakest point in this belief structure is our lack of understanding of the origin of life...if a broadly based life principle exists...then some signs of its handiwork should be detectable on the other worlds of our system."

Dr. Shapiro admits to some "weak" points in his "belief structure"

Dr. Shapiro states that the "weakest point in this belief structure is our lack of understanding of the origin of life...etc." Before analyzing this weak point, let's briefly review (from the above cited passage in Shapiro's book), the actual *content* of this "belief structure" that he is referring to. It consists of:

A) The discovery of life on another planet.
B) The existence of something called "The Life Principle" which favors generation of life.
C) An understanding of how this "Life Principle" causes life to arise naturally.

D) Based on **A**, **B** and **C** – understanding the history of the universe and societal development according to a process called "Cosmic Evolution" and a "new vision" built around this "Cosmic Evolution" that "provides a sense of purpose for our own future."

Here are the "weak" points in Dr. Shapiro's belief structure

A) There is no meaningful evidence at all that life exists on other planets, and even if there were, there would still be no scientific clarity as to how it got there.
B) There is no empirical evidence of something called "The Life Principle" which drives inanimate matter to organize itself into living organisms.
C) There is no empirical evidence that life can arise naturally from inorganic matter
D) Since the concept of "Cosmic Evolution" is built on the truth of **A**, **B** and **C**, there is no evidence that such a thing as "Cosmic Evolution" exists.
Besides that, Shapiro's "belief structure" is pretty sound.

Dr. Shapiro's bold prediction

At the beginning of 2006, Dr. Shapiro predicted the following:

> We shall understand the origin of life within the next five years...two very different groups will find this development dangerous...many scientists have been attracted by the RNA World theory....they would not be pleased [if Shapiro's **"Metabolism First"** theory of origin of life turned out to be true]...Those who advocate creationism and intelligent design would feel that another pillar of their belief system was under attack...A successful scientific theory would leave one less task for God to accomplish: the origin of life would be a natural (and perhaps frequent) result of the physical laws that govern this universe... [74]

I have to admit that it is quite bold of Shapiro, not only to predict that within five years (before January 2011) a naturalistic explanation of the origin of life will be discovered, but he even tells us who will be upset when this happens. What makes it bold is the fact that at the present time no meaningful evidence at all exists for his theory. Perhaps you'll recall from Chapter 3 that on January 22, 2008, Dr. Leslie Orgel published an article claiming that Shapiro's theory was based on "if pigs could fly" chemistry. To complicate matters further, an article on the *Science Daily* website (January 9, 2010) appeared with the following headline: "New Study Contradicts the "Metabolism First" Hypothesis." My question is: Who will be upset if the origin of life is *not* understood by January 2011? I don't think it will make any difference at all. No committed believer in the dogmas of Scientific Naturalism is going to allow something that trivial to shake their faith.

Objection #3 — Science Will Find an Answer (i.e. be patient we're working on it)

What follows below is not a joke:

www.us.net/life/ — "The Origin of Life Prize"
Description and Purpose of the Prize
Lifeorigin.info

"The Origin-of-Life Prize", will be awarded for proposing a highly plausible* *mechanism* **for the spontaneous rise of** *genetic instructions* **in nature sufficient to give rise to life. To win, the explanation must be consistent with empirical biochemical, kinetic, and thermodynamic concepts...and be published in a well-respected, peer-reviewed science journal.**

The one-time prize will be paid to the winner(s) as a twenty year annuity...the annuity consists of $50,000 per year for twenty consecutive years, totaling one million dollars in payments. [emphasis in original]

The fact that until now no scientist has been able to present a "highly plausible" explanation for the naturalistic origin of life is the atheist's and agnostic's problem, not mine. If you discover a way to empirically and plausibly demonstrate that life could have originated from inorganic matter naturally,

---

* "plausible" – *having an appearance of truth or reason; seemingly worthy of approval or acceptance; credible; believable* (from Dictionary.com)

give me a call (and enjoy the fifty grand a year).

In the meantime, I hope you'll excuse me if I don't sit breathlessly by the phone like some teenage girl who is waiting for a boy to call and ask her to the prom.

Chapter 5

Actually, The Watchmaker Has 20/20 Vision

(Objection #4) Philosophical Objections to "The Argument from Design"

The simplest and easiest to understand of all the arguments ever offered by believers is the *Argument from Design*. The argument is remarkably simple, and though a good portion of Chapter 3 dealt with the *Argument from Design*, we will restate it here in a slightly different form. It goes as follows: The existence of a suit implies the existence of the tailor who made the suit. The existence of a bicycle implies the existence of the mechanic (or mechanics, or a factory with workers), who put the bicycle together. The existence of a poem on a piece of paper implies the existence of the poet who created that poem. In other words, the *suit itself* is the proof of the existence of the intelligent creator of the suit (the same principle, of course, applies to the bicycle and poem), no other evidence is necessary. There are levels of design, sophistication, and functional complexity that the human mind simply refuses to accept could be accounted for by any undirected process. How to precisely define such levels is not our topic of discussion. It is clear however, that a suit, bicycle, poem by Robert Frost, and *a living bacterium*, are certainly well over that line.

The entire plot of the classic film, *2001: A Space Odyssey* is based on this obvious principle. At a dramatic moment in the film, when a rectangular monolith is discovered buried on the moon, it is clear to those who discover it (and accepted as absolutely logical and reasonable by everyone watching the movie) that this is unmistakable proof of alien life. After all, a precisely measured monolith couldn't possibly have made itself or "evolved naturally." The rest of the film is about the search for the aliens who constructed and buried the monolith in the first place.

The human body is an incredible piece of machinery; who put it together? It certainly required a great deal more sophistication to build a human being than to construct a rectangular monolith. The existence of highly sophisticated living organisms implies a highly sophisticated designer of these organisms. Believers call this designer, *the Creator or God*. What could possibly be the flaw in such an argument?

Extremely Important: Nobody disagrees with The Argument from Design

Before we actually deal with the objections raised by atheists and skeptics, I want to repeat what I wrote in the subtitle of this paragraph: *Nobody disagrees with the Argument from Design.* There is nobody in their right mind who does not understand that the existence of the suit itself proves the existence of the tailor who made the suit and that the poem itself proves the existence of the author of that poem. In the debate between skeptics and believers the disagreement is not about the validity of the Argument from Design. The argument itself is undeniably true. The point of contention is the following: Does the incontrovertibly true Argument from Design apply to living organisms? Skeptics raise two basic objections to applying the Argument from Design to the world of living systems: **1)** ideas found in the writings of a highly influential 18th century Scottish philosopher by the name of David Hume, and **2)** Darwinian Evolution. We will deal with both shortly.

David Hume and Dialogues Concerning Natural Religion

Dr. Frank Sonleitner and Dr. Julian Baggini claim that Hume's philosophy invalidates any attempt to apply the Argument from Design to the living world:

> Hume, in his book *Dialogues Concerning Natural Religion*, shows that the Argument from Design...is illogical and contrived. Norman Kemp Smith, late professor of metaphysics at Edinburgh, in his introduction to Hume,

explicitly points out that organisms are not like designed, manufactured objects.[1] (Sonleitner, NCSE Website)

Furthermore, as David Hume points out, we can only hypothesize [a designer of a watch], because we know by experience what the cause of watches are. We have no experience of causes of the universe, so we are not justified in making any assumption about who or what they might be.[2] (Baggini)

Hume's argument is simple; we can know clearly that a suit is made by a tailor, because we have *experience* of suits being made by tailors. However,

Will any man tell me with a serious contrivance that an orderly universe must arise from some thought and art...because we have **experience** of it? To ascertain this reasoning, it were requisite, that we had **experience** of the origin of worlds...[3] (Hume, *Dialogues Concerning Natural Religion*)

Hume is completely irrelevant to our discussion

I find it hard to believe that any intelligent person could seriously consider Hume's argument as having any relevance to the matter at hand. We are not discussing the "causes of the universe" or the "origin of worlds," *i.e.,* things of which we have no experience.* We are talking about highly complex living organisms that are meticulously studied, catalogued, and experimented on day and night by scientists all over the world. Let me give a few simple examples.

The Filter and the Pump — Most Definitely Within Our Experience

Suppose someone is unfortunate enough to suffer from impaired kidneys and must be hooked up to a dialysis machine several times a week. In a moment of frustration he barges into the R & D department of a biomedical engineering firm and demands that they manufacture an artificial kidney that can be inserted where a normal kidney goes. The sympathetic engineer

---

* For arguments sake I am assuming that Hume's argument makes sense. I have purposely left aside the philosophical/academic point as to whether or not Hume's argument is actually valid on its own merits.

tells him that our current technology is unable to produce such a device and the best we have to offer is the dialysis machine.

It would be foolish to suggest that the construction of the filtering device we call a kidney is out of our experience when we actually build kidneys; we just call them dialysis machines. They perform the exact same function as real kidneys, which are essentially nothing more than highly sophisticated filters, except that we experience and understand them well enough to know that they are primitive compared to an actual kidney. Experience teaches us that highly sophisticated filtering devices do not make themselves, any more than suits make themselves. Clearly, Hume's argument is not applicable.

There is another mechanical device that is well within our experience: the electric pump. Electric pumps do not make themselves. The human heart is nothing more and nothing less than an electric pump. It operates on the exact same principles of physics as every other electric pump on the planet Earth. Our bio-medical engineering firms also build "primitive" pumps to replace the heart. It is absurd to invoke Hume's argument when we are discussing the heart.

There are endless examples of systems of which we have experience

The truth, of course, is that the kidney and heart are just two of many examples of systems that exist in the living world of which we have experience. We could have mentioned the navigational systems of birds and sea turtles, the sonar of bats, and the electrical generating systems of eels and other animals to name just a few. The rational conclusion must be that these incredibly complex systems could only have been designed and constructed by a super-intelligent creator. Eliminating Hume from the picture brings us to the second argument that skeptics use to claim that the Argument from Design does not apply to the world of living systems: Darwinian Evolution. I do not want to spend much time on this topic because I am going to keep my word. I did say, at the beginning of Chapter 3, that for arguments sake I would concede the fact of Neo-Darwinian Evolution. *Done!*

Before Darwin even Richard Dawkins could not deny the existence of a Creator

Before the theory of evolution, however, one needed an enormous amount of almost fanatical determination *not* to believe in a creator. Remember, Darwinian evolution does not invalidate the Argument from Design; it simply offers an alternative explanation for the functional complexity of living systems. Christopher Hitchens begrudgingly concedes that before Darwin, the "default position" of a creator was reasonable:

> Before Charles Darwin revolutionized our entire concept of our origins...many scientists and philosophers and mathematicians took what might be called the default position and...professed...that the order and predictability of the universe seemed indeed to imply a designer...This compromise was a logical and rational one for its time...[4]

Richard Dawkins also admits to the obvious truth of this point. However, unlike Hitchens (a non-scientist) who downplays pre-Darwin belief in God by describing it as a "default position" and a "compromise;" Dawkins states categorically that before Darwin he "could not imagine" being an atheist:

> I feel more in common with the Reverend William Paley** than I do with the distinguished modern philosopher, a well known atheist, with whom I once discussed the matter at dinner. I said I could not imagine being an atheist at any time before 1859, when Darwin's Origin of the Species was published. "What about Hume?" replied the philosopher. "How did Hume explain the organized complexity of the living world?" I asked. "He didn't" said the philosopher, "Why does it need any special explanation?" Paley knew it needed a special explanation; Darwin knew it, and I suspect that in his heart of hearts, my philosophical companion knew it too. [5] [author's note: I would also add that no *Origin of Life* chemist or microbiologist – people who deeply and intimately understand the fantastic complexity of the simplest living organisms – takes the esoteric arguments of David Hume seriously.]

Dawkins tells us that Darwin made it possible to be an "intellectually fulfilled atheist." [6] However, we shall soon see that just as Hume is irrelevant to our question, so too Darwin is irrelevant

---

** Rev. William Paley, an 18th century religious philosopher who authored one of the classic presentations of the Argument from Design.

to our question (regarding the existence of a creator). Even assuming the truth of Neo-Darwinian theory, the atheist will still find himself sitting naked and shivering, bereft of any intellectual clothing.

The amazing microscopic digital information system

In *River Out of Eden,* Dawkins describes the intricate functioning of genetic coding in the living cell:

> After Watson and Crick we know that genes themselves...are living strings of pure digital information. What is more they are truly digital, in the full and strong sense of computers and compact discs, not in the weak sense of the nervous system. The genetic code is not a binary code as in computers...but a quaternary code, with four symbols. **The machine code of the genes is uncannily computer-like.** Apart from differences in jargon, the pages of a molecular biology journal might be interchanged with those of a computer engineering journal. Our genetic system, which is the universal system for all life on the planet is digital to the core...DNA characters are copied with an accuracy that rivals anything modern engineers can do...**DNA messages...are...pure digital code.** [7]

Dr. Paul Davies on the same subject:

> In a living organism we see the power of software, or information processing, refined to an incredible degree...the problem of the origin of life reduces to one of understanding how encoded software emerged spontaneously from hardware. How did it happen? How did nature "go digital?" [8]

Microsoft CEO Bill Gates, echoes Dawkins' and Davies' description of the genetic coding in the cell, "DNA is like a computer program but far, far more advanced than any software we've ever created." [9]

Darwinian Evolution Simply Begs the Question

For the truth-seeking individual, the very best that Darwinian evolution can tell us is the following: Once you have in place a fantastically complex piece of molecular machinery called a living cell, which has at it's core an astonishingly sophisticated self-replicating system, which is based on the storage, retrieval, and decoding of enormous amounts of pure digital information – given enough time – the *interactions* between this nanotool filled organism, its "uncannily computer-like" genetic code and its environment (interactions we call "natural selection") are able to produce an astounding variety of forms of biological organisms. All varieties of life are possible – if, and only if – this amazing piece of machinery is in place. *How did it get there?*

Lest anyone have the impression that the compelling and profoundly significant nature of this line of reasoning can only be appreciated by those with inclinations toward religion, here is distinguished philosopher Thomas Nagel (who describes himself as being "just as much an outsider to religion as Richard Dawkins"):

> The entire apparatus of evolutionary explanation therefore depends on the prior existence of genetic material with these remarkable properties...since the existence of this material or something like it is a precondition of the possibility of evolution, evolutionary theory cannot explain its existence. We are therefore faced with a problem...we have explained the complexity of organic life in terms of something that is itself just as functionally complex as what we originally set out to explain. So the problem is just pushed back a step: how did such a thing come into existence? [10]

The Argument from Design does not disappear with Darwin: it is simply refocused with a vengeance

As it turns out, Darwinian evolution is not, as the skeptic would have us believe, a testimony to what can emerge from undirected processes; it is a testimony to the unimaginably awesome capabilities and potential contained in the first living cell and its genetic code. A paradigm-shifting insight emerges from all this: Contrary to popular belief, not only is Darwinian evolution not the *cause* or *explanation* of the staggering complexity of life on this planet; Darwinian evolution itself is a process which is the *result* of the staggering complexity of life on this planet. Human beings who are seeking the truth about the existence of a Creator should stop wasting their time and energy arguing about Archaeopteryx and the 2nd Law of Thermodynamics. It is all beside the point. Darwinian evolution most definitely *does not* provide an escape hatch from the challenge that Dawkins articulated to his atheist philosopher colleague: "How [do we] explain the organized complexity of the living world?" All existing life is nothing more than a variation on a theme. All the "organized complexity" of life is a variation on the "organized complexity" of the first living organism. This is what Professor Emeritus of Chemistry at New York University, Dr. Robert Shapiro, meant when he said that "The difference between a simple mixture of chemicals and a bacterium, is much more profound than the gulf between a bacterium and an elephant." The *Argument from Design* does not disappear with Darwin; it is simply refocused with a vengeance:

> What stands out as the central unsolved puzzle in the scientific account of life – is how the first microbe came to exist. Peering into life's innermost workings serves only to deepen the mystery. The living cell is the most complex system of its size known to mankind…ingenious marvels of construction and control, with a fine-tuning and complexity as yet unmatched by any human engineering…The problem of the origin of life reduces to one of understanding how encoded software emerged spontaneously from hardware. How did it happen? How did nature "go digital?"…How did something so immensely complicated, so finessed, so exquisitely clever, come into being all on its own? How can mindless molecules, capable of only pushing and pulling their immediate neighbors, cooperate to form something as ingenious as a living organism? (Dr. Paul Davies)

The only relevant question is: *How did life begin?* Darwin has nothing at all to say on the subject. Darwinian evolution does not even pretend to address the issue. Chance, as we've seen, is not an answer. Science simply has no answer. Just as the suit itself is the proof of the tailor, and the poem itself is proof of the poet, the astoundingly complex microbe *itself*, with its fully digital software, is the proof of *its* creator. The who's-buried-in-Grant's-tomb, right-in-front-of-your-eyes, wake-up-and-smell-the-coffee, it's-staring-you-in-the-face answer is that life is *created*.

The Last Stand of Richard Dawkins

In the final analysis, the atheist's denial of God,* despite his propagandist smokescreen to the contrary, has nothing to do with *Science*. We have shown clearly that the two giant battleships in the scientific arsenal of the atheist, Darwinian evolution and Origin of Life, are nothing more than floundering, leaky rowboats (if even that much). Evolution is irrelevant, and Origin of Life clearly points to a creator. As it turns out, the ultimate battle between believer and non-believer will not be fought in the scientific arena at all. Stripped of the mighty sword of Darwinism and his Scientific Naturalism body armor, the atheist retreats and barricades himself in his ideological version of the Alamo. "Dawkins Last Stand" will be fought with the only weapon remaining: a *philosophical* argument that he calls "The Ultimate Boeing 747 Gambit."

Fly the friendly skies of Dawkins Airlines; The Ultimate Boeing 747 Gambit

This argument's intriguing name derives from the following analogy used by Sir Fred Hoyle to describe the extreme improbability of a chance origin of the first living organism on earth:

> A junkyard contains all the bits and pieces of a Boeing 747, dismembered and in disarray. A whirlwind happens to blow through the yard. What is the chance that after its passage a fully assembled 747, ready to fly, will be found standing there? So small as to be negligible, even if a tornado were to blow through enough junkyards to fill the whole Universe. [11]

Before we present Dawkins' actual argument, let's summarize Hoyle's argument and its logical consequences. Sir Fred is telling us that the probability of life originating on earth by chance is as probable as a tornado sweeping through a junkyard and assembling a 747. Therefore, if you find yourself face to face with a fully assembled Boeing 747 you can be absolutely certain it was not assembled by a tornado; it was assembled by an Intelligent Designer. Carrying the analogy to its logical conclusion: If you

---

* I want to again remind the reader what I stated in Chapter 2; this book deals with the existence of God, not the truth or falsehood of any particular religious faith.

find yourself face to face with a living bacterium (which is at least as functionally complex as a 747), you can be absolutely certain it was not assembled by random forces "sweeping through" a bunch of chemicals. It was assembled in the same manner as a 747, namely, by an intelligent designer. It's really a very simple and easy to understand analogy. Somehow, Dawkins manages to turn it into an impenetrable smokescreen.

And now Dawkins:

> Actually the argument from improbability properly deployed, comes close to proving that God does not exist. My name for the statistical demonstration that God almost certainly does not exist is the Ultimate Boeing 747 Gambit...Hoyle said the probability of life originating on earth is no greater than the chance that a hurricane, sweeping through a scrap yard, would have the luck to assemble a Boeing 747...However statistically improbable the entity you seek to explain by invoking a designer, the designer himself has got to be at least as improbable. God is the ultimate 747. [12]

Dawkins further clarifies the idea:

> Seen clearly, intelligent design will turn out to be a redoubling of the problem. Once again, this is because the designer himself immediately raises the bigger problem of his own origin...Any entity capable of intelligently designing something as improbable as a Dutchman's Pipe [a type of flower], would have to be even more improbable than a Dutchman's Pipe...chance and design both fail as solutions to the problem of statistical improbability, because one of them is the problem, and the other regresses to it. [13] *(The God Delusion)*

Mayday! Mayday! Boeing 747 going down!

There is an obvious flaw in the logic of the Ultimate Boeing 747 Gambit. Let's rephrase the above cited paragraph from *The God Delusion* and apply Dawkins' logic to the Texas Instruments business calculator that is sitting on my desk as I write these words. It will immediately become clear that something has gone terribly wrong with Dawkins' attempt to cling to his non-belief:

Seen clearly intelligent design will turn out to be a redoubling of the problem. This is because the designer himself immediately raises the bigger problem of his own origin. Any entity capable of designing something as improbable as a *Texas Instruments business calculator* would have to be even more improbable than the business calculator itself...chance and design both fail as solutions to the problem of statistical improbability, because one of them is the problem, and the other regresses to it.

Of course we know this is ridiculous. An intelligent entity purposefully and consciously designed and built the calculator. Applying the same logic to a bacterium is more absurd, in light of the fact that a bacterium is extraordinarily more functionally complex than a calculator. Only a willful designer could produce a digitally controlled self-replicating molecular machine like a bacterium.

The confusion in Dawkins' argument stems from his subtle, but significant misrepresentation of Hoyle's analogy. Here is how Dawkins presents Hoyle's words: *"Hoyle said the probability of life originating on earth is no greater than the chance that a hurricane sweeping through a scrap yard, would have the luck to assemble a Boeing 747."* That is not what Hoyle said. Hoyle said that the probability of life originating on earth *by chance* is comparable to the probability of a hurricane assembling a 747 *by chance*. However, the probability of a 747 being assembled *by design* and the probability of life originating on earth *by design* is extremely high. If we keep that in mind the rest of Dawkins' argument makes sense. In other words, if it is statistically improbable that a 747 could have originated *by chance*, then it is an even greater statistical improbability that the *designer* of the 747 originated *by chance*. I agree wholeheartedly. Both the 747 and the human creators of the 747 are here not by chance, but *by design!*

The problem is not if the bacterium is designed and created; it is as obviously designed and created as much as a laptop computer is obviously designed and created. There is no escaping that simple fact. Just as there clearly exists a designer of the 747, and just as there clearly exists a designer of the calculator, so too, there clearly exists a designer of the first bacterium and its genetic code. The philosophical problem that must be addressed is the following: *How do we escape from the dilemma of the infinitely regressing series of creators (i.e.,* whoever created me would have to be at least as complex and sophisticated as I am, and therefore he would also need someone to create him, and so on.)? To state this dilemma in a slightly different way: Since all agree that at one time life did not exist and now it does exist, there must be an actual *beginning* to the process, it cannot go back infinitely.

Only complex "material" configurations need a creator

One of the skills stressed in Talmudic learning is that when posing a logical difficulty, one must struggle to formulate the question as precisely as possible. Many times, the largest part of finding a solution to a difficulty is asking precisely the right question. Dawkins did not accurately pose the question; therefore it is not surprising that he is getting inaccurate answers. Properly presented, the question is as follows:

Any functionally complex and purposefully arranged form of physical matter (i.e., a Boeing 747, a calculator, or a bacterium), must itself have a creator at least as complex as the object in question. How do we (or can we) escape an infinite regression of creators?

That which demands and requires a preceding creator is a complex arrangement of *physical matter*. With this precise formulation of the question, the answer becomes obvious. At some point in the progression, we are faced with the inescapable conclusion that there must be a creator who is not physical matter at all; a creator who does not need to be created; a creator who is not subject to the limitations of cause and effect. There must be a creator who is the first, who is the beginning of it all. There must be a creator who is outside of the physical universe. A creator who is outside of the physical universe, not existing in time and space, and composed of neither matter nor energy, does not require a preceding creator. There is nothing that came before him. He *created* time, he does not exist in time; there *is* no "before". ("What happened before the big bang? The answer is there was no "before". Time itself began at the big bang." [14] Physicist, Dr. Paul Davies) *We* are created; along with time, space, matter, and energy. *We* are subject to the limitations of a time/space bound series of causes and effects. The creator simply *is*.*

Dr. Robert Shapiro and I are in agreement about a supernatural creator

In fact, in 1986, a year before Dawkins' *The Blind Watchmaker* was published, Dr. Robert Shapiro had already presented the same argument and reached the same conclusion as myself:

> Similarly, the existence of bacteria and other living beings, all of which are much more complex than a watch, implies the existence of a creator, as only a higher being could design creatures so fit for their function...If a watch is complex, then the watchmaker must be even more complicated. A being with the capacity to create a watchmaker would be the most complex of the lot. **By following this line of reasoning, we have made our problem more difficult... and we can resolve it only by introducing supernatural forces.** We must look for another solution if we wish to remain within science. [15] (Shapiro, Origins)

This is exactly what I stated above. The conclusion is that there must be a creator who is not part of the physical universe at all (*i.e.,* a supernatural creator). Inasmuch as Dr. Shapiro is a self-declared agnostic, he obviously rejects this conclusion. Why?

If you'll notice, Shapiro does not in any way whatsoever attempt to explain to us why this "line of reasoning" is flawed. He does not point out any logical inconsistencies, mistaken assumptions, or any other glitches that would cause a rational,

---

* See Chap. 9, for a fuller explanation of this concept of God. The following description of the universe "before" the Big Bang was written by physicist Dr. Gerald Schroeder. I placed the word *before* in quotation marks because as a result of the human inability to grasp and describe a state of being without the existence of time – a state of being where the words "before" and "after" have no meaning in the sense that we normally understand them to have – I have no choice but to use highly inadequate terms and descriptions: "At the moment of the Big Bang everything, the entire universe, you included was part of a homogeneous speck – no divisions, no separations ...and before this there was neither time nor space nor matter. That speck was the entire universe. Not a speck within some vacuous space. A vacuum is space...There was no other space. No outside to the inside of the creation. Creation was everywhere at once." (*The Hidden Face of God*, Schroeder, Touchstone Books, 2002, pg. 3)

truth seeking individual to reject this "line of reasoning." He simply dismisses it because he does not like where it leads; namely, to the conclusion that the source of the first living organisms must be a supernatural force. In his own words: "...we can only resolve it by introducing supernatural forces." So I ask you Dr. Shapiro, what is so terrible about that?

In fact, the rational truth seeker would pose the following to Dr. Shapiro: All agree that the process which resulted in the formation of the first living organism required a beginning. There are two possible beginnings, **A)** a supernatural creator who is composed of neither matter nor energy, and does not exist in time and space, or **B)** a naturalistic process that started with non-life and ended with life. The evidence for a supernatural creator is obvious. Just as the suit itself is proof of the tailor and the poem itself the proof of the poet, the bacterium itself (which is exponentially more sophisticated than either of the other two), is proof of its creator. As it turns out, logic leads us to the conclusion that *this* creator must ultimately be supernatural, but a creator nonetheless. What plausible, empirical evidence can you offer for alternative **B),** that life arose from non-life by a naturalistic process? Instead of admitting to the simple truth that there is no plausible evidence that life arose from non-life naturalistically, Shapiro, like many of his colleagues, dodges the issue: "We must look for another solution if we wish to remain within science." Dr. Shapiro, you can choose to remain "within science" if you so desire; I choose the truth.

The reality of a Creator is part of our inner essence

Not only is a supernatural creator the reasonable and logical solution to our question, I would suggest that we are "hard wired" to both understand and *experience* the reality of this concept. It is part of our inner essence. Richard Dawkins himself expresses this inner reality, and despite himself, is unable to contain this genuine reaction to the wonders of nature:

> I think that when you consider the beauty of the world and you wonder how it came to be what it is, you are naturally overwhelmed with a feeling of awe, a feeling of admiration...and you almost feel a

desire to worship something...I feel this...I recognize that other scientists such as Carl Sagan feel this, Einstein felt it, we all of us share
a common kind of religious reverence for the beauties of the universe,
for the complexity of life, for the sheer magnitude of the cosmos, for
the sheer magnitude of geological time...and it's tempting to translate
that feeling of awe and worship...into a desire to worship some particular thing, a person, an agent...you want to attribute it to a maker,
to a creator. [16] (from a debate with Dr. John Lennox)

What is Dawkins describing, if not the experience of a reality that is indescribably greater than ourselves, that transcends
our own being? That the beauties of the universe, the unfath-
omable complexity of life, the sheer magnitude of the cosmos,
inspire in us a desire to reach out somehow and connect with
that ultimate greatness. A desire to not just connect, but a primal understanding that this ultimate "maker" is a being we want
to *worship*. What stops him from taking that step? In Dawkins'
own words:

What Science has now achieved is an emancipation from that impulse
to attribute these things to a creator...It was a supreme achievement of
the human intellect to realize there is a better explanation...that these
things can come about by purely natural causes...we understand essentially how life came into being. [17] (from the Dawkins-Lennox debate)

**"We understand essentially how life came into being"?! –
Who** understands? Who is **"we"?**
Is it Dr. Stuart Kauffman? "Anyone who tells you that he or she
knows how life started...is a fool or a knave." [18]

Is it Dr. Robert Shapiro? "The weakest point is our lack of
understanding of the origin of life. No evidence remains that we
know of to explain the steps that started life here, billions of
years ago." [19]

Is it Dr. George Whitesides? "Most chemists believe as I do that
life emerged spontaneously from mixtures of chemicals in the
prebiotic earth. How? I have no idea...On the basis of all chemistry I know, it seems astonishingly improbable." [20]

Is it Dr. G. Cairns-Smith? "Is it any wonder that [many scientists] find the origin of life to be utterly perplexing?" [21]

Is it Dr. Paul Davies? "Many investigators feel uneasy about stating in public that the origin of life is a mystery, even though behind closed doors they freely admit they are baffled...the problem of how and where life began is one of the great outstanding mysteries of science." [22]

Is it Dr. Richard Dawkins? Here is how Dawkins responded to questions about the *Origin of Life* during an interview with Ben Stein in the film *Expelled: No Intelligence Allowed:*

Stein: How did it start?
Dawkins: **Nobody knows how it started,** we know the kind of event that it must have been, we know the sort of event that must have happened for the origin of life.
Stein: What was that?
Dawkins: It was the origin of the first self replicating molecule.
Stein: How did that happen?
Dawkins: **I told you I don't know.**
Stein: So you have no idea how it started?
Dawkins: **No, No, nor does anyone else.** [23]

"Nobody understands the origin of life, if they say they do, they are probably trying to fool you" [24] **(Dr. Ken Nealson, microbiologist and co-chairman of the Committee on the Origin and Evolution of Life for the National Academy of Sciences)**

Nobody, including Professor Dawkins has any idea "how life came into being!" Is there any clearer example of the "atheistic disconnect" that I described in the first chapter of this book? It is only this self-deceiving view of reality that allows Dawkins to declare that science has emancipated him from the impulse to attribute the astounding wonders of the living world to a creator. There is no human intellect on the face of the earth that has achieved a "better explanation." We have shown conclusively that no chemist, physicist, biologist, nor any other type of scientist has any real clue how life could have come about through "natural processes." Scientists do **not** understand how life "essentially" (or nonessentially for that matter), came into being. Only a "fool," a "knave," or an individual who is soaked through to the bone with arrogance or ignorance could make such an outrageous claim.

Perhaps it is time for these scientists to express not awe, not admiration...but humility. To stand back from their lab tables, their beakers, pipettes, and Bunsen burners, and reflect on the words of the Psalmist: **My heart was not proud, and my eyes were not haughty, nor did I pursue matters too great and wondrous for me...** *(Psalms 131)*

Professor Dawkins stated in his debate with Dr. Lennox, "...it is *tempting* to translate that feeling...into a desire to worship some particular thing...you want to attribute it to a maker, a creator." My advice to Richard Dawkins and his atheistic colleagues? Don't go to church, don't go to synagogue, don't plan a trip to Mecca, or India, or Nepal, or for that matter to Salt Lake City. Just do it, give in to temptation. And if you find yourself unable to kneel and worship at the very least stand bowed in humility before your Creator.

Part III

Man's Search for Meaning and Spirituality

— Chapter 6 —

The Existence of a Personal God

— Chapter 7 —

*"Spirits in the Sky":
The World of Spirituality*

Chapter 6

*The Existence of a
Personal God*

While experiencing the slightly manic and frenetic state of mind that gripped me as I wrote this book, a relative of mine who had read up until this point in the manuscript made the following sobering comment: "The really important question for me is what does God have to do with me? Is there anything to indicate that he is important to me on a personal level?"

Keeping with the spirit of his comments, I think it appropriate to change gears slightly. While it is still essential to point out the anamorphic attitudes and mindsets that pervade the world of atheistic thinking, it is clearly time to present an approach to a clear intellectual awareness of not just the existence of God as Creator, but of the reality that our whole being and purpose in life revolves around seeking a relationship with this God. In my opinion, the most effective approach to this subject matter is a careful and measured dissection of certain key ideas that are found in *atheistic writings*.

The Three Big fundamental issues

The three fundamental philosophical and metaphysical issues that believers constantly point to in their ongoing debate with skeptics, are **1)** man's search for meaning, **2)** the seemingly non-material (i.e. spiritual) realities that permeate our lives (for example the mind/brain duality), and **3)** morality. At first glance, each of these concepts suggest a reality that extends beyond the material universe, a reality that exists in time but not space; a reality that profoundly affects our lives, but cannot be quantified or detected by any conceivable material yardstick or measuring device. In fact, this is to be our working definition of the spiritual: A reality that exists in time but not space, has a clear effect on our lives, and is undetectable and unmeasure-able by physical means.

When confronting these issues skeptics and freethinkers tend to view themselves as having a virtual monopoly on the commodities of rational discourse and contemplation. The following passage from Dr. Julian Baggini's book, *Atheism: A Very Short Introduction*, conveys the attitude just described:

> Most atheists see themselves as realists – their atheism is a part of their willingness to square up to the world as it is and face it without recourse to superstitions or comforting fictions about a life to come or a benevolent power looking after us. [1]

I would argue that skeptics love "comforting fictions"

I would agree that, generally speaking, atheists do not resort to actual superstitions in order to "square up to the world as it is." However, I would suggest that in order to keep their non-belief intact they routinely *do* turn to "comforting fictions." I contend that a careful analysis of these "comforting fictions" will lead us to an extraordinary insight. We will see that in his very remonstrations against religious belief, the atheist in fact testifies that the deepest drives and impulses in the human psyche can only be understood as functions of the inner need to seek and relate to a transcendent God. Paradoxically then, over the next few chapters we will use atheistic philosophy itself as a sort of radio beacon to navigate a course to a rendezvous with our Creator. To begin the journey we present *Richard Dawkins and The Meaning of Life.*

Richard Dawkins: What is your purpose? Why were you born? (and What is Your Favorite Color?)

In an article written for *Scientific American* (1995), Dawkins, the High Priest of Atheism in our day, informs us in blunt, raw language his existential view of reality, "The universe that we observe has precisely the properties we should expect if there is, at bottom, no design, no purpose, no evil, no good, nothing but pitiless indifference." [2] I don't think I would be going out on a limb by opining that the universe described in the above statement is not a universe that would inspire the average person to jump for joy (it might however, inspire him to jump off a tall building). How does a prominent atheist like Richard Dawkins deal on an emotional and psychological level with what is ostensibly a horribly depressing and despair-inducing view of reality? In my opinion, it can be best illustrated by the following joke:

> *A young woman approaches her parents and explains how sorry she is to have to tell them that she has died. At first the parents think she is joking, but it soon becomes apparent that the girl is absolutely convinced that she is dead. They become quite alarmed and decide to take her to a world famous psychologist. After a lengthy conversation with the girl the psychologist says, "Look, we both know that being dead means that your heart has stopped beating, right?" The girl nods her head. He continues, "If you cut the finger of a dead person, it won't bleed because the heart is not pumping blood, right?" Again the girl nods her head. "So if I make a small cut on your finger and you start bleeding, that means your heart is pumping and you are actually alive, right?" She nods once more. The psychologist makes a small cut on her finger and of course, blood starts flowing freely out of the cut. The girl stares dumbfounded at her finger and says, "I don't believe it, dead people **do** bleed!"*

At first it seems as if Dawkins is exemplifying the atheistic ideal described by Baggini. He is willing to "square up to the world as it is" without seeking comfort in imaginary constructs. He admits the simple truth, that the world of the atheist is one that has no purpose or value, only "pitiless indifference." But that still does not answer the question I posed above. How does he deal with it? In fact, he deals with it the same way that almost all atheists deal with it; he rushes headlong into the embrace of a "comforting fiction." Lo and behold, just like our girl in the story, Dawkins stares at his bloody finger and proclaims:

> "...isn't it a **noble**, an **enlightened** way of spending our brief time in the sun, to work at understanding the universe, and how we have come to wake up in it?...isn't it sad to go to your grave without ever wondering **why you were born?** Who, with such a thought, would not spring from bed, eager to resume discovering the world and rejoicing to be a part of it? [3] (Dawkins, *Scientific American*)

Noble – "of an exalted moral or mental character" (*Random House Dictionary, 2010*), **enlightened** – "having knowledge and spiritual insight, characterized by full comprehension of the problem involved" (*American Heritage Dictionary of the English Language, 2006*). How is it possible to say in one breath that our universe has "no design, no purpose...nothing but pitiless indifference," which explicitly means that the universe is totally devoid of all significance, and a moment later describe devoting one's life to understanding that *same* universe as a "noble" and "enlightened" way of life, adjectives that are literally bursting with implications of significance? Why would anyone be "eager to resume discovering [a] world, and rejoicing [to be part of a world]" that has neither design nor purpose?

The unbearable agony of meaninglessness

What does it mean when we say something has no purpose? A water bucket whose bottom is full of holes has no purpose. Would anyone dream of examining or trying to understand a bucket that is full of holes or would you simply throw it in the garbage? Imagine assigning a worker the task of filling up such a bucket with water. How long before he would throw the bucket against the wall cursing, and walk away?

Let's focus on a skycap at an airport whose job essentially consists of putting tags on luggage and then placing that tagged luggage on a conveyor belt. It may not be a job that requires advanced education but it is certainly an honest and honorable way to support one's family and earn a living. He can work for an airline for thirty years, retire, and live off his pension. Take the same skycap, tell him to put tags on luggage, put the luggage on a conveyor belt that goes around in a circle, and when the luggage comes back around his job is to take it off and start all over again. Can you imagine doing *that* for eight hours a day for 30 years?! How long would it take before he would start howling at the sky like a raving lunatic? What is the difference between the two scenarios? In the first, the skycap feels there is some *purpose and meaning* in what he is doing. People travel to different locations for business and/or pleasure. They also need their luggage transported to their destination and the skycap is part of this process. In the second scenario he is doing the *same work,* but it is purposeless and meaningless. An ox can turn a millstone for its entire life without caring if there is grain under the millstone or not, as long as he is fed and gets adequate rest. Put a human being to work at a purposeless task for a long enough period of time and he will most likely go stark raving mad.

I once read the account of a survivor of the Soviet Gulag who described how inmates were marched out in the dead of winter and told to dig a long narrow ditch. The ground of course, was frozen solid and the work was excruciatingly difficult. The inmates returned to the prison camp exhausted beyond description. The next morning they were marched to the same spot and were ordered to fill in the ditch with the same dirt. Which was easier work; digging the ditch or filling it in? Which was more painful? To order sick and malnourished men to dig a ditch in the middle of a Siberian winter will break men's bodies; to have them fill it in the next day and to realize that all that backbreaking work was absolutely purposeless will crush men's spirits and souls (which of course is exactly what it was designed to do).

This then, is the authentic human reaction when confronted with purposelessness, whether it is in the form of filling a hole-riddled bucket with water, putting luggage on a conveyor belt going nowhere, or filling in a ditch with dirt. When faced with a purposeless situation, human beings do not see it as *noble and enlightened;* they do not approach it *eagerly and joyfully.* Purposelessness is a state of being that is unbearably painful for the human being. People who **truly** feel that life is purposeless will either take drastic steps to block out that reality and the accompanying pain (with drugs, alcohol, etc., or a "comforting fiction") or when despairing of a solution will end the agony with suicide.

You can't have it both ways Professor Dawkins

A universe with "no design, no purpose, no evil, no good, nothing but pitiless indifference", is essentially one giant cosmic conveyor belt going around in meaningless circles. In "Mr.

Dawkins' Neighborhood" we are all a bunch of skycaps trapped in a Twilight Zone-like surrealistic horror film. The universe of Richard Dawkins is one that offers a life filled with agonizing despair. On the other hand, a life that is "noble and enlightened", a life that is approached with "joy and eagerness" is a life rich with *purpose and meaning*. It is the type of life that can only be lived in a universe that has been created with ultimate goals and ultimate purposes. Does Richard Dawkins actually believe that he lives in a meaningless world and then psychologically and emotionally covers it up with his "comforting fiction" (which consists of a fantasy about the nobility of the pursuit of scientific knowledge); or in his heart does he really believe there is an ultimate purpose to our lives and simply avoids having to confront his Creator by calling himself an atheist?

"Isn't it sad to go to your grave without ever wondering why you were born?" (Richard Dawkins)

Is it actually possible that the above question was propounded by Richard Dawkins, perhaps the most articulate, outspoken, passionate, and loyal disciple of Charles Darwin alive today? The late Dr. Stephen J. Gould, world renowned paleontologist, has already told us the obvious answer to this question:

> We are here because one odd group of fishes had a peculiar fin anatomy that could transform into legs for terrestrial creatures; because the earth never froze entirely during the ice age; because a small and tenuous species, arising in Africa a quarter of a million years ago, has managed so far to survive by hook and by crook. We may yearn for a higher answer – but none exists. [4]

In other words Professor Dawkins, you were born for *no reason at all*. You were born because of a meaningless series of coincidences and happenstance. You are a flaming accident! You started from nothing and you are going nowhere. Is Richard Dawkins a Darwinist or some Eastern mystic seeking to unravel the mystery of the universe and our existence?

How are we to understand this philosophical version of a Dr. Jekyll/Mr. Hyde-like dichotomy in the world outlook of Richard Dawkins? On the one hand the existentialist atheist who sees a purposeless, insignificant, indifferent, pitiless world, and on the other hand the bedazzled awestruck child, the mystical seeker who yearns to understand the universe, why we are here, and what is our unique place in it? How is it possible for one person to have two such diametrically opposed views of the world at the same time? Is there any way of harmonizing these two separate identities or is this just another example of the atheistic disconnection from reality? (Guess how I would answer that question) Let's examine how this seemingly irresolvable tension expresses itself among other atheist writers and philosophers.

Futility: The atheistic way

Sigmund Freud: *The moment a man questions the meaning and value of life he is sick, since objectively neither has any existence.* [5]

Christopher Hitchens: *...why care? Why do I bother? That's a very good question. It...doesn't have a conclusive answer.* [6]

Steven Weinberg: *...the more we know of the cosmos, the more meaningless it appears.* [7]

Richard Dawkins: *...the universe...has...no design, no purpose ...nothing but pitiless indifference.* [8]

Dr. James Watson: *I don't think we're here for anything, we're just products of evolution. You can say, gee, your life must be pretty bleak if you don't think there is a purpose; but I'm anticipating having a good lunch.* [9]
[Alimentary, my dear Watson...]

Stephen J. Gould: *...we may yearn for a higher answer – but none exists.* [10]

Jean Paul Sartre: *Life has no meaning the moment you lose the illusion of being eternal.* [11]

<u>Carl Sagan</u>: *The very scale of the universe….speaks to us of the inconsequentiality of human events in the cosmic context.* [12]

<u>G. Gaylord Simpson</u>: *Man is the result of a purposeless…..process…* [13]

<u>Emile Cioran (Romanian Philosopher)</u>: *I'm simply an accident, why take it all so seriously?* [14]

<u>Will Provine</u>: *There is no hope whatsoever in there being any… meaning in life.* [15]

To sum up the atheistic viewpoint on the meaning and purpose of life in their own words:

There is no reason to care about anything, no reason to bother with anything; All meaning in life is based on an illusion. We are here by accident; there is no reason to take it seriously. We live in a purposeless, insignificant, indifferent, pointless universe. Life has no objective value or meaning; our deeds and doings are inconsequential, we are not here for anything at all, there is no hope of finding meaning in life, we are products of a blind and directionless evolutionary process, and it makes a man sick to think about it…We may yearn for a higher answer – but none exists.

I did not make these statements, *they did.* All of them, in one way or another, exhibit the same schizoid behavior that we pointed out above in Richard Dawkins. Why are these people writing books? Why are these people giving lectures? Why do they all seek achievement? Why are they chasing awards and honors (other than to give Steven Weinberg's mother the chance to say, "My son the Nobel Prize winner!")? There is no logical or rational reason for the atheist to do any of these things. Pointless means *pointless.* **No point** means there is **no point.** It means that the lectures don't matter; it means the books are inconsequential, it means the values hold no significance – there is **no point** to it. Jean Paul Sartre, the French philosopher and author, spent his entire lifetime writing books explaining why there is really no meaning to writing books, giving lectures about how there is no real point to giving lectures, and teaching students that there is no real purpose in teaching students. The atheistic passion to achieve is an object lesson in theatre of the absurd.

When Sigmund Freud awoke in the morning and looked in the mirror did he say, "Remember Ziggy, don't think about the value and purpose of your life, because in reality it has none. If you keep thinking about it you are going to need a psychiatrist! So *don't* think about it"? Do you think I am gratuitously mocking Freud? I wasn't the one who said that when a man thinks about the meaning and value of life he becomes sick, because in fact there is no meaning and value to life; *Freud said it.*

Perhaps the following is the most glaring question of all for the atheist ideologue: For what possible reason would you care if people believe in God and religion or not? Dr. Steven Weinberg, a brilliant physicist, has declared that, "The more we know of the cosmos, the more meaningless it appears." [16] He then turns around and says, "Anything that we scientists can do to weaken the hold of religion should be done, and may in the end be our greatest contribution to civilization." [17]

What upsets Weinberg about religion? If Richard Dawkins is allowed his comforting fiction, why can't religious people have their comforting fiction? It certainly is not because life is necessarily more pleasant without religion. Many people are very happy living a religious lifestyle. The simple historical fact is that atheist tyrants and their societies have been *at least* as tyrannical, vicious, and destructive as any repressive religious society (How about North Korea? The former Soviet Union? Red China? The former East Germany? Cambodia under the Khmer Rouge? North Viet Nam? Cuba?) In fact, many scientists *themselves* have been guilty of the most horrible atrocities in recent history.

Is it because religion teaches that there is a meaning to the universe and Weinberg demands that everyone "cry uncle" and admit that it's really meaningless? If it's meaningless, then what is the point to caring what anyone believes? What does he mean by "our greatest contribution to civilization"? That everyone should agree to the atheist doctrine that civilization itself is pointless and meaningless? Is this the great intellectual and ideological victory that Weinberg dreams of? This type of thinking borders on madness. But perhaps I have misunderstood; perhaps the *universe* is pointless and meaningless, but we can fashion our own meaning for *human civilization.*

Can the atheist create his or her own meaning?

Atheistic philosophers tell us that the only escape is to create our own *subjective* meaning and purpose in life:

> Human life has no meaning independent of itself...the meaning of life is what we choose to give it. [18] (Paul Kurtz, Humanist philosopher)

> Life has no meaning a priori...it's up to you to give it a meaning, and value is nothing else but the meaning you choose...man is alone...abandoned on earth...with no other aim than the one he sets himself. [19] (Jean Paul Sartre)

Before analyzing what Kurtz and Sartre have proposed, it is instructive to actually define what "subjective" means: "proceeding from or taking place in a person's mind rather than the external world...existing only within the experiencer's mind... existing only in the mind, illusory" *(American Heritage Dictionary)*

The idea of creating our own subjective meaning and purpose in life may sound very profound in the lecture hall of the existentialist atheistic philosopher or in some late night university dorm rap session. However, when stripped of its philosophical camouflage what it really means is the following: *make something up that gives your life purpose and pretend that it's real. Create a fantasy world, an illusion in your mind so that you will not, in the words of T.C. Boyle, have to face the "naked howling face of the universe."*

We have now come full circle from the statement of Julian Baggini that was cited at the beginning of this chapter: "...their atheism is part of their willingness to square up to the world as it is...without recourse [to] comforting fictions..." It has now become crystal clear that what the atheist philosopher truly preaches is exactly the opposite. In other words, do <u>**not**</u> "square up to the [meaningless] world as it is." In other words, hold on tight to a "comforting fiction." In other words, hook yourself up to "The Matrix" and attempt to live a blissful hallucination. The sum total of all the anguished, harrowing probing of the human psyche by philosophers like Sartre and Kurtz is really nothing more than an active expression of Freud's observation – *i.e.,* figure out a way to avoid confronting the absolute meaningless and valueless reality of our existence lest, as Freud puts it, you become "sick" (or decide to take a long walk off a short ledge).

Victor Stenger attempts to solve the problem, but fails miserably in his hypothesis

Since our discussion is getting quite heavy, for some comic relief I thought we'd take a look at how physicist, Victor Stenger, in *God: The Failed Hypothesis,* faces this dilemma of the ages. Stenger admits that in the world of the atheist, ultimately nothing we do matters. However, he offers what he believes is an ingenious solution to the problem:

> Philosopher Erik Wielenberg tells of a gym teacher who would calm things down when tempers flared...by saying, ten years from now will any of you care who won this game? Wielenberg recalls thinking that a reasonable response would be "does it really matter <u>now</u> whether any of us will care in ten years?" He quotes philosopher Thomas Nagel in the same vein, "It does not matter now that in a million years nothing we do now will matter." In other words what matters now is what happens now. [20]

For a moment it seemed that Stenger was going to disappoint us and actually say something insightful, but in the end he snatches victory from the jaws of defeat and manages to come through with a very respectable level of atheistic nonsense. Let's expand on Stenger's penetrating insight that "what matters *now,* is what happens *now*":

It doesn't matter <u>now</u> that I haven't attended any classes all semester, haven't opened a book, and will be expelled from school; what matters <u>now</u> is that I am partying and having a great time. It doesn't matter <u>now</u> that I'm taking heroin and will become a broken down junkie within months; what matters <u>now</u> is that I am on a high. It doesn't matter <u>now</u> that if I commit murder I might get caught and be in jail or the electric chair ten years down the road; what matters <u>now</u> is that I am killing the liquor store owner and getting $1000 out of the cash register. It doesn't matter <u>now</u>, that as you face the end of *your life, <u>like all of us will one day</u>, you might be confronted with a paralyzing thought: **What was the point to all this? What difference did it all make?** After all, if you don't think about it, you can pretend the question doesn't exist.*

While in the midst of a tantrum, a three-year-old is not expected to see beyond right now. However, one of the characteristics that distinguishes adults from children is the ability to understand the consequences and implications of their ideas, beliefs, and actions. What is Stenger's solution to the profound existential dilemma that the greatest intellects in human history have grappled with for millennia? *It doesn't matter that in objective reality everything you are doing is insignificant and meaningless. Don't think about that, push it out of your mind. What difference does it make how you will feel about your life in five years, or ten years, or twenty years? The only thing that matters is **now**!* In fact Stenger's brilliant new philosophy is really a very old philosophy: "Eat, Drink, and be Merry, for Tomorrow We Die." Thank you Victor Stenger for sharing; your particular atheistic "comforting fiction" is *very special!*

The Secret Life of Atheists — Seeking meaning in a meaningless world

When addressing the meaning of life, Sartre, Dawkins, Weinberg, Freud, etc., bear an unmistakable resemblance to a group of dogs going around in circles chasing their proverbial tails. The universe of Dawkins is purposeless, ("the universe...has no design...no purpose") but he finds great purpose in studying it and writing one book after the other about it. The universe of Dr. Steven Weinberg is meaningless ("the more we know of the cosmos, the more meaningless it appears"), but he finds great meaning in devoting his life to investigating it and winning a Nobel Prize in the process. In Freud's evaluation human life has no value, ("the moment a man questions the meaning and *value of life* he is sick, since objectively neither has any existence"), but he found it immensely valuable to study human behavior and publish prolifically on the subject. It is clear that these men are driven to define their lives in the context of some meaningful and purposeful activity, even though their espoused atheistic ideology explicitly denies, as Dr. Will Provine put it, even the "hope" of the existence of such a thing. They are unable to escape this relentless, inexorable drive. Why?

We have already pointed out that unlike the ox that goes in circles around the millstone and could care less about why or what he is accomplishing, the human being simply cannot live without purpose. The human need for meaning is as real an ' as critical as our need for oxygen, water, and food. It goes even -ther than that. Our need for meaning is *greater* than our nee. oxygen, water, and food. It is greater than our need for friendship, love, or happiness. Human beings will *sacrifice their lives* for what they believe is meaningful. This is not some abstract, intellectual concept; it is hardcore everyday reality. People all over the world are dying, and are prepared to die for what they believe in. It cuts across all doctrines and belief systems. It applies to religious ideologies and atheistic ideologies. Whatever a particular individual believes is the essential reason for, and central meaning of his existence – whether it is to defend one's family, honor, country, or faith – that individual will be prepared to give up his or her life for it. (At the very least, the potential is there for this individual to give up his or her life.) What need could possibly be so powerful as to be more important than life itself?

Meaning and purpose beyond physical existence

The meaning and purpose we are talking about here is not the utilitarian type of purpose to acquire food or fulfill some other practical necessity. That type of drive we share with all living things. We are talking about someone who has every physical need taken care of and still yearns for something "more."* It is the type of meaning that Sartre refers to when he says, "Life has no meaning the moment one loses the illusion of being eternal." It is the type of meaning that Freud talks about when he says that a man becomes sick when he realizes that there is no objective meaning to his life. It is the type of meaning that

---

* Imagine a healthy, robust, well fed ox turning a millstone and suddenly thinking to himself, "I want *more* from my life."

Holocaust survivor Dr. Victor Frankl* writes about, "What man actually needs is not a tensionless state, but rather the striving and struggling for some goal worthy of him. What he needs is…the call of a potential meaning waiting to be fulfilled by him." It is the type of meaning human beings crave so powerfully, that a split second after an atheist declares human existence and the universe to be void of all significance; that very same atheist is driven to declare his passionate commitment to investigating and understanding human existence and the universe. This burning hunger for meaning and purpose has no atomic structure, no molecular configuration, and no chemical formula with which it can be satiated. The only "food" which satisfies this ravenous desire is some transcendent goal or quest. It is this deep yearning that drives Jean Paul Sartre to exclaim, "That God does not exist I cannot deny, that my whole being cries out for God, I cannot forget." [22]

How can we need transcendence, when it has no actuality in the fabric of existence?

Where does an avowed materialist and atheist like Sartre get the idea of a God that his "whole being cries out for?" What achingly profound inner need is at work inside him that he understands that if God existed, that's what he is looking for? How is it possible for an outspoken atheist like Sam Harris to make the following statement: "There is clearly a sacred dimension to our existence and coming to terms with it could well be the highest purpose of human life." [23] What could the phrase "sacred dimension to our existence" possibly mean to an atheist? For that matter, what could the phrase "higher purpose" mean to Sam Harris? We have already seen that prominent atheists declare to us that life has no purpose at all! What forces are churning inside the soul of Richard Dawkins that would produce these words: "When you consider the beauty of the world, and you wonder how it came to be…you are naturally overwhelmed with a feeling of awe, a feeling of admiration, and you

---

*Frankl was an Austrian neurologist and psychiatrist who created *Logotherapy*, and authored a famous chronicle of his life in the Nazi death camps entitled *Man's Search for Meaning.*

almost feel a desire to worship something...you want to attribute it to a maker, a creator." [24] Dawkins, Harris and Sartre speak for billions of other human beings when they express that their whole being cries out to connect with something beyond this world, which transcends this world, to worship "a maker, a creator," to experience a "sacred dimension" and a "higher purpose" that would provide them with the fulfillment and significance that they feel is lacking.

Where is there room for such thoughts and concepts in a purely physical universe? In the atheistic view of reality there isn't anything beyond this world, there is no such thing as transcendence. None of these things have any existence or reality. To propose an answer that primitive man dreamed up God or gods to explain the powerful forces of nature, is shamelessly begging the question. *Why* would primitive man, or for that matter, why would modern man even bother to think of such a question? From what part of a person springs the *need* to seek some ultimate explanation of himself and the world around him. Why does it eat at him and relentlessly drive him? Why can't people be happy and satisfied to live purely physical, material lives like the purely physical primates that we *actually are* in the atheistic worldview?

Can a man be thirsty if liquid does not exist?

Imagine if the laws of physics and chemistry in our universe were slightly different and precluded the existence of the state of matter we call liquid. Could anyone conceive of a thing called "liquid"? Try right now to conceive of a state of matter that could not by definition exist in our universe. To attempt to do so would be ridiculous; you can't possibly have any idea of what you're trying to conceive of! It's like asking the blind-from-birth man, to conceive of a flag made from red, white, and blue. Colors are simply not part of his reality. Actually we can take it a step further. Imagine if our entire universe only consisted of "black and white." *Nobody* would ever talk about or even dream about red, green, or blue. If the state of matter we call "liquid" did not exist, it would be absurd – in fact it would be impossible – to talk of a living creature being "thirsty."

Our thirst for meaning inescapably implies the existence of meaning

We cannot have a drive and need for something which has no actuality and existence. In a purely materialistic universe, there is no such thing as "purpose" or "meaning", only atoms, light waves, and the laws of physics. *They would simply and absolutely not have any place in the fabric of reality; including our thoughts and imagination* (In other words we would all be like the ox turning the millstone, perfectly content as long as our physical needs were taken care of). I reiterate: "meaning" cannot be metamorphosed, transfigured, or expressed as a function of any material formula. It is just as absurd for a living creature to need meaning in an absolutely material world, as it would be for that same creature to be thirsty if the laws of physics and chemistry did not allow for the existence of liquid. In this sense, the fact that I get thirsty incontrovertibly testifies to the existence of a state of matter called liquid. In the same way, my overwhelming "thirst" for meaning testifies to the existence of a thing called "meaning."

Our desire for meaning is real; we "cry out" for meaning. The urgent compulsion to seek meaning is more powerful than life itself – *we will trade our lives for meaning.* Meaning exists. The cosmos is not "meaningless", as Steven Weinberg put it. It is not true that "we're not here for anything." The universe has *purpose,* and we are most definitely here for *something.* We are inescapably hard wired to seek a meaning that transcends our physical existence. A search for meaning that ultimately can only find it's fulfillment in a connection to something "noble and enlightened," to a "sacred dimension," a "higher purpose," a "maker...a creator"...the eternal, One God. It is as futile to attempt to escape this implacable urge and the transcendent reality that implicitly must exist, as it is to attempt to escape the need to eat and breathe.

As we have illustrated, our quest for meaning eloquently testifies to the existence of a higher realm; however, the concept of spirituality needs to be explored at a deeper level. Is it really possible to account for the entire spectrum of day-to-day human experience within the purely material paradigms of the atheistic conception of reality? Or is there perhaps — more?

Chapter 7

"Spirits in the Sky":
The World of Spirituality

In his book *Atheism: A Very Short Introduction,* Dr. Julian Baggini addresses a controversy that continually bedevils the atheist/materialist. What is the nature of "consciousness" and "self awareness?" Are they manifestations of a non-material/spiritual reality, or are they explainable and under-standable as purely material phenomena? In his discussion of this subject Baggini displays the extreme narrow-mindedness that typifies much of atheistic thought:

> What best explains the correlation between consciousness and brain activity...[the] atheist hypothesis that consciousness is a product of brain activity or an **implausible tale** about how non-material souls exist alongside brains and somehow interact with them? [1]

What is "implausible" about a non-material soul?

The classic example of a declarative statement in the *form* of a question is, "when did you stop beating your wife?" When Baggini queries about the "implausible" existence of the soul, he is clearly making a statement, not posing a question. Why did he feel it necessary to frame the question in this manner? Why is it an "implausible tale" to consider the existence of a non-material soul? *Roget's II: The New Thesaurus* lists the following as some of the synonyms for *implausible:* "flimsy, improbable, inconceivable, weak, unconvincing, thin, shaky." *Random House Unabridged Dictionary:* "not having the appearance of truth or credibility." *WordNet 3.0:* "having a quality that provokes disbelief," "a far-fetched excuse." If the viewpoint of the believer on this issue is "improbable," "not having the appearance of truth or credibility," "shaky," "weak," or in other words, if it is so obvious that the athe-istic explanation is much more sensible, why not just pose the question in a neutral manner (as follows below), and let the reader come to the obvious conclusion?:

What best explains the correlation and relationship between consciousness or self awareness, and brain activity? The atheist claims that consciousness is a product of brain activity and is wholly explainable as a material phenomenon. The believer claims that consciousness and self awareness represent a non-material dimension of the soul that clearly interacts with the brain and our physical being, but still expresses a separate aspect of human experience and existence.

Once we read a neutral formulation of the question the reason why Baggini felt compelled to add the words "implausible tale" becomes rather obvious. When posed neutrally, it is apparent that the suggestion that consciousness and self awareness are manifestations of a separate non-material reality is not really "far-fetched," "having a quality that provokes disbelief," "inconceivable," "flimsy," or implausible at all. To cavalierly dismiss the notion of a non-material soul as implausible, when billions of human beings from every conceivable race, culture, geographical location, and level of education claim an intuitive and experiential connection with its reality, is a flagrant display of intellectual laziness and pompousness. It is absolutely clear that no matter what conclusion is eventually reached the honest thinker must consider both sides. Baggini of course, wants to avoid opening *that* can of worms. With his calculated fashioning of the question he eliminates the need to consider another point of view. Not only does he not offer any logical or scientific explanation for his *a priori* rejection of the soul, but on the contrary, he explicitly informs us that this conclusion has been reached via a leap of faith:

> What most atheists do *believe* is that although there is only one kind of stuff in the universe and it is physical, out of this stuff comes minds, beauty, emotions, moral values. [2]

"What most atheists do *believe*"?! – Is it possible that a strictly rational, logical, skeptical, scientific, atheist is using the "B" word? Do atheists have "Beliefs"? I thought only medieval, backward, superstitious, religious people had "Beliefs." Atheists deal only in scientific and empirically proven "facts." Is Baggini implying that he really does not *know* if the only "stuff" in the universe is physical and from that physical "stuff" comes minds (*i.e.* consciousness and self awareness), beauty, and morality? I want to point out that Richard Dawkins cites this paragraph verbatim in the *The God Delusion*. [3] It seems that Dawkins also does not really *know* if this statement is true or not. Praise Darwin! Baggini and Dawkins are *true believers*.

No Spirituality Allowed: An atheistic "article of faith"

The simple truth is that of course they don't *know* if the only thing in the universe is physical "stuff." They have no idea whatsoever if love, beauty, and emotions can be defined in terms of some purely material configuration. If anyone knew the chemical or molecular formula for love they would've patented it and become billionaires many times over. For them it is an *article of faith*. Once they have chosen to deny the existence of God, they have no choice but to also deny that there can be any type of reality besides one that is exclusively material. According to them nothing exists besides atoms, molecules, chemicals, light waves, and the laws of physics. Thus, beauty, emotions, and morality must also be defined in physical terms, no matter how counterintuitive or bizarre that seems.

I would like to suggest a completely different reason why it's possible for the skeptic to deny the actuality of the spiritual world. In the same way that a fish may never notice the water because it is completely immersed in it, it is also possible for people to fail to notice the spiritual side of life because our whole life and being is so completely immersed in a spiritual existence. Let's now take a little plunge into the ocean of our spiritual world.

Who is "I"?

Let's imagine for a moment that all the thoughts and pictures in our heads can be defined physically. Perhaps they are arrangements of electrons like the picture on a T.V. screen. This would mean that as I think and I see things inside my head, it's like watching a type of cerebral T.V. The essential mystery that must be solved, however, is in the statement, "I am watching a cerebral T.V. screen." Who is doing the watching? No matter how we explain it, *somebody* is certainly watching *something*. Is the "I" also a configuration of electrons? Electrons watching electrons? Do the other electrons stare back?

The "I" is clearly separate from everything else going on in my head. At the very least, that is the way that every human being perceives it and until demonstrated otherwise there is no reason to doubt it. I have a brain, but "I" am not a brain. I have a body, but "I" am not a body. I feel emotions but "I" am not an emotion. I think thoughts but "I" am not a thought. Who is doing the thinking? Who is doing the feeling? Who is doing the perceiving? Who is this *inescapable* "I?" The existence of the "I" does not need to be proven. The "I," in fact, needs nothing at all to assert, justify, or confirm its own reality. The "I" simply is. It would seem that the classic Cartesian formulation, "I think therefore I am," would be more precisely stated as "I *am,* therefore I think;" "I *am,* therefore I feel;" "I *am,* therefore I perceive."

According the atheistic/materialistic view of reality, how does a chemical, atom, or molecule suddenly step back and look at itself? Do the liver cells in my body wonder why they aren't kidney cells? Do the kidney cells wonder why they didn't end up as part of the optic nerve? Do they chalk it up to kismet, destiny, or karma? Molecules and chemicals don't have "identity." A human body that is only composed of material elements is nothing more than a machine – a machine does not have self-awareness. It seems nonsensical to suggest such a thing and at the very least is profoundly counterintuitive. Even atheistic bio-chemist Dr. Stuart Kauffman chafes at such a notion:

> The second predominant view among cognitive scientists is that consciousness arises when enough computational elements are networked together. In this view, a mind is a machine, and a complex set of buckets of water pouring water into one another would become conscious, I just cannot believe this. [4]

That of course is the reason why Baggini and Dawkins declare that "most atheists....*believe*" that out of the exclusively physical "stuff" comes consciousness, emotion, morality, beauty, etc. For some reason they expect us to accept this idea on their authority.

The Problem (?) of Consciousness

That the "I" is spiritual is the most obvious and elegant solution to the "problem of consciousness," as Philosopher Daniel Dennet, of Tufts University, calls it. (It's a "problem" for him because he *a priori* has made the decision that there cannot be a non-material soul.)

The human *body* is essentially a sophisticated machine. For example, the heart is nothing more than a pump. The kidney is a filter, *etc.* Our bio-engineering firms are able o produce replacement parts for the "human machine." Although relatively primitive, we have manufactured artificial limbs, knee joints, lungs, kidneys, and hearts. It is entirely conceivable that with advances in technology we will produce a pump that is superior to the human heart. The same is true for all of the aforementioned parts of the human body. However, it is the "I" that distinguishes the human being from the human "machine."

Not only is our technology totally incapable of building a machine that possesses a conscious "I," we shall soon see that science hasn't even a clue where to begin to attempt to accomplish such a feat. The only entity capable of projecting a conscious human "self" *is the "self" itself!* I would like to suggest to the reader a simple reason why the "I" cannot be duplicated by a machine; because the "I" is not an atom, molecule, or chemical; that the "I" exists in time but not in space; that the "I" constantly interacts with and affects the physical world (particularly the brain) but is itself undetectable and unmeasurable by any material means of detection or measurement; that the "I" is the soul. Not only does this answer mesh with the deep, powerful intuitive feeling of most human beings, it is unmistakably the simplest, clearest, and easiest answer to the question. At the very least, there is no good reason why the honest skeptic should not seriously consider the possibility.

When confronted with an uncomfortable idea, deny, deny, deny...

What we actually find, however, is that many skeptics and atheists are unable to approach the issue with open minds; they seem incapable of even *considering* such a possibility and simply go into denial. In a preposterously distorted argument, they claim that since no one can *physically locate* the "self" or the "soul," the logical conclusion must be that it does not really exist:

> Despite our every instinct to the contrary, there is one thing that consciousness is not; some deep entity inside the brain that corresponds to the "self", some kernel of awareness that runs the show, as the "man behind the curtain" manipulated the illusion of a powerful magician in The Wizard of Oz. After more than a century of looking for it, brain researchers have long since concluded that there is no conceivable place for such a self to be located in the **physical brain, and that it simply doesn't exist.** (Journalist Michael Leminick, *Time Magazine*) [5]

Atheist author Sam Harris puts it this way:

> There is no discrete self or ego lurking like a Minotaur in the **labyrinth of the brain.** There is no region of cortex or stream of neural processing that occupies a privileged position with respect to our personhood...In subjective terms, however, there seems to be one...What are we conscious of?...**We are – we think – conscious of ourselves in our bodies.** After all, most of us don't feel merely identical to our bodies. We feel, most of the time, like we are riding around inside our bodies, as though we are an inner subject that can utilize the body as a kind of object. This last representation is an illusion... [6]

Dr. Steven Pinker shares his perspective:

> ...the intuitive feeling we have that there's an executive "I" that sits in a control room of our brain...is an illusion. Consciousness turns out to consist of a maelstrom of events distributed across the brain. [7]

How, "despite every instinct to the contrary" do we *know* that consciousness is not really a "self," that there is no "man behind the curtain" or "executive I" that runs the show, and that our perception of ourselves as being separate from our physical bodies is an illusion? Simple, declares the atheist: since scientists have not found a particular *physical location* for the "self" inside the brain, then obviously there is no self!

The distorted thinking process that has actually transpired is the following: Instead of examining the data and evidence and then deciding if a spiritual/non-material dimension is plausible, the atheist declares *a priori* that there is no such thing, and proceeds to evaluate all data in light of that declaration. The deeply flawed syllogism goes something like this:

A) Atheists propose as a premise, effectively as an article of faith, that there *cannot* be any spiritual, non-material dimension of existence:

• "My fundamental premise about the brain is that its workings – what we call "mind", are a consequence of its anatomy and physiology and nothing more." [8] (Carl Sagan, astronomer)

• "Everything, including that which happens in our brains, depends on these and only on these: A set of fixed, deterministic laws." [9] (Marvin Minsky, renowned expert in artificial intelligence)

• "Resolutely shunning the supernatural...it **must** be in virtue of some natural property of the brain that organisms are conscious. There just **has** to be some explanation for how brains [interact] with minds...Consciousness, in short, **must** be a natural phenomena." [10] (Colin McGinn, philosopher)

• "Our behavior is [solely] the product of physical processes in the brain." [11] (Steven Pinker, cognitive Scientist)

B) Therefore if the "self" exists, it *must* have a physical, material location inside the brain.

C) Since we cannot find a specific physical location for the "self" inside the brain, the "self" does not actually exist and is an illusion created by the brain.

Even a brilliant scientist will follow faulty reasoning when it suits his agenda

Renowned sociobiologist and entomologist, Edmund O. Wilson, travels even further down this path of deeply flawed reasoning, "The brain and its satellite glands have now been probed to the point where no particular site remains that can reasonably be supposed to harbor a *non-physical soul*." [12]

Did Wilson actually presume to discover a non-material soul with *physical* "probes"? Did he expect to find the soul by measuring electro-magnetic waves? Was he searching for tiny, unexplained footprints in the grey matter of the cerebral cortex, as if the soul was some little elf running and hiding inside our skulls? By definition, it is impossible to find something non-material by using material measurements; by definition it is not something that can be seen, heard, touched, smelled, measured, or weighed. Its *effect* on our physical being can be seen and measured, which is why they were "probing" for it in the first place, but not the soul itself.

Perhaps it's time for the atheist to quit being so dogmatically narrow-minded and think a little outside the box. Perhaps the reason why every human being who has ever lived is so certain that their "self" is real, is because it is real. Perhaps the obvious conclusion to draw from the fact that scientists have been unable to identify a physical location for the "self" is not that it is an illusion, but that the very real existent self, in fact *has no physical location*; that it exists in time but not space, that the "self" is spiritual. How is it possible for a brilliant man like Wilson not to realize, that the most compelling reason of all to seriously consider the possibility that the "self" is spiritual *is the very fact that we perceive and experience its effects so clearly and pervasively in our lives, while at the same time we are thoroughly incapable of measuring, defining, or quantifying it by any conceivable material method or standard?*

A simple method for the atheist/materialist to conclusively prove his viewpoint

Nobody harbors any illusions that even the most sophisticated computer game on the market is anything other than the result of purely material processes. A skilled computer engineer is able to explain how all the high definition graphics – the soldiers, criminals, athletes, and other assorted characters running around in a computer game – are functions of algorithms and principles of electronics and physics. Keeping this in mind it becomes obvious that the atheist has a very simple way to prove that there is no soul or self that is separate from the physical brain. All he has to do – just like the computer engineer – is to explain the chemical and molecular processes in the brain that produce consciousness, self awareness, and the illusion of the executive "I" who runs the show. Alternatively, he could build a *machine* that has consciousness and self awareness, thus demonstrating that physical processes alone are responsible. Could any assignment be simpler and clearer than that? (Good luck, Dr. Pinker!) As it turns out, it is one of those things much easier said than done. What insights does the world of science actually have to offer us on this subject? Consider the following:

Nobody has the slightest idea how anything material could be conscious. Nobody even knows what it would be like to have the slightest idea about how anything material could be conscious. [13] (Dr. Jerry Fodor, Professor of Philosophy and cognitive scientist, Rutgers University)

The problem of consciousness tends to embarrass biologists. Taking it to be an aspect of living things, they feel they should know about it and be able to tell physicists about it, **whereas they have nothing relevant to say.** [14] (Dr. George Wald, Nobel Prize winning biologist)

Consciousness seems to me to be wholly impervious to science. It does not lie as an indigestible element within science, but just the opposite: Science is the highly digestible element within consciousness... [15] (Dr. George Wald)

The Hard Problem...is why there is first-person subjective experience. The Hard Problem is explaining how subjective experience arises from neural computation. The problem is hard because no one knows what a solution might look like **...everyone agrees that the hard problem remains a mystery.** [16] (Dr. Steven Pinker)

The human brain is the most complex object in the known universe...No scientific problem compares to it...One challenge is that **we are still clueless about how the brain represents the content of our thoughts and feelings.** [17] (Dr. Steven Pinker)

What is consciousness? Well, I don't know how to define it. **I think this is not the moment to attempt to define consciousness, since we do not know what it is.** [18] (Sir Roger Penrose, mathematical physicist)

Science's biggest mystery is the nature of consciousness. It is not that we possess bad or imperfect theories of human awareness; we simply have no such theories at all. About all we know about consciousness is

that it has something to do with the head, rather than the foot.[19]
(Dr. Nick Herbert, Physicist)

If the phenomena of consciousness and self awareness are such profound scientific mysteries, it would stand to reason that scientific opinions about the nature of the "self" (which is at the very center of consciousness and self awareness) if expressed at all, would be offered in the most humble, guarded, and tenuous of terms. However, even after admitting that he has no meaningful understanding of the "self" and consciousness, that he has "nothing relevant to say" on the topic, and despite the fact that it is a subject which is "wholly impervious to science", the skeptic recklessly and obliviously drones on...

Steven Pinker declares, "There's no sense that we can make of that..."

Dr. Steven Pinker, cognitive scientist, informs us of the following:

> I don't believe there is such a thing as...a ghost in the machine, a spirit, or a soul, that somehow reads the TV screen of the senses and pushes buttons and pulls levers of behavior. There's no sense we can make of that...our behavior is the product of physical processes in the brain. [20]

The only things here that don't make sense are Pinker's incoherent statements about the nature of human behavior. If what Pinker says is true, then *"who"* analyzed the evidence and reached the conclusion that "our behavior is the product of physical processes in the brain?" *"Who"* decided that there is no soul and that the "self" is an illusion? *"Who"* is *fully aware and conscious* of the fact that there is no distinct self pushing buttons and pulling levers? If there is no *"who"* evaluating and deciding, all that is left is raw data and sensory information; in other words, what remains is a *"what,"* not a *"who."* Information cannot understand, evaluate, or make decisions by itself, *because it has no self*; it has no power, it has no ability to act, it has no faculty of will. This is self-evidently true whether the information and data in question are photographs from the Hubble Space Telescope, test results from a hospital laboratory, or sensory data and information stored in a human brain. Data and information are totally inert and useless unless perceived, examined, evaluated, and acted upon by a *"who," i.e., a self.* To suggest that the brain automatically analyzes data and issues instructions like a sophisticated computer controlling a factory assembly line would be a flagrant begging of the question. The computer itself is useless without the assistance of a very real *"who"* in the form of a programmer or software engineer that gives the computer instructions. Pinker is very aware of the significance of this dilemma, but is determined at all costs not allow a separate self to skulk into the picture. When asked in an interview how we *know* that there is no "ghost in the machine," *i.e.,* a spirit and soul that makes decisions, Pinker responded with the following:

> Well, we certainly can't prove it [translation: he really **doesn't** know] but on the other hand we have no reason to believe it either...the brain has a mind boggling complexity, 100 billion neurons, connected by 100 trillion synapses which is fully commensurate with the mind boggling complexity of the human mind. If we opened up the skull and the brain was just spam or oatmeal, with no structure, we'd really have to think there is some magical extra ingredient. When you look at the staggering complexity of the neural network **you immediately see that it's capable of doing computations that we can't even dream of working out right now**, but the physical basis is there for complex intelligence. [21]

In other words, even though "nobody has the slightest idea how anything material could be conscious," even though scientists have "nothing relevant to say" on this topic, even though "everyone agrees that [consciousness] remains a mystery," *even though we have no idea whatsoever how it works,* the non-oatmeal/spam brain has such incredible "mind boggling" complexity that you can "immediately see" that it's capable of accomplishing astounding feats. Thus, Pinker deduces that the brain is even capable of pulling off the fantastic trick of self awareness, of fooling us into thinking that there is "someone" making decisions, and even creating the illusion that we are aware of ourselves making these decisions (gee, what a sparkling example of strictly scientific reasoning based on empirically established facts). In short, what is Pinker's answer to the dilemma we posed above? *Abrakadabra, Cerebral Magic!* I don't begrudge Dr. Pinker the right to his belief in the magical, mystical abilities of neurons and synapses; that right is protected by the Constitution of the United States of America. However, I think he does display more than a little bit of chutzpah by trying to palm these conclusions off as Science.

The root cause of this spiritual-phobia on the part of the skeptic is wonderfully illustrated in this recounting by Ernest Becker – in his Pulitzer Prize winning book, *The Denial of Death* – of a conversation between Sigmund Freud and one of his closest disciples, Alfred Ernest Jones:

> Once while discussing psychic phenomena, Jones made the remark, "If one could believe in mental processes floating in the air, one could go on to a belief in angels," at which point Freud closed the discussion with the comment, "Quite so, even der liebe Gott." [22]

Once the possibility of a separate self is on the table, we are only a short step away from the possibility of God himself. In a TIME magazine article entitled "The Mystery of Consciousness", (January, 2007) Dr. Pinker tells us, "No one knows what to do with the Hard Problem [how something material could be conscious]. Some people may see it as an opening to sneak the soul back in." Someone should inform the distinguished Dr. Pinker that we do not need to "sneak" the soul back in, because – despite the desperate and foolish atheistic assertions to the contrary – we never got rid of it in the first place. If the skeptic is not prepared to accept the idea of a spiritual soul that is separate from the brain, at least an unconditional acknowledgment of ignorance or lack of clarity on the matter would be a refreshing and admirable demonstration of intellectual integrity. Instead – much like a child who sticks his fingers in his ears while obnoxiously chanting, "I can't hear you" – the skeptic/atheist/materialist triumphantly declares that the "self" obviously *does not exist!*

To remain a non-believer the atheist is prepared to deny our very grasp on reality

Atheists are prepared to burrow very deep down the materialist rabbit hole in order to avoid any possible confrontation with the spiritual. How deep? Deep enough to cast doubt on our very connection with reality...The skeptic claims that neuroscience provides evidence that there is no spirit or soul controlling our actions, and that the intuitive notion that there resides within us a separate "executive" self is an illusion. Leaving totally aside the issue of whether or not that assessment of the neuroscientific data is accurate, there is a much more fundamental question that must be addressed. *By what unique entitlement, privilege, or faculty does the skeptic confidently disavow as illusory the all-pervasive notion of a separate "self," yet simultaneously justify his absolute trust in his own perceptions and analysis regarding the "scientific" examination of the brain, that led him to reach that conclusion in the first place?*

In other words, the crippling flaw of the atheist/materialist position is starkly highlighted by a simple fact: our awareness of possessing a unique sense of consciousness (*i.e.,* the "self") does not lie within our brain, *our awareness of possessing a brain lies within our unique sense of consciousness.* The "self" is not a projection of the brain. *Our knowledge of the brain is a projection or perception of the "self."*

Our entire interface with what we perceive and define as reality starts with our awareness of self and is processed through the self; if that is an illusion, what is to stop us from concluding that everything we perceive is an illusion, including scientific research? By declaring the self as illusory, the materialist has breached the walls that protect our grip on a coherent sense of reality. Our entire concept of reality presupposes a distinction between the perceiver and the perceived. It is axiomatic that it is the "self" or the "executive I" who evaluates, discerns, and decides what is real and what is fantasy; once that is gone, our access to reality has been obliterated. All that remains is a series of perceptions and sensations whose true source and nature are unverifiable. There is no longer any distinction between "me" and what I perceive. There is no longer any difference between our "illusory" perception of the self, our "illusory" perception that we possess a brain, and our "illusory" perceptions about a scientific examination of that brain. Everything is now up for grabs, including our ability to make decisions. Atheist academic Dr. Susan Blackmore informs us that,

> The self is not the initiator of actions, it does not "have" consciousness and it does not "do" the deliberating. There is no truth to the idea of an inner self inside my body that controls the body and is conscious. Since this idea is false so is the idea of my conscious self having free will...[it is a] false idea that there is someone inside who is in charge...Free will, like the self who "has" it, is an illusion. [23]

It may seem hard to believe, but there is certain logic behind this madness. Once you have accepted on faith that "our behavior is [solely] the product of physical processes of the brain," then it follows that not only is the "self" an illusion, but the intuitive feeling that the self is making choices, is also an illusion. Blackmore is in distinguished company. Nobel laureate, Bertrand Russell concurs regarding the illusory nature of free will:

> The first dogma which I came to disbelieve was that of free will. It seemed to me that all notions of matter were determined by the laws of dynamics and could not therefore be influenced by human wills. [24]

The above statement by Russell is not just nonsense of a *high* order; it is nonsense of a *cosmic and celestial* order! If there is no free will, not only would it be absurd to suggest that a person could "come to disbelieve" anything, it would be absurd to suggest that one could "come to *believe*" anything either. Everything is "determined" by the "laws of dynamics," like a series of billiard balls hitting each other. Just as the billiard ball has no control over its direction, velocity, or the force with which it collides with the next ball, a person has no control over what he or she believes or doesn't believe. If one believes in God, it is because an inescapable series of causes and effects determined that belief. If one is an atheist, it would be the result of exactly the same type of process. When Russell believed in free will, it had nothing to do with his understanding or choices, and when he ceased believing in free will it had nothing to do with his understanding or choices as well. It was *inevitable* that he would deny the dogma of free will. In fact, if we follow this line of reasoning to its logical conclusion, all discussion, argument, evidence, debate, and even scientific investigation on any subject would be completely useless and pointless. Everything we believe, perceive, understand, contemplate, all conclusions we reach, *etc.,* are ineluctably ordained as the inevitable results of a series of causes and effects which are governed by the laws of physics and chemistry. After coming to the above conclusions, I made the pleasant discovery that on this point I am in distinguished company. The famed British philosopher of science, Sir Karl Popper writes that:

> ...physical determinism is a theory which, if it is true, is not arguable, since it must explain all our reactions, **including what appear to us as beliefs based on arguments, as due to purely physical conditions.** Purely physical conditions, including our physical environment, make us say or accept whatever we say or accept... [25]

According to the atheistic/materialistic view, we do not really think our own thoughts, experience our own lives, or decide our own actions. It is all just an inescapable series of deterministic events. If this sounds so outrageously absurd that one feels hard pressed to believe that such an opinion could actually be expressed, think again. Here is atheist author Sam Harris:

> While most of us go through life feeling like we are the thinker of our thoughts and the experiencer of our experiences, **from the perspective of science we know that this is a false view.** [26]

Gee, I wonder...are we the *speakers of our speakings and the writers of our writings?* In the confused world of the atheist, the "self" is an illusion, free will is an illusion, we don't think our own thoughts, we don't experience our own experiences, and in fact, outside of our own thoughts there is no verifiable reality at all. All of this provides an illuminating backdrop for the following episode that is described by Dr. David Berlinski in his classic work (which I highly and enthusiastically recommend), *The Devil's Delusion: Atheism and Its Scientific Pretensions,*

> In a recent BBC program entitled "A Brief History of Unbelief", the host, Jonathan Miller, and his guest, philosopher Colin Mcginn, engaged in a veritable orgy of competitive skepticism, so much so that in the end, the viewer was left wondering whether either man believed sincerely in the existence of the other. [27]

To be fair, not every atheist flatly denies the existence of free will as do Bertrand Russell, Susan Blackmore, and Cornell University's Will Provine. Prominent atheist/materialists such as Daniel Dennet and Richard Dawkins desperately struggle to straddle both sides of the fence and retain some concept of free will (unsuccessfully, as far as I'm concerned), while at the same time carefully trying avoid the "trap" of admitting the existence of a "self" (which is exercising that will) that is separate from the brain. I would also add that even those atheists who express these ridiculous ideas don't actually live their lives as if they are true.* From their pulpits in the rarified world of the university lecture hall, they declare the "self", free will, thoughts, and experience as illusory, and then go back to everyday living like the rest of mankind. In other words, they continue living and acting as if their "self" is absolutely real, as if they have free will, and as if their own thoughts and experiences truly belong to them.

Is there a scientific basis for a materialist view of consciousness?

What *is* the "scientific" basis for a strictly materialistic view of the brain and consciousness? Dr. Steven Pinker briefly summarizes his approach in an article entitled "The Mystery of Consciousness" that appeared in TIME Magazine in January, 2007:

> Scientists have exorcised the ghost from the machine not because they are mechanistic killjoys, but because they have amassed evidence that every aspect of consciousness can be tied to the brain. Using functional MRI, cognitive neuroscientists can almost read people's thoughts from the blood flow in their brains. They can tell, for instance, whether a person is thinking about a face or a place or whether the picture the person is looking at is of a bottle or a shoe...And consciousness can be pushed around by physical manipulations. Electrical stimulation of the brain during surgery can cause a person to have hallucinations that are indistinguishable from reality, such as a song playing in the room or a childhood birthday party. Chemicals that affect the brain, from caffeine and alcohol to Prozac and LSD, can profoundly alter how people think, feel and see. [28]

It's very difficult to understand what relevance any of this has

---

* Imagine Susan Blackmore buying paint for her living room. The clerk asks her if she would like the peach color or the off-white. She answers, "I *must* choose the peach!"

to the question of the existence or non-existence of a separate self or a soul.

A) I decide to have a conversation with a friend. A cognitive neuroscientist in another room monitoring the brain activity correctly assesses that I am involved in a conversation. I then decide to end the conversation and begin contemplating a mathematical problem that has been bothering me for a long time. The neuroscientist again correctly assesses that I am now involved in abstract reasoning. How does that prove that I don't have a soul or make free will decisions? While there is no doubt that the brain is involved in the process of both the conversation and my contemplation of mathematics, it is also clear that more is going on than just the sum total of neural and cerebral activity. It was "my" decision (*i.e.* my soul) to have a conversation that caused a particular part of my brain to light up; it was "my" decision to think about mathematics that caused a different part of my brain to light up. This points clearly to a separate self who is in control. The crucial issue is not the fact that scientists can identify the different parts of the brain that are involved in different functions, but what is the connection between my decision and my brain? How does my brain know to switch cerebral circuits, when I decide to switch my activity? How and why does my will turn on and off different parts of the brain? How does "my" brain convey information to "me"?

B) A specific part of my brain is electrically stimulated during surgery and I vividly relive the experience of my mother singing a lullaby to me when I was a child. Again I ask, what does this have to do with the existence of the soul and again Pinker has ignored the essential point. The issue that needs to be addressed is not *that* I experience the song when the brain is poked in the right way, but "who" is experiencing the song right now, "who" experienced the song in childhood, and how is it possible for anything material to be conscious and self aware of experiences like lullabies to begin with?

C) *"Chemicals that affect the brain...can profoundly alter how people think, feel, and see."* What is Pinkers' point here? That artificial manipulation of the brain affects me? Was that actually ever in question? If getting punched in the stomach affects my brain and can alter how I think, feel, and see, why would I expect a lesser result if the brain itself is artificially manipulated? Is he trying to tell us that before the advent of modern neuroscience nobody ever noticed that alcohol affects people's behavior? A slight rephrasing of Pinkers' words highlights the truly relevant issues that are being ignored: "chemicals that affect the brain...can profoundly alter how "I" think, feel, and see." "Who" is thinking, "who" is feeling, "who" is seeing (and "who" is getting drunk and stoned?), and how is it possible for me to think, feel, and see in the first place?

D) In truth, everything that Pinker writes above is an outstanding example of the "atheistic disconnect." How is it possible for him to state on the one hand, that it is a total "mystery" how "first-person subjective experience...arises from neural computation;" that "we are still clueless about how the brain represents the content of our thoughts and feelings;" and then a moment later state that scientists have "amassed evidence that *every aspect* of consciousness can be tied to the brain." Yes Dr. Pinker, *every* aspect of consciousness except **what it is, how it works, and how such a thing could be possible in the first place!** The evidence that he presents only tells us that the physical brain is *involved* in many aspects of consciousness (which frankly, is not such an earth shattering revelation); it does not even begin to tell us what consciousness is and it does not in any way contradict the notion of a separate self or soul that works in tandem with the brain. In fact, all the "scientific evidence" that Pinker presents is nothing more than an elaborate repetition of what physicist Nick Herbert had already stated so simply and elegantly: "About all we know about consciousness is that it has something to do with the head and not the foot."

Mind over matter: "I" can use my free will to change my brain

As we have discussed at length, the atheist claims that the "self" who is in control of decision-making is an illusion created by the brain. If that were true, then it would certainly be impossible for me to physically affect my brain through my own willful decisions. How could an illusion created by the brain actually turn around and alter brain function in a way that could be scientifically documented? It would be as if a character in a computer game actually turned around and changed the program, function, and hardware of the game itself – a wonderful idea for a science fiction story or an episode on *The Twilight Zone*, but impossible in the real world. Evidence of such phenomena would be a crushing blow to the materialist view of reality.

Via the latest brain imaging technology, Canadian neuroscientist Dr. Mario Beauregard, among others, has documented that "I" can actually change the patterns of activity in my brain through the exercise of my will. In the following passage he briefly summarizes some of his findings:

> Materialists must believe that their minds are simply an illusion created by the workings of their brain and therefore that free will does not really exist and could have no influence in controlling any disorder. But nonmaterialist approaches have clearly demonstrated mental health benefits...Jeffrey Schwartz...a UCLA neuropsychiatrist, treats obsessive-compulsive disorder – a neuropsychiatric disease marked by distressing, intrusive, and unwanted thoughts – by getting patients to reprogram their brains. Their minds change their brains. Similarly, some of my neuroscientist colleagues at the University of Montreal and I have demonstrated, via brain imaging techniques, the following:
>
> • Women and young girls can voluntarily control their level of response to sad thoughts, though young girls found it more difficult to do so
> • Men who view erotic films are quite able to control their responses to them, when asked to do so.
> • People who suffer from phobias such as spider phobia can reorganize their brains so that they lose the fear.
>
> Evidence of the mind's control over the brain is actually captured in these studies. There *is* such a thing as "mind over matter". We do have will power, consciousness, and emotions, and combined with a sense of purpose and meaning, we can effect change.[29]

Dr. Reuven Feuerstein is an educational and cognitive psychologist who studied under one of the great pioneers in cognitive psychology, Dr. Jean Piaget. Feuerstein is the founder and director of the International Center for the Enhancement of Learning Potential (ICELP) in Jerusalem. The staff and faculty of ICELP, putting into practice the protocols and techniques developed by Feuerstein, have achieved astounding results in restoring function and dramatically increasing learning potential in people with conditions such as: autism, Down syndrome, and those who have suffered brain damage in terrorist attacks, strokes, drownings and car accidents. In November of 2008, Feuerstein addressed the National Urban Alliance:

> Human beings are modifiable and not just modifiable in terms of their behavior...not just the structure of their behavior can be modified, but actually the neural system can be modified, and marvelously, miraculously. We can point out the fact that the behavior which we impose on our brain, modifies our brain. It means it's not only the brain which shapes our behavior; **our behavior shapes the nature of the hardware of our brain.** [30]

As the aforementioned Dr. Jeffrey Schwartz so appropriately concludes, "The time has come for [those who advocate a purely materialistic view of] science to confront the serious implications of the fact that directed, willed mental activity can clearly and systematically alter brain function." [31] The actuality of a "self" that is separate from our physical being is not the end point of our exploration of spirituality, it is just the beginning. The spiritual ocean we swim in is quite large...

Soul Power: Communication through speech

Have you ever stopped to ask yourself what is happening when you have a conversation with another person? We do it so often and naturally that it is taken for granted. If you have children then you have watched your children learn how to talk. Did they think thoughts before they learned how to talk? In what language were they thinking? How does a young child conceive the thought that he wants a drink, when he does not know any words at all? After all, children who do not know how to speak a language still are able to communicate (and they still get thirsty). They can make it very clear to their parents or care-givers that they have wants and needs. My three-year-old daughter many times would translate for us when we could not understand what her one-year old brother wanted. He would be making sounds that to us were incomprehensible and somehow she could tell he wanted a particular toy, or a drink, etc. The critical question however, is what was going on in *his* head as he was speaking this incomprehensible language? No matter what explanation you may offer, it's clear he was thinking ideas that he did not yet know how to translate into language.

"Words" and "ideas" are two separate things

The *thought* "I want a drink," is not the same thing as the *words* "I want a drink." In fact, the two in a certain sense have absolutely nothing to do with each other. My daughter under-stood by certain sounds her little brother made that he was thinking inside his head "I want a drink," even though he could not yet speak the words, and in fact he was even too young to *think* the words. *The words themselves mean nothing at all.* They are simply arbitrary sounds that we use to express an idea. The obvious proof of this is that if someone says "I want a drink" in a foreign language we have no idea what they are talking about.

"Words" are meaningless sounds — the "idea" or "information" is clear and specific

I have a thought in my head: "I desire to imbibe liquid into my body." I then proceed to form a series of *arbitrary, intrinsical-ly senseless* sounds with my mouth. These sounds travel through the air where they are heard by another person, who then decodes them and understands to bring me a glass of water. We take it for granted because we do it all the time, but what is tran-spiring is nothing short of miraculous. I am taking *ideas* in my head and sending them through the air to other people. *I am attaching ideas to sound waves.* Remember, the sound, or word, is not the same as the idea, or the particular information I am communicating. The word is an arbitrary, meaningless sound, but the information or message is very specific and very meaningful. They are two completely unrelated things and yet somehow I am able to bind them together. Let's try to understand this from the perspective of the atheistic scientist.

What parts of a conversation will he be able to measure and quantify in the laboratory? He can monitor the brain activity from the person speaking, he can measure the sound waves as they travel through the air, and he can monitor brain activity in the person listening to the words. Can the scientist measure, quantify, or define the "idea," the "information," or "message" that passes between two people? Can he "touch" the idea? Can he "smell" the idea? Can he "see" the idea? Can he "taste" the idea? In truth he cannot even "hear" the information. He can only understand what is being said if he also speaks the language, but that is just begging the question. The idea itself, "I want a drink of water," is not accessible through any of our physical senses, nor can it be quantified or measured, for the simple reason that it is not physical or material in any way. If I speak complete gibberish in the same tone and for the same amount of time, the measurements of the scientist will be the same: electrical activity and sound waves. Evolutionary biologist George Williams put it this way, "You can speak of galaxies and particles of dust in the same terms because they both have mass and charge and length and width. [But] you can't do that with *information* and matter...Information doesn't have mass or charge or length in millimeters..." [32]

Even Dr. Steven Pinker, the highly celebrated Harvard professor specializing in cognition and linguistics, can barely contain his wonder and awe when contemplating the human capacity for language. This self-declared "proud atheist" manages to seamlessly weave the "m" word into his description of that remarkable faculty called language in the very first paragraph of his award winning book, *The Language Instinct: How the Mind Creates Language*:

> You are taking part in one of the wonders of the natural world. For you and I are members of a species with a remarkable ability...That ability is language...The ability comes so naturally that we are apt to forget what a **miracle** it is. [33]

A miracle, indeed! All day long we are involved in binding together the spiritual reality of ideas and thoughts, with the physical reality of sound. Speech is nothing less than one soul relaying a spiritual message to another soul through the physical medium of sound. We are just so used to it, that we never take the trouble to think about what is actually happening.

The Miracle of Written Language

Many years ago, I saw a film about a Catholic missionary who was sent to the Native Americans living in the Great Lakes area of the North American Continent.[34] The story takes place in the early part of the 17th century. These Indians had no written language. In one scene they express their bewilderment as to what the white men are doing scratching strange symbols on pieces of paper. The priest finds that he cannot explain it to them conceptually, so he asks one of the Indians to say a word. He says "canoe". The priest writes the word, and then he and the Indians who are watching walk 10 or 15 yards over to another of the white men. The priest then asks this man to read the word. He reads "canoe." The Indians jump back in horrified astonishment. They start screaming at the priest that what he just did could only be the work of a demon.

Of course we just shake our heads and condescendingly smile at these primitives who would mistake something as simple and as elementary as written words for witchcraft or the work of a demon. However, the reason we do not share their horror and awe is not because the written word is so simple and elementary, it is only because we have become so used to the mind boggling, fantastic notion of written language.

I can send my thoughts across the ocean

I have a thought in my head. I have an emotion that I am feeling. I have ideas I want to communicate. I want someone across the ocean to know how I feel, to know what I am thinking, to understand what I understand. How can I possibly accomplish such a feat? Very simple; I take a pen or pencil, scratch a few lines on a piece of paper, and someone thousands of miles away knows my thoughts and feelings. If I scratch the right symbols I can bring a person to tears, to feel joy and happiness, to feel anger or disappointment. Not only can I attach non-material ideas and feelings to sound waves, I can attach them to lines on a piece of paper, or for that matter to symbols on a computer screen. I again bind the spiritual and physical.

Just like the sounds of a spoken language, letters mean *absolutely nothing.* They are random, arbitrary markings made with a pen, pencil, crayon, or keyboard. An English speaker looking at Arabic or Chinese writing for the first time would have no idea if he was looking at an alphabet or the random doodling of a child. Renowned Hungarian scientist and philosopher Michael Polanyi put it this way:

> A book transmits information. But the transmission of the information cannot be represented in terms of chemical and physical principles. In other words, the operation of the book is not reducible to chemical terms... [35]

Imagine the most sophisticated and advanced laboratory that exists in the world today, and have the scientists there analyze the paper and the markings on the paper. They can tell you the chemical composition and the molecular structure of the paper and the ink, but they cannot ever hope to measure or quantify the ideas and feelings that are contained in the words *and yet they are there nonetheless.* The only monitor capable of detecting the ideas, concepts, and emotions contained in the sound of a human voice or in the writing of a human poet, is the "monitor" called the human soul.

We have the ability to send messages on light waves

Not only can I bind a non-material/spiritual idea or piece of information to markings on a piece of paper and FedEx it to you overnight (or instantaneously by email); not only can I attach emotions, concepts, and information to a sound wave and send it to you at the speed of sound; I even have the ability to attach non-material messages to a light wave and send it to you at the speed of light without the aid of a video camera, satellite, telephone, or computer. Does it sound too fantastic to believe, like science fiction? It is just another illustration of how routine and habit can dull our awareness to the miraculous things going on around us all the time.

A loved one is in surgery. You are anxiously awaiting word on the outcome of the delicate and critical procedure. At the other end of the waiting room you see the chief surgeon emerge still dressed in his scrubs. He catches your eye, flashes a big wide smile, gives you the thumbs up, and then disappears back behind the swinging doors. You breathe a sigh of relief and whisper a prayer of thanks (if you're not an atheist). What just happened?

If I were to offer a scientific description of this event it would go something like this: *Light waves traveling at app. 186,000 miles per second were reflected off the figure in surgical scrubs, were perceived by your eye, and via your optic nerve were sent to your brain where the image was analyzed. Your brain told you that you were looking at a surgeon with his lips pulled back exposing his teeth and his thumb extended upward. You concluded that the doctor was conveying to you a message that the surgery was successful and the patient will be fine.* How was the doctor able to send you the message and how were you able to understand the message?

As strange as it may sound, what happened was that the doctor attached a spiritual entity (a message) to a light wave and sent it to you. His physical gestures were the language, but it was a language that arrived via light. The information was *not* "somebody's lips pulled back exposing their teeth" (a smile); the information was *not* "an extended thumb" (thumbs up). The information was that *the surgery was successful and the patient is doing fine.* One of the powers of the human soul is to take spiritual ideas and information, and bring them into the material world by attaching them to a physical gesture.

All thoughts, ideas, and information are spiritual entities that can only be brought into our material word by being attached to a material entity (*i.e.* writing, sound, gestures, etc.) Imagine someone under a type of anesthesia where he is fully conscious, but cannot move (except to breathe) or speak. Despite the fact that this person's head is filled with all kinds of thoughts, information, and feelings, no one else can possibly be aware of what they are. This simple reason is because the tools needed to bring these spiritual entities into our physical universe are inoperable. I repeat, the thoughts, ideas, feelings, and information exist, but they are "trapped" in the spiritual realm.

Self Esteem: A projection of our spiritual essence

Most of us have skeletons in our closets. It may be something very big, or perhaps relatively small, but just about everyone has done things that they hope and pray no one ever finds out about. Picture in your mind that particular "skeleton" and imagine being at a joyous public gathering of those who are close to you (birthday party, engagement party, wedding, etc.), and someone reveals to everyone assembled the exact details of that terrible thing that you did. That terrible, horrible deed that you had hoped would stay secret for all eternity. What is your reaction? Most likely, an indescribably painful feeling of humiliation. If you were hooked up to an array of body sensors, they would certainly record a sudden, profound change in your body chemistry, heart rate, brain waves, etc.

What exactly happened that caused your physical bodily functions to go haywire? Did someone inject a chemical into your body? Did you inhale a gas? Did you ingest a solid or liquid? *Was there any change at all in the physical universe?* The only thing that changed was that something you had done, which up until now was a secret, became public knowledge. Is there a scientific measurement for quantifying when a secret is not a secret anymore? For that matter, is there a scientific measurement for a secret altogether? Is there any possible way to scientifically detect such a thing? How is it possible to destroy someone's self esteem with cruel words and insults? Are there tiny pieces of chemicals that enter into the person along with the offending words? How is it possible to lift somebody with a genuine compliment or kind words? Are there mysterious molecular structures that float through the air which enter a person's body along with the heartfelt praise and acknowledgement? I defy any scientist to demonstrate that there is a material, chemical, or molecular basis to explain why vicious or compassionate words, scrawlings on a piece of paper, or physical gestures, can have such a profound effect on another human being.

The spiritual/non-material dimension of life is very plausible

It has become quite clear that when Baggini depicts the non-material world of the soul as an "implausible tale" he is grossly mistaken. Not only is it not an "implausible tale" but it is palpably and unmistakably an integral part of the reality in which we exist, as evidenced by our sense of self awareness, the ability of the "self" to reprogram brain patterns, our relentless quest for transcendent meaning, the spoken word, written language, non verbal communication, and our sense of self-esteem. It is also unquestionably true that the spiritual and physical interact and affect one another.

It is the atheist/materialist who must prove that it does *not* exist. It is the atheist who must demonstrate that the flow of ideas and information between human beings – whether in the form of the written word, spoken word, or physical gestures – can be accounted for and understood within the strict parameters of the laws of chemistry and physics. When I reveal an unpleasant secret about another human being, the atheist must demonstrate that a "secret" has material, chemical and molecular properties that cause the physical and mental reactions we call "humiliation." It is the atheist who must demonstrate that consciousness, the self, ideas, thoughts, concepts, emotions, communication, and self esteem are definable wholly in terms of physical "stuff." It is the atheist who must produce a plausible, empirically demonstrable alternative to the self evident reality of the ocean of spirituality in which all mankind is immersed.

We have thus far seen Richard Dawkins and his cohorts attempting to escape the inescapable drive for transcendent meaning and chasing "comforting fictions" while trying to make sense out of their senseless atheistic lives. We have also analyzed the failed attempts by Julian Baggini, Steven Pinker, and other skeptics to pigeonhole all human experience into the world of materialism. We will now investigate the last, and in a certain sense, the most crucial of the three major concepts that were mentioned at the beginning of Chapter 6: Morality. Over the next three chapters we will discover a rather astonishing fact about the relationship between moral values and atheism; namely, that there is none! Moral values have no place at all in the atheistic worldview, or perhaps it might be more precisely stated that for the atheist, moral values have no objective significance. Since the atheist claims we are nothing more than upright walking primates, human values are qualitatively no different and certainly no more significant than the "values" that guide the lives and behavior of our jungle dwelling relatives. We will see that true moral principles can only exist in a Godly universe; in a universe where the human being is inherently different than all other creatures. In the world of the atheist there is neither morality nor immorality, only **amorality...**

Part IV

Atheism and Morality

— Chapter 8 —

*The Amoral World
of Atheism*

— Chapter 9 —

*Euthyphro:
A Philosophical Dinosaur*

— Chapter 10 —

*The Source of the Inborn
Moral Imperative:
One God*

Chapter 8

*The Amoral World
of Atheism*

The Two-Legged Darwinian "Animal Farm"

One obvious and inescapable implication of atheism is this: We are qualitatively no different than any other animal. George Gaylord Simpson, paleontologist and highly influential evolutionary biologist expressed this idea in the following manner:

> Man is the result of a purposeless and materialistic process that did not have a human in mind. He was not planned. He is a state of matter, a form of life, a sort of animal, and a species in the order of primates, akin nearly or remotely, to all life, and indeed, to all that is material. [1]

"Amoral": A) neither moral nor immoral; B) outside the bounds of that to which moral judgments apply (Webster's Third New International Dictionary)

The world of the animal is *amoral.* The world of the animal is "outside the bounds of that to which moral judgments apply." When a lion pulls down and kills a zebra, the lion has not done anything "moral nor immoral." That is simply the way nature operates, the way things are. If it is true that we are part of the animal world, there is no difference between a lion killing a zebra, a person killing a zebra, and a person killing a person. Why is one viewed as the way nature operates and one suddenly labeled immoral? The intellectually honest atheist knows that morality is nothing more than a *word* that an individual or society assigns to behavior that it subjectively has decided it prefers. Subjective morality has no inherent significance. In other words, the fact that the zebra quite clearly prefers, subjectively, not to be eaten by the lion in no way at all changes the amoral nature of the act. In the same way, if a particular "human animal" would prefer not to be harmed by another "human animal" it does not magically create a mysterious entity called morality. For the atheist there is no real meaning to the word "morality." *It means whatever the individual or the particular society wants it to mean.*

> Morality is the custom of one's country and the current feelings of one's peers. Cannibalism is moral in a cannibalistic country. [2] (Samuel Butler)

I would add to the above that just as cannibalism is moral in a cannibalistic country, so too, slavery is moral in a country that has slaves, lynchings are moral in a society that accepts lynchings, and killing unwanted female infants is moral in a society where females are considered inferior and undesirable.

The absolutely subjective nature of atheistic morality is inescapable

Morality for the atheist is just another way of saying, "Different Strokes for Different Folks." No particular society is "right," and no particular society is "wrong." Each society establishes, maintains, and modifies its values to suit its own needs. It is absurd for the atheist to suggest that any particular individual or society has the authority to dictate to all human beings what their values should or shouldn't be; it is even more absurd to suggest that the pronouncements of a particular individual or society in any way *obligates* others to behave accordingly. An atheist can say that a certain system of behavior does not appeal to his taste, that he doesn't *like* it, but not that it is *immoral*. A more precise way of putting it would be that what the atheist really means when he labels something as "immoral" is that he subjectively doesn't like it. In the words of one of the most prominent atheistic philosophers of the 20th century, Bertrand Russell:

> I cannot see how to refute the arguments for the subjectivity of ethical values, but I find myself incapable of believing that all that is wrong with wanton cruelty is that I don't like it. [3]

Russell's incredulousness notwithstanding, for the atheist that's exactly the way it is. For Bertrand Russell the only thing that could possibly be wrong with torturing and molesting children is that he subjectively doesn't like it. In fact, a prominent 21st century atheist philosopher, Dr. Joel Marks, confirms this proposition:

> Even though words like "sinful" and "evil" come naturally to the tongue as a description of, say, child-molesting, they do not describe any actual properties of anything...There are no literal sins in the world because there is no literal God...I now maintain nothing is literally right or wrong because there is no Morality...Yet we human beings can still discover plenty of completely-naturally-explainable internal resources for motivating certain preferences. Thus, enough of us are *sufficiently averse to the molesting of children, and would likely continue to be so...* [4]

I am thrilled, on behalf of Dr. Marks' neighbors, that at the present time his personal *"preferences"* are *"likely"* to prevent him from molesting children. However, a word to the wise if you live in his area: Just in case Dr. Marks' personal *"preferences"* change (as is wont to happen with human beings), keep a close watch on your young children!

Is it possible for the atheist to have a meaningful system of morality?

In *Atheism: A Very Short Introduction,* Dr. Julian Baggini explains that, "...religion is a human construct that does not correspond to any metaphysical reality." [5]

Let's assume for arguments sake that the above cited assertion by Dr. Baggini is true. How then would we view religion? Baggini's obvious point is that if religion is just a human construct – with no connection to a higher reality – why should anyone take it seriously? It is just another product of the creative human imagination and has no intrinsic value or meaning at all. It corresponds to nothing except to the imaginative energy and the subjective reality inside the head of its human creator. Baggini then goes on to try to convince us that the atheist can actually have a meaningful set of moral values:

> However, many people think that atheists believe there is no God and no morality...there is nothing to stop atheists from believing in morality, a meaning for life, or human goodness. [6]

If Baggini's ears would only listen to what his own mouth is saying he would see how completely disconnected from reality his position actually is. Not only are *all* atheistic systems nothing more than "human constructs" that do not correspond to any "metaphysical (beyond the physical) reality," the atheist explicitly denies there *is* such a thing as a metaphysical reality. The only things that exist are atoms, molecules, and chemicals. (Dr. Baggini is living in a material world, and he is a material boy!) If, as atheists claim, religion is a human construct that has artificially created concepts such as "God," "revelation," and "commandment," then atheistic ideologies are human constructs that have artificially created concepts such as "values," "meaning," and "morality." In other words, a system of values based on an atheistic world view is in essence another form of "religion" that has at its source nothing more significant than the imagination of its human creator.

Atheism denies a Grand Divine Plan, leaving us with Cosmic Chaos

I present you with another excerpt from Christopher Hitchens' lecture at Sewanee University, "The Moral Necessity of Atheism:"

> If it was true...that we are all part of a grand divine design...What would it actually mean?...It would mean a regime of permanent supervision and surveillance over our lives and personalities...an inescapable authoritarian control...It would be like living in a celestial North Korea...why would you want such a thing to be true?! What a hideous realm of permanent total inescapable unfreedom is being proposed to you...the struggle to throw off this servility is the precondition for liberty, whether personal, intellectual, or moral. [7]

He's absolutely right. How frightening to think about a world with a grand divine design; that would imply that there is actually a real purpose to our existence. How unnerving to think of a world with divine supervision and authority; after all, that would mean we might actually be held accountable for what we did with our lives. That would not be very much fun would it? *Real Purpose? Accountability for our actions?* I mean it almost sounds as if the way we would have to conduct ourselves is…is…like responsible adults! (Gasp!)

I'm sure there are readers who thought I was indulging in hyperbole or literary license when I said that atheists tend to disconnect from certain obvious truths and realities to maintain their non-belief. I want to make it clear that I meant it exactly the way I wrote it in the first chapter. Did anyone notice which government Hitchens describes as the epitome of authoritarian repression? North Korea, *an officially atheistic regime*. Mazel Tov! *Now* I understand the moral necessity of atheism. In truth though, I'm really not being fair. The reason why the government of North Korea is so murderously repressive is because they only speak Korean. If they spoke English, they could watch Hitchens' lecture on YouTube like I did and they would finally find out that "the struggle to throw off this servility [of a grand divine design] is the precondition for liberty, whether personal, intellectual, or moral!!"

Hitchens can jabber on about personal liberty but he and other atheists will never admit the obvious truth: that throwing off the yoke of divine authority simply means that I am "free" to do whatever the hell I please (as long as I can get away with it of course). The world of the atheist is the world that exists in the novel *The Lord of the Flies:* a group of wild children who ultimately are responsible to no one and accountable to no one but themselves. The Talmudic phrase in Aramaic that describes this very old ideology is *Leis Din, V'leis Dayan* — "There is No Judgment and there is No Judge." The only inescapable, inviolable, and relentless rule of existence is that "ol' black magic" called survival of the fittest.

The True Amoral Face of Atheism

The true face of Atheism shines through in all its amoral glory in the following statements by a number of well-known atheists:

With savages, the weak in body and mind are soon eliminated; and those that survive commonly exhibit a vigorous state of health...there is reason to believe that vaccination has preserved thousands, who from a weak constitution would formerly have succumbed to small pox. Thus the weak members of civilized societies propagate their kind. No one who has attended to the breeding of animals will doubt that this must be highly injurious to the race of man...but excepting in the case of man itself, hardly any one is so ignorant as to allow his worst animals to breed." [8] (Charles Darwin)

Darwin, by explicitly equating the development of humans with the breeding of animals, has established the philosophical and ideological basis for the horrors that follow.

The men of the New Republic will not be squeamish, either, in facing or inflicting death...they will have an ideal that will make killing worthwhile...they will contrive a land legislation that will keep the black, or yellow, or mean white squatter on the move...this thing this euthanasia of the weak...is possible...it will be permissible, and I have little or no doubt that in the future it will be planned and achieved. [9] (H.G. Wells, British author of *The Time Machine, The Invisible Man, and War of the Worlds*)

Wells passionately advocated the implementation of the Darwinian principle of survival of the fittest by killing off "unfit" humans. Wells, who some called the "father of Science Fiction," also seemed to have a prophetic streak in his soul. His noble vision of euthanasia was planned and achieved by the Germans less than 40 years after he wrote this in 1902. In Nazi Germany the Darwinian inspired ideal was carried out with typical German meticulousness and efficiency. Close to 300,000 individuals identified as "useless eaters, persons devoid of value, worthless people, superfluous people, misfits, undesirables, cripples, schizophrenics, idiots, *etc.*" were put to death in a plan carried out by a chain of mental hospitals, professors of psychiatry, and directors and staff members of mental hospitals (from *A Sign For Cain: An Exploration of Human Violence*, Frederic Wertham, (Hale, 1968)

The moment we face it frankly we are driven to the conclusion that the community has a right to put a price on the right to live in it...If people are fit to live, let them live under decent human conditions.

If they are not fit to live, kill them in a decent human way. [10] (George Bernard Shaw, awarded the Nobel Prize for Literature in 1925)

G.B. Shaw, a great playwright, a great atheist, a great Darwinist, and...he had a heart of gold. What a shame he wasn't a Nazi, he would have made sure that people in Auschwitz were murdered "in a decent human way."

> Just as in cancer the best treatment is to eradicate the parasitic growth as quickly as possible, the eugenic defense against the dysgenic effects of afflicted subpopulations is of necessity limited to *equally drastic measures*...when these inferior elements are not effectively eliminated...they destroy the host body as well as themselves. [11] (Dr. Konrad Lorenz, awarded the Nobel Prize for Medicine in 1973)

Gee, with Nobel Prize winners like these, who needs war criminals?

> Even when war is totally abolished, there is still a place in morality for killing...that is to say by killing the unfit...it is one of the unfortunate results of Christianity among us today...that we were led to reject infanticide...We know in the back of our minds that we only do it out of quaint superstition. [12] (Havelock Ellis, an ardent supporter of the Darwinian inspired Eugenics movement)

Hitchens is right, religion *does* poison everything. Imagine how many good, decent, hard working people never experienced the thrill of killing babies because of those silly religious superstitions about the sanctity of life!

It's really a quite natural flow and progression: We are animals, *and* the animal kingdom is driven by natural selection and survival of the fittest, *therefore* let's use our evolutionary gift of intelligence to make our species *more fit* by eliminating the *unfit*.

The truth, of course, is that an individual atheist is not *obligated* to agree with his Nobel Prize winning atheist brothers and murder "unfit" humans. (But he should at least express his kinship by reciting, "Hail Darwin, Father of us all!" with appropriate reverence.) Remember, once the chains of divine authority are broken and true liberty has been achieved, he is free to choose any value system he desires. What will be the basis for his choice?

Ultimately, the only basis for atheistic "morality" is personal preference

In the amoral world of the atheist, the only possible basis for a system of values is "that's the way I like it." Why are the value systems of George Bernard Shaw, Sam Harris, Christopher Hitchens, Fidel Castro, Marquis De Sade, Vladimir Lenin, Jean Paul Sartre, Pol Pot, Julian Baggini, all atheists, so different? For the simple reason that they all have different tastes and personalities. Just like different people like different types of food, different people like and dislike different types of behavior, or for that matter, different types of ideologies. Some enjoy power, some enjoy money, some enjoy hedonism, some enjoy family life, some enjoy academic and intellectual pursuits, some enjoy a humanistic approach, and some enjoy cruelty. None are "right," and none are "wrong." They are all just doing their own thing.

In his introduction to *The Portable Atheist*, Christopher Hitchens makes it very clear that what motivates him is his own personal preference, not moral principles. To put it a different way, what determines his moral principles are his personal preferences. In other words, the two terms are completely interchangeable:

> When I give blood for example, I do not lose a pint, but someone else gains one. There is something about this that appeals to me, and I derive other satisfactions as well from being of assistance to a fellow creature. [13]

His essential motivation is that "something about this appeals to me" not because it is the right thing to do, not because of a moral principle obligating him to help others. If molesting children "appealed" to him – *i.e.,* if he had the physical desires of a pedophile – he would do that (unless of course he was afraid of being caught); if it "appealed" to him to run scams on lonely widows he would do that. Thank God, it "appeals" to him to *give* blood, not *shed* blood like one of his atheist brothers, Pol Pot, the ruler of Cambodia in the late 70's. It "appealed" to Pol Pot to murder millions of Cambodians in order to create a classless Communist society, so that's what *he* did. In the final analysis, the morality of the atheist will always be a function of what "appeals" to him. What else is there? After all, we are animals, and the only thing an animal can do is follow preprogrammed instinct and seek its own personal satisfaction.

Jackals are not immoral; dogs are not moral

Please don't get me wrong, there certainly are atheists whose nature is to be gentle and compassionate; that's what "appeals" to them, but their behavior has nothing to do with morality or moral principles. Keep in mind that dogs, cats, goats, cows, sheep, deer, *etc.*, are all gentle and relatively harmless animals. Some "human animals" are like that too. Sheep are not harmless because of moral principles; that is their nature. To reiterate the point: There is nothing *immoral* about a cheetah killing a gazelle, and there is nothing *moral* about a gazelle being shy and harmless, or for that matter there is nothing *moral* about a beagle being friendly to children.

Josef Stalin, Mao Tse Tung, and Pol Pot (and other Communist despots), who were proponents of the atheistic ideology of Communism, caused more human misery and were responsible for the spilling of more innocent blood in a seventy-year period, than all religious fanatics combined were able to cause, with their wars and atrocities, in the 1000 years preceding Communism. **Mao Tse Tung** *(China)* – murdered 50-70,000,000, **Stalin** *(Soviet Union)* – 20-30,000,000, **Pol-Pot** *(Cambodia)* – about 2,000,000 (but in his defense we should point out that he only had the small country of Cambodia to work with). In the amoral jungle of the atheist world, Stalin, Mao, and Pol Pot are the jackals, hyenas, and wolves, the animals of prey. On the other hand, Sam Harris, Richard Dawkins, and Christopher Hitchens are the goats, cows, and field mice. Jean Paul Sartre expressed this idea quite candidly and lucidly, "It disturbs me no more to find men base, unjust, or selfish, than to see apes mischievous, wolves savage, or the vulture ravenous." [14] (Jean Paul Sartre – French atheistic existentialist philosopher)

A pragmatic "social contract" is not morality

For the atheist, rules and regulations governing behavior are just a function of the "social contract" that different societies make in different ways at different times. Group cooperation is not morality. People in a village cooperate and make rules or else life becomes intolerably stressful. That's being practical, not moral. However, there is no problem attacking, looting, and pillaging the *neighboring* village. In fact, to attack other villages and plunder their wealth can be extremely practical. Not only do you benefit from their wealth, possessions, women, and livestock, but it provides a sense of purpose and accomplishment. This is especially true if you outnumber them, have better weapons, and have stronger fighters.

The religious person, on the other hand, believes that there is a *transcendent* source for his values, namely God. Ultimately, it is not really relevant if doing the right thing is "appealing" to him or not. The believer understands that he must subordinate his behavior and his feelings to God's moral code. This is not to say that professing a belief in God alone will make a person moral and saintly; however, it does provide the only possible rational, philosophical, and spiritual basis for becoming moral and saintly. (The issue of atrocities and evil committed in the name of religion will be explored in the last chapter.) Even if the believer fails in his quest to live up to a divinely commanded morality because of human weakness, he still knows that God's moral commands are greater than, and more important than himself. Moral values for the believer are not determined by personal preference, public opinion polls, and what the latest "progressive" trend happens to be. They are from the absolute being of the infinite, eternal God. There is no question that moral values can only be real and meaningful if their source is the transcendent God. In fact, only the believer can use the word "morality" in a meaningful and authentic way. The crucial issue which must be addressed, which I pointed out in Chapter Two, is how does one know that his values actually are what God has commanded?

Humanism: Another Red Herring created by atheists

"Ethical" atheists like to fool themselves and others by preaching "humanistic" values. I would suggest that what prevents the "humanistic" atheist from committing murder with impunity is one of three factors: A) He has no *desire or reason* to commit murder; for example, he might be very gentle by nature. B) If he does have a motive, he is afraid of getting caught, or C) He has been conditioned by his society with Judeo-Christian values (thank God), and is psychologically unable to jettison them. **Extremely Important to Note:** There can also be a fourth reason: he actually does believe that there are transcendent values that supersede his own personal preferences. In other words, he's not really an atheist but does not yet realize it. He simply has not put two and two together.

It's easy to talk about humanism when you are feeling good. What does the humanist atheist do when he is overwhelmed with burning anger, jealousy, lust, greed, *etc.,* and he concludes that the most effective remedy to relieve the situation is murder? What would possibly stop him – besides the psychological conditioning that I mentioned above – if he feels he can get away with it? The hero of the atheist is the evolutionary biologist, like G. Gaylord Simpson. He has already told us that man is "purposeless...a sort of animal...a species in the order of primates." There is no essential difference between a man and a squirrel. If we kill squirrels when it suits us, then why not kill a man when it suits us? In the atheistic view we are, in the previously cited words of Dr. Peter Walker, "...a carbon based bag of mostly water, on a speck of iron silicate dust revolving around a boring dwarf star." [15]

What could possibly be wrong with killing a purposeless, directionless primate, who anyway is just a "carbon based bag of water" revolving pointlessly around a "boring dwarf star?" A moments thought will tell you that for the atheist nothing is intrinsically wrong with murder. If an Orthodox Jew or evangelical Christian – who truly believes that God has explicitly forbidden him to murder – is unable to control himself in the face of some enormous temptation and actually commits murder, it would be *despite* everything he believes in and stands for. If the atheist commits murder it would be *entirely consistent* with what he believes in and stands for. When I say it is "entirely consistent," I do not mean that an inevitable consequence of his being an atheist is that he will commit murder.

I mean that it is "entirely consistent" with his philosophy that there is nothing intrinsically wrong with committing murder. Don't forget, in the final analysis the atheist is accountable to no one but himself.

One man's "Deep Moral Feeling," is another man's "Indigestion"

In order to escape the inherent and undeniable *amorality* of an atheistic worldview and the subsequent need to turn to a transcendent God for meaningful moral values, many "ethical" atheists promote the pathologically naive idea that humans have some sort of *natural* morality inside their molecular structure somewhere. Hitchens, in his introduction to *The Portable Atheist*, puts it this way:

> ...the working assumption [of believers] is that we should have no moral compass if we were somehow not in thrall to an unalterable and unchallengeable celestial dictatorship. What a repulsive idea...The so-called Golden Rule is innate in us. [16]

In other words, we don't need moral direction or guidance from a Supreme Being; just be true to the voice of the "innate Golden Rule" and all moral issues will magically resolve themselves. It is hard to imagine a statement that more savagely violates human reason and common sense.

If Hitchens grew up in ancient Rome, wouldn't he be at the Coliseum along with all the other "good" Roman citizens, cheering wildly as gladiators killed each other, and those awful, superstitious, rebellious Christians were eaten by lions? If he grew up in India, wouldn't he solemnly throw the widow on the funeral pyre just like any "good" Indian? If he was raised in the Hitler Youth, wouldn't he "know" beyond any doubt whatsoever that it is the supreme, master Aryan race *uber alles?* If he were raised in Mississippi in 1930 wouldn't he be mugging for the camera at a lynching just like everyone else did in those good old days? If he grew up in Saudi Arabia, wouldn't he proudly murder his own sister or daughter if she dishonored the family by her unchaste conduct? If he was raised in the atheistic doctrine of Communism in the Soviet Union, wouldn't he "know" that morality is subordinated to the needs of the proletariat Republic and inform on his parents like a good comrade of the workers paradise? Which human being has the authority to decide which of these value systems is right or wrong? Don't the followers and advocates of these systems "innately" know the truth?

Doesn't everybody "innately" know that killing an unborn child is murder? Millions do know just that...and millions of others "innately" know that the noblest thing that can be done for women everywhere, and for all humanity, is to make abortion a Constitutional right. If the pro-life side is actually right, we are guilty of mass murder; if the pro-abortion side is right, all those opposed to abortion are cruel and heartless, hell bent on enslaving woman and stripping them of their most basic human rights. Both sides are certain that they "know" the truth. Both sides have the Golden Rule "innately!" Don't all decent, sensitive, compassionate, animal loving people everywhere "innately" know that bullfighting is a terribly inhumane, cruel sport?...Can 50,000,000 Spaniards and 100,000,000 Mexicans really be "innately" wrong? *OLE!* It seems that the voice of the "innate Golden Rule" gives radically different messages to different people in different places and times. Hitchens, not surprisingly, responds with the ultimate cop-out answer to this simple and obvious problem:

> The so-called Golden Rule is innate in us, or is innate except in the sociopaths who do not care about others and the psychopaths who take pleasure from cruelty. (Introduction to *The Portable Atheist*)

In other words, everyone who agrees with the value system of Christopher Hitchens is good and moral, and anyone who disagrees is by *definition* a psychopath or a sociopath! No need to deal with the obvious reality that the headhunter's and cannibal's version of morality are just as valid as any other. No need to deal with the simple fact that psychologically healthy Romans thought that watching people kill each other was incredibly exciting and simply great entertainment (and besides, only criminals and illegal Christians were fed to the lions, by court order!) No need to acknowledge that people who participated in lynchings loved their children, wives, friends, and were otherwise healthy, productive members of their communities. They just understood (like everyone around them did) that the "colored" had to be taught their proper place in society.

It is critical to point out how Hitchens' desire to promote his atheistic agenda distorts his reasoning process. In order to sidestep the *amorality* of atheism and the self-apparent truth that human moral sensitivities are notoriously subjective and fickle, Hitchens simply labels adherents of value systems that conflict with his own as "psychopaths" and "sociopaths." He would have us believe that no sane, psychologically healthy person would ever justify the murder of a helpless baby; after all, our "innate Golden Rule" would never allow it. Nothing could be further from the truth. In 1978, anthropologist Laila Williamson, of the American Museum of Natural History in New York City, reached the following conclusions after a study on the prevalence of infanticide:

> Infanticide has been practiced on every continent and by people on every level of cultural complexity, from hunters and gatherers to high civilization, including our own ancestors. Rather than being an exception, then, it has been the rule. [17]

I would add that infanticide is still a common practice in India and China, particularly when the baby is female. Are we to conclude then that all these people were, and are "psychopaths" or "sociopaths?" Dr. Steven Pinker, in an article entitled, "Why They Kill Their Newborns," directly addresses the issue of the psychological state of baby killers:

> Neonaticide, many think, could be only the product of pathology...But it's hard to maintain that neonaticide is an illness when we learn that it has been practiced and accepted in most cultures throughout history. And that neonaticidal women do not commonly show signs of psychopathology...Several moral philosophers have concluded that neonates are not persons, and thus neonaticide should not be classified as murder. Michael Tooley has gone so far as to say that neonaticide ought to be permitted during an interval after birth. [18]

If the "innate Golden Rule" is unable to prevent the justification of the murder of millions of babies "on every continent" and "every level of cultural complexity", and is even unable to prevent so called "moral philosophers" at the University of Colorado, such as Dr. Michael Tooley, from concluding that murdering babies should be a legal option in the 21st century, *what exactly does this "innate Golden Rule" actually do anyhow?*

As long as we are on the subject, what about "psychopaths" and "sociopaths" like Plato, Aristotle, Seneca, Cicero, George Bernard Shaw, and H.G. Wells, all of whom casually and matter-of-factly endorsed the practice of infanticide? The Roman historian, Cornelius Tacitus (whom we have no reason to believe was psychologically unhealthy), counted among the "sinister and revolting" practices of the Jews the fact that they considered it a "deadly sin to kill a born or unborn child." [19] Rabbi Yaakov Weinberg once observed, "Nobody ever let something as trivial as facts and logic interfere with their agenda; if the facts and logic don't fit, then the facts and logic will just have to fend for themselves." [20] Hitchens has made it clear that when it comes to his own atheistic philosophy, "the facts and logic will just have to fend for themselves."

Why is it so difficult for these "ethical" atheists to realize that nearly all human beings, irrespective of their psychological health, experience a powerfully "innate" feeling that their own particular value system, *no matter what it may be*, is perfectly moral and good? Simply put, just about everybody is "innately" positive they are doing the right thing. ("All of a man's ways are proper in his own eyes…" *Proverbs 21:2*) And when I say everybody, I mean *everybody*. The following is from a translation of a speech made by Reichsfuhrer-SS Heinrich Himmler (among the top three or four most powerful men in Nazi Germany), at Poznan, Poland on October 4, 1943 to a gathering of SS Officers (on the website listed in the endnotes you can also hear the original recording of the speech):

> I also want to mention a very difficult subject before you here, completely openly. It should be discussed amongst us, and yet, nevertheless, we will never speak about it in public…I am talking about the Jewish evacuation, the extermination of the Jewish people. It is one of those things that is easily said, The Jewish people is being exterminated. Every Party member will tell you: perfectly clear, it's part of our plans, we're eliminating the Jews, exterminating them, ha! a small matter.

And then along they come, all the 80 million upright Germans, and each one has his decent Jew. They say: all the others are swine, but here is a first-class Jew. And none of them has seen it, has endured it. Most of you will know what it means when 100 bodies lie together, when there are 500, or when there are 1000. And to have seen this through, and – with the exception of human weaknesses – to have remained decent, has made us hard and is a page of glory never mentioned and never to be mentioned.

Because we know how difficult things would be, if today in every city during the bomb attacks, the burdens of war and the privations, we still had Jews as secret saboteurs...and instigators...We have taken away the riches that they had, and I have given a strict order, which Obergruppenfuhrer Pohl has carried out, we have delivered these riches, completely to the Reich, to the State. We have taken nothing from them for ourselves...he who takes even one Mark of this is a dead man. A number of SS men have offended against this order. There are not very many, and they will be dead men – without mercy! We have the moral right, we had the duty to our people to do it, to kill this people who wanted to kill us, but we do not have the right to enrich ourselves with even...one cigarette...with anything. That [right] we do not have. Because at the end of this, we don't want, because we exterminated the bacillus, to become sick and die from the same bacillus.

I will never see it happen, that even one bit of putrefaction comes in contact with us or takes root in us...**But altogether we can say: We have carried out this most difficult task for the love of our people. And we have taken on no defect within us, in our soul, or in our character.** [21]

Kind of stirring, isn't it? "Ethical" atheists everywhere, including of course Christopher Hitchens, can take great comfort in the fact that Himmler did not ignore his Darwinian gift of a genetically encoded Golden Rule, even as he was slaughtering millions of people. He was very careful to "remain decent," to only do that which he had a "moral right" to do, not to forget the "love of his people," and in an extraordinary display of virtue and ethical sensitivity, he and his SS colleagues scrupulously avoided taking on "defects" in their soul or character. Perhaps *The Guinness Book of World Records* should contain a category called: "The most insignificant, hollow, meaningless statement made by a well known atheistic author." There you would see the following: "*The so-called Golden Rule is innate in us.*"

The significance of the inborn "moral compass" and its relationship to Himmler's speech

In truth, when all is said and done, I agree with Hitchens; we *do* have an inborn "moral compass." It is regarding the significance and function of this "moral compass" where our opinions and worldviews radically diverge. As a believer, my position is that moral values and our inborn "moral compass" have actual metaphysical existence. Although moral principles emanate from God and are spiritual, existing in time but not space, they are as much a part of our reality as gravity, chemical bonds, and electromagnetic forces. That is why I find it extremely significant that Himmler felt the need to morally justify his actions. Even Himmler could not totally escape the moral voice that God implanted in the soul of every human being. What is absolutely clear, however, is that the inborn moral voice *by itself* is almost useless. A ship at sea on a stormy night can only navigate accurately towards its destination by homing in on the beacon from a lighthouse situated on the firm foundation of dry land. Unless our inner "moral compass" is guided to seek its moral objectives by homing in on an absolute and immutable system of God-given moral values and principles, there is literally no perversion or corruption imaginable that cannot be justified by our inner "moral compass." I am certain that the overwhelming majority of those reading this book would agree that Himmler perverted and abused his innate moral sense. However, the absolute, transcendent moral laws that he violated still remain eternally in place. Despite the horrific deviations of Himmler from the moral path, the God-implanted moral sense in every human being and the God-given moral principles still retain their ultimate significance and function.

From the viewpoint of the atheist however, Himmler's speech only underscores how hollow and insignificant this inborn "moral compass" is, no matter what its chemical, genetic, or evolutionary source. For the atheist, moral principles have no actual existence. They are products of human desire, human construct, and human imagination. Since all human preferences, including moral values are purely subjective, the "moral compass" will obviously lead an individual wherever he or she subjectively would like to go; including morally justified infanticide – or for that matter, mass murder – committed for the noblest of reasons. When the atheist honestly confronts the fact that this "moral compass" can produce a Himmler and a Stalin on the one hand, a humanist atheist on the other, and everything in between, he must be struck with an obvious question: what difference does this "compass" really make? *All of them feel equally strongly that their behavior is morally justified and ethically noble.* I would even take it a step further. In the atheistic worldview it would be quite reasonable to conclude that the *whole evolutionary purpose* of our evolved inborn "moral compass" is to give us the ability to justify and feel good about any system of values we choose to follow, no matter what it may be!

Atheists Tend to be Overachievers When it Comes to Mass Murder

Richard Dawkins, the atheist equivalent of The Big Kahuna, lamely attempts to disassociate himself from the mass murder committed by atheist tyrants with the following: "The bottom line of the Stalin/Hitler debating point is very simple. Individual atheists may do evil things, but they don't do evil things in the name of atheism." [22]

He's absolutely correct. Nobody makes wars or commits mass murder in the name of atheism. The reason for this is the same reason that nobody makes a war in the name of tiddly-winks. In order to do "great" things, you need a "great" idea. You cannot inspire people to fight a war in the name of tiddlywinks because it is trivial. Atheism is the most trivializing idea of all. In fact atheism represents the negation of everything great in humankind. Atheism implies that we are all just a bunch of purposeless, meaningless, glorified bacteria spinning around in space. How could you possibly arouse the masses to do *anything* in the name of atheism?

However, while the concept of atheism itself negates any form of greatness, being an atheist does not eliminate the inner need of the human being to seek greatness. Once an individual has thrown off divine moral restrictions by declaring himself an atheist, he can now use all his ambitions, talents, energy and passion to achieve "great" things, *without any moral boundaries whatsoever.* H.G. Wells, Konrad Lorenz, George Bernard Shaw, and the Nazis did not advocate murdering unfit humans in the name of something as trivial as atheism. They advocated these policies in the name of the glorious cause of "creating a race of thoroughbreds," as Margaret Sanger, founder of Planned Parenthood so eloquently termed it, or building a "New Republic," or "perfecting the human species," or "creating a Master Race." It was atheism, however, that intellectually, psychologically, and spiritually allowed them to justify the use of any means necessary, without "the inescapable authoritarian control" of divine moral restrictions, to achieve their goals.

Josef Stalin, Mao Tse Tung, and Pol Pot absolutely and literally applied the words of Lenin, "Our morality is entirely subordinated to the interest of the proletariat's class struggle," [23] and those of atheist Mikhail Bakunin, one of the founders of the Anarchist movement, "To [the revolutionary] whatever aids the triumph of the revolution is ethical; whatever hinders it is unethical and criminal." [24] (*Catechism of the Revolutionist*)

How can atheists be so blind to the consequences of freedom from Divine morality?

What is absolutely incredible is the blindness and obtuseness of atheists like Dawkins, Harris, and Baggini to the obvious consequences of "liberty" from divine morality. Contrast this to the simple elegance with which the book of Genesis sums up the entire concept. In Genesis 20, Abraham pretends that his wife Sarah is his sister, and Avimelech, the Philistine king sends royal messengers to take her to the palace to be his wife. God appears to the king in a dream and warns him that Sarah is the wife of Abraham. Avimelech confronts Abraham, aghast that Abraham would precipitate a situation "that would bring a great sin on our kingdom." He asks Abraham, "What did you see that you did this thing?" Abraham replies, "I said [to myself], the only thing missing here is fear of God, and therefore they will kill me to get my wife." Keep in mind – as you contemplate the following statements by several well known atheists – that the obvious lesson of the story in Genesis 20, is that once the divine moral fences have been destroyed, any agenda can be rationalized and justified....

> I hope that every kind of religious belief will die out...although I am pre-
> pared to admit that in certain times and places it has had some good
> effects. I regard it as belonging to the infancy of human reason, and to a
> stage of development which we are now outgrowing. [25] (Bertrand Russell,
> *Selected Essays*, 1928)

This remark was published in 1928. Atheist mass murderer
Josef Stalin became Secretary General of the Communist Party
in 1922.

> ...ideas which divide one group of human beings from another, only
> to unite them in slaughter, **generally** have their roots in religion. [26]
> (Sam Harris, *The End of Faith*)

Harris would do better in the future to avoid speaking in *gener-
alities,* because *specifically* the greatest mass murderers have
been his fellow atheists.

> The unbelievers as I have read history have done less harm to the world
> than the believers. They have not filled it with savage wars...with cru-
> sades, or persecutions, with complacency or ignorance. They have
> instead, done what they could to fill it with knowledge and beauty,
> with temperance and justice, with manners and laughter. [27] (Carl Van
> Doren, Professor of English Literature at Columbia University, and
> Pulitzer Prize winning author)

The "knowledge and beauty" of Stalin and the Soviet Politburo
as they murdered tens of millions and enslaved their own people in the Gulag, the "temperance and justice" of Mao Tse Tung
("political power grows from the barrel of a gun") as he killed
over 50,000,000 of his own Chinese people, and the "manners
and laughter" of the great unbeliever Pol Pot as he soaked
Cambodia with the blood of millions. Can you believe this guy
actually got tenure at Columbia University?

> To what heights the philosophy of Atheism may yet attain, no one can
> prophesy. But this much can be predicted; only by its regenerating fire
> will human relations be purged from the horrors of the past. [28] (Emma
> Goldman – The Philosophy of Atheism)

I have no comment; I just don't know whether to laugh or cry.
"Atheism...is the only sure way to regard our fellow creatures as

brothers and sisters." [29] (Christopher Hitchens) Like in North Korea! The only sure way to regard our fellow creatures as brothers and sisters is to believe and live by the words of the Declaration of Independence as they echo the words of Genesis that "man was created in the image of God." – "We hold these truths to be self-evident, that all men are created equal, that they are endowed by their Creator with certain unalienable rights." If the Declaration of Independence had been written by an atheist it would have read as follows:

We hold these truths to be self-evident, that all men, women, children, animals, fish, insects, bacteria, etc., are here because meaningless blind chance, combined with the purposeless, yet existent laws of physics and biology, produced living organisms on this planet. Neither man nor beast has any objective value or purpose, and neither does our rebellion against England, but it sure beats sitting around on a Saturday night with nothing to do. VIVA LA REVOLUCION!

Introducing Sam Harris

Sam Harris is the author of a best selling atheist manifesto entitled *The End of Faith: Terror, Religion and the Future of Reason*. In 2005, (the year after its publication), his book won the PEN American Center/Martha Albrand award. In 2006, Harris authored *Letter to a Christian Nation*, which Wikipedia described as a "rejoinder to the criticism his first book attracted."

Harris takes a rather novel approach in his attempt to overcome the insurmountable dilemma faced by all atheists: the problem of "the subjectivity of ethical values" (as Bertrand Russell so aptly phrased it). He claims that *Science* will provide the answers:

> **There will probably come a time when** we achieve a detailed understanding of human happiness and of ethical judgments themselves at the level of the brain...**There is every reason to believe that** sustained inquiry in the moral sphere will force convergence of our various belief systems in the way that it has every other science... [30]

In the passage above, Harris provides us with two powerful reasons to believe that science holds the key to solving this dilemma: *A) "There will probably come a time when..."* and *B) "There is every reason to believe that..."* How is that for compelling, rational evidence? I didn't realize how easy it was to establish a fact. You don't need to present evidence, logic, or construct a reasonable argument. All you have to do is preface your agenda with "there will probably come a time when (<u>fill in the blank</u>)" or "there is every reason to believe that (<u>fill in the blank</u>)" and you're good to go! I think I will try it myself. *There is every reason to believe, that there will probably come a time when* even Sam Harris realizes that intractable philosophical problems cannot be solved by invoking flimsy pronouncements such as "there is every reason to believe that..." and "there will probably come a time when."

Harris claims that believers have an inherently distorted perception of morality and ethics

Not only does Harris present us with the totally unsupported article of faith that science will settle all metaphysical questions regarding morality, but in *The End of Faith* he also indicates that a God-based view of the world necessarily includes a distorted perception of morality and ethics:

(Harris, quoting philosopher Bertrand Russell): *"There is something odd about the ethical evaluations of those who think that an omnipotent deity...would consider himself adequately rewarded by the final emergence of **Hitler, Stalin, and the H-Bomb**."* Harris then offers his commentary on this statement by Russell: *"This is a devastating observation, and there is no retort to it."* [31]

I have no objection to Harris raising the very real challenge that evil and suffering pose to the believer. Theologians and religious philosophers have pondered the question for millennia. It is so important that an entire book of Scripture – *The Book of Job* – is devoted exclusively to this subject. What I find objectionable is Harris' comment that "This is a devastating observation, and there is no retort to it." Frankly, it smacks of smugness and arrogance. In Harris' mind, pointing out the crimes of Hitler and Stalin and the existence of H-Bombs conjures up images of vanquished theologians and clergy helplessly thrashing in the mud, while cultivated, broad-minded atheists like himself continue climbing the path to enlightenment. It's as if Harris actually believes he was the first person to think of the question.

Is it really true that Russell's observations about Hitler, Stalin, and the H-Bomb are so "devastating" that the believer has "no retort?"

Perhaps Harris and his fellow skeptics should consider the following:

Hitler – "Struggle is the father of all things...he who wants to live must fight, and who does not want to fight in this world where external struggle is the law has no right to exist." [32] (*Mein Kampf*) "The stronger must dominate and not blend with the weaker...only the born weakling can view this as cruel...*for if this law did not prevail, any conceivable higher evolution of organic living beings would be unthinkable.*" [33] (*Mein Kampf*)

Stalin – An atheist who was one of the most evil men who ever walked the face of the earth

H-Bomb – In the world of the atheist, who are the aristocrats, the priestly class, the Brahman caste? It is the "rational," "logical," "truthful" Scientist. Who created the H-Bomb? ...Scientists!

Let us sum up: **Hitler** – Darwinist par excellence; **Stalin** – Atheist mass murderer; **H-Bomb** – Created by the elite of the atheistic world: Scientists. *That*, Mr. Harris, is a devastating observation and there is no retort to it.

In his heart of hearts, the atheist knows he is morally bankrupt

In short, the world of the atheist is the amoral world of the jungle, the forest, the anthill, and the sea. An atheist who refers with awe to Thomas Paine and the "Rights of Man" is confused and deluded indeed. (At the risk of being repetitious; if what appeals to a particular atheist is Thomas Paine, that's fine, just admit that it is a completely subjective personal preference; kind of like choosing the chocolate cream pie over the black forest cake.)

If there is any doubt at all as to the amorality of the atheistic faith, I introduce to you Dr. Peter Singer, world famous atheist philosopher and intellectual father of the animal rights movement. Professor Singer, who is a native Australian, was named Humanist of the Year in 2004 by the Council of Australian Humanist Societies and is currently the DeCamp Professor of Bioethics at Princeton University. His appointment drew protests from some Princeton students, because Singer advocates infanticide in certain cases. In an article entitled "Heavy Petting," Singer gave his stamp of approval to bestiality as long as the animal is not harmed in any way (unless, of course, the animal is into S&M).

In a videotaped interview with journalist William Crawley, Singer was asked if he thought that pedophilia was "just wrong." Singer became what might be described as mildly indignant and responded:

> I don't have intrinsic moral taboos. **My view is not that anything is just wrong**...You're trying to put words in my mouth...I don't think that this moral method of saying it's just wrong is a method we should rely on, neither in this case [pedophilia], nor any other. [34]

Singer went on to say that he is a "consequentialist." This is a clear case of lunacy masquerading as ethical philosophy. Every mafia hit man is a "consequentialist." If there is a policeman around and he is afraid of getting caught (*bad* consequences), he will not commit murder. Seals at a circus show, waiting for their trainer to throw them a fish after they have successfully completed a trick, are also "consequentialists." (Perhaps Singer should join the circus.)

In light of the fact that Peter Singer is a professor of *Ethics* (!) at Princeton University, I feel compelled to record here my slightly revised version of a stingingly insightful statement by the late William F. Buckley Jr. I have simply substituted "Princeton University" where Buckley originally had written "Harvard University": "*I would rather entrust the government of the United States to the first 400 names in the Boston telephone directory than to the faculty of Princeton University.*"

Singer is not the only atheistic thinker who comes right out and admits to the non-morality of atheism

Richard Dawkins – **A)** *The universe that we observe has precisely the properties we should expect if there is, at bottom, no design, no purpose, no evil, no good, nothing but pitiless indifference.* [35]

B) *Why do we vent such visceral hatred on child murderers, or on thuggish vandals, when we should simply regard them as faulty units that need fixing or replacing? Presumably because mental constructs like blame and responsibility, indeed evil and good, are built into our brains by...Darwinian evolution. Assigning blame and responsibility is an aspect of the useful fiction of intentional agents that we construct in our brains as a means of short-cutting a truer analysis of what is going on in the world in which we have to live. [i.e., that evil and good, blame and responsibility are in truth nothing more than "useful fictions"]...we shall eventually grow out of all this and even learn to laugh at it.* [36]

Jean Paul Sartre – *The existentialist finds it extremely embarrassing that God does not exist, for there disappears with him all possibility of finding values in an intelligible heaven.* [37]

Dr. Michael Ruse – *...there are no grounds whatsoever for being good... Now that you know that morality is an illusion put in place by your genes to make you a social cooperator, what's to stop you behaving like an ancient Roman [raping Sabine women]? Well, nothing in an objective sense...morality has no foundation.* [38]

Julian Baggini – **A)** *[I] caution against the expectation that one can hope to find a simple source for morality, a reason to be moral that every rational person should recognize.* **I would argue that such a source cannot be found.** *The best attempt to find such a source is the Kantian endeavor...but despite their inventiveness, and ingenuity, such attempts do not, I think, ultimately succeed.* [39] [emphasis mine]

B) *...we can provide no logical proof that the atheist ought to behave morally.* [40]

Dr. Will Provine – *[as an atheist] you give up the hope that there is an imminent morality...you can't hope for there being any free will [and there is]...no ultimate foundation for ethics.*

Dr. Joel Marks – *I have given up morality altogether! [I] have been laboring under an unexamined assumption, namely, that there is such a thing as right and wrong. I now believe there isn't...I experienced my shocking epiphany that the religious fundamentalists are correct; without God there is no morality...Hence I believe there is no morality...The long and short of it is that I became convinced that atheism implies amorality; and since I am an atheist, I must therefore embrace amorality...*[42] (Dr. Marks, Prof. Emeritus of Philosophy at U. of New Haven, gets a gold star – along with Joseph Stalin – for being intellectually consistent. The next quote is from a man who could have been one of Dr. Marks' most devoted disciples.)

Jeffrey Dahmer – *I always believed the theory of evolution as truth that we all just came from the slime...if a person doesn't think there is a God to be accountable to then what's the point of trying to modify your behavior to keep it within acceptable ranges?* [43]

Mike, EvilTeuf, atheist blogger – *Atheism...doesn't carry any obligation to any kind of political or moral system. In that sense it is amoral...What the amorality of atheism entails is a lack of obligation to any system of morality...An atheist can have any system of morality he or she wishes...you should always remember that no morals are absolute and that you always have a choice.* [44] (mwillet.org/atheism/moralsource.htm)

I have a simple question. If they admit to the amorality of atheism; if an atheist can choose any system of morality he or she wishes (ranging from Nihilism to Confucianism to Nazism); if as Baggini says there is no rational reason for the atheist to be moral; if as Dawkins explicitly states, that evil and good are "useful fictions;" if as Will Provine explains, there isn't even any hope of ethics or morality for the atheist; if morality is simply an "illusion" without any foundation as Michael Ruse describes it, and "in an objective sense" you can rape and murder with impunity; if as Peter Singer informs us (leaving nothing at all to the imagination), there are no "intrinsic moral taboos," that *nothing* "is just wrong," why do Hitchens, Harris, Dawkins, and Baggini all keep prattling on about the morality of the atheist? Why on earth did Hitchens call his lecture at Sewanee University "The Moral Necessity of Atheism," when it should have been called *No Morals are Absolute, Nothing is Intrinsically Wrong, and Religious Fundamentalists are Correct: Without God there is No Morality?*

These authors' attitudes are classic examples of the "atheistic disconnect" from reality. They take their own version of a "leap of faith" and consider themselves unbound by rules of logical consistency and reason. Those atheists who self-righteously speak of noble moral principles are simply espousing ideals and values that only make sense if a transcendent Creator exists. They then continue on their merry way, ignoring the fact that without a transcendent God there is no rational foundation for anything they are saying.

In order to cover up their own glaring moral nakedness, atheists throw up a smokescreen and point a finger at religious people. Oddly enough they will accuse believers of being "no better than we are." With this then, we are ready to introduce one of the most potent – and what will turn out to be illusory – weapons in the atheist arsenal: A philosophical concept with the quaint Greek name of EUTHYPHRO.

Chapter 9

Euthyphro:
A Philosophical Dinosaur

As we discussed at length in the last chapter, in a universe without God there simply are no real, binding, moral principles. The truth of this proposition is so clear, in my opinion, that anyone who fails to grasp it either has not thought it through properly or perhaps is psychologically and emotionally unable to accept the implications of this simple truth.

Atheist thinkers strike back

Atheist philosophers reply that designating God as the moral lawgiver still does not solve the problem of discovering true moral principles. In other words, they contend that both the believer and atheist sit on the horns of the same philosophical/moral dilemma. Dr. Julian Baggini states this idea explicitly, "Of course, it can still be said that we can provide no logical proof that the atheist ought to behave morally, but neither can we provide such a proof for theists." [1]

The first part of Baggini's statement, that there is no logical reason for an atheist to behave morally is obviously true as we have pointed out. However, what does Baggini mean when he writes, "But neither can we provide such a proof for the theists"? Why doesn't the theist, or believer in God, have a logical, rational reason to behave morally? If I believe that the infinite Creator of the universe commands me to behave in a certain way, isn't that a logical reason to behave morally? What Baggini is referring to is the atheistic challenge found in the works of Plato, in a dialogue entitled EUTHYPHRO. From this point on it will be referred to as the Euth. Argument.

The Euth. Argument has been presented by many atheists in various formulations. Bertrand Russell, in a work entitled

Why I Am Not a Christian, presents one version. In a debate with Dennis Prager, Professor Jonathan Glover used this argument to challenge Prager's assertion that morality must be God-based. It was also used by atheist philosopher Kai Nielsen in a debate with Dr. William Lane Craig. I even once saw it written up in the religion column of the *Chicago Sun-Times*. The argument is well known to theologians and philosophers of religion.

At first glance, the argument seems very powerful. At least one blogger, *Snaars.blogspot*, July 2005, seems to indicate that it was instrumental in converting him from believer to atheist:

> When I saw this argument for the first time, I was stunned. I had been firmly of the belief that morality did depend on God's command! Eventually, I accepted the point of the argument. [*i.e.*, that morality, if it exists at all, has nothing to do with God's command]

The Euthyphro Argument

I present below two versions of the Euth. Argument. The first is the one formulated by Julian Baggini, and is taken from his book *Atheism: A Very Short Introduction*:

> Plato made the point extremely clearly in a dialogue called Euthyphro...Plato's protagonist, Socrates, posed the question...**A)** do the gods choose what is good, because it is good, or **B)** is the good, good, because the gods chose it? If the first option is true, that shows that good is independent of the gods (or God, in a monotheistic faith). Good is just good, and that is precisely why a good god will always choose it.

> But if the second option is true [*i.e.*, it is good because the gods choose it], then that makes the very idea of what is good arbitrary. If it is God's choosing something alone that makes it good, then what is there to stop God from choosing torture, for instance, and thus making it good [or murder, or hatred, *etc.*]...to recognize this, however, is to recognize that we do not need God to determine right or wrong. Torture is not wrong just because God does not choose it..." [2]

Here is a drier, more "mathematical" presentation of the same argument. Some readers might find this version easier to understand:

THE EUTHYPHRO ARGUMENT AGAINST THE DIVINE COMMAND THEORY OF MORALITY (DCT)

DCT states: Actions are wrong if, and only if, God commands us not to perform them.

1. EITHER: **A)** God commands us not to steal, murder, lie, *etc.*, because these actions are wrong; or **B)** these actions are wrong because God commands us not to do them.
2. If **A)** is true, then there is a standard of morality separate from God's commands and DCT is false
3. If **B)** is true, then either: **C)** God has reasons for commanding us to avoid these actions; or **D)** God has no reasons for commanding us to avoid these actions
4. If **C)** is true, then it is these reasons, whatever they are, that make these actions wrong, not God's commands, and DCT is false
5. If **D)** true, then God's commands are arbitrary and effectively meaningless
6. Thus, either DCT is false, or divine moral rules are arbitrary and meaningless

It seems that the believer is in the same patch of quicksand as the atheist. My contention though, as indicated by the title of this chapter, is that no matter how convincing it may sound at first, the Euth. Argument is really nothing more than a philosophical dinosaur. It belongs in a Museum of Philosophy, in the section that displays ancient philosophical fossils of ideas that used to walk the earth, but in reality crumbled into dust a long time ago. In truth this argument was obsolete even before the time of Plato. It died with the appearance of Abraham and his introduction* to the world of the revolutionary concept of Monotheism.

The reason that the Euth. Argument is still talked about is a combination of two factors: **1)** atheistic philosophers have not

---

*Actually, from the perspective of Jewish theology, Abraham reintroduced Monotheism into the world.

realized, or have chosen not to realize, that the argument only applies to the pagan gods of Plato and the rest of the ancient world, but not the One God of Monotheism; and **2)** none of these philosophers ever bothered to formulate an actual meaningful *definition* of good, as opposed to simply presenting certain types of actions that they believe are good, and certain types of actions they believe are bad (for example: murder is bad, kindness is good). In the absence of these two factors the argument crumbles, as I will demonstrate.

To paraphrase a dictum of Talmudic study and apply it to philosophy: the most effective and complete way to answer a philosophical problem is to show that the question never really was a question in the first place. It was all based on a fundamental misunderstanding of one sort or another. As we shall see, this is exactly the case with the Euth. Argument. Before I proceed, however, it is very important to restate and explicitly clarify the problem we are trying to solve. I have found that unless this is done many people become confused during the presentation.

A Clarification: What the Issue Is, and What the Issue Isn't

Please bear with me as I briefly review some of the things we have discussed. The believer argues that in a world without God, there are no objective moral truths. Every person, or group of people, will make up guidelines to live by as they see fit. The particular guidelines will reflect the tastes and opinions of different individuals and different societies at different times and places. For what human being or society has the authority to declare to all mankind what is right or wrong? Only a transcendent moral being can formulate and command moral truths which bind and obligate all humanity. (It is extremely important to note that even if this argument is true, it does not necessarily prove the existence of such a Being. It would only prove that without such a Being, there could be no objective moral truths.) The atheist, of course, answers back using the Euth. Argument, that *even if God exists,* morality does not depend on God. Moral truths either exist independently of God or they are arbitrary and meaningless.

To summarize: When we are discussing the Euthyphro

Argument, the issue at stake is **not:** *Does God exist?* The issue at stake **is:** *Do we require the existence of God in order to have meaningful, absolute, objective moral truths.* Please keep this distinction in mind as we proceed.

Value judgments involve comparisons

Invariably, value judgments involve comparisons. In other words, if I say someone or something is good or bad, it is in comparison to something which acts as a standard. For example, if I talk about a major league baseball pitcher as being "good," I am essentially comparing him to a theoretical model of what a pitcher is supposed to accomplish. The more strikeouts, fewer earned runs, more games won, *etc.,* the "better" the pitcher. I can also make a comparison to great pitchers of the past or present.

Let's say I own a factory where I want to produce "excellent" CD players. At the end of the assembly line I will compare the CD players to a certain list of specifications: sound quality, frequency response, *etc.* If the unit matches my specifications, I consider it an "excellent" system. Imagine the absurdity of a situation where I demand from my workers production of excellent electronics, but I give no specifications as to what excellence is. Without the standard of comparison, the whole concept becomes meaningless.

When we talk about "good" or "bad" people, or "good" or "bad" behavior, there must be a standard to which we are comparing the people or behavior. If the standard is one that is subjective or arbitrarily chosen, the meaning of "good" or "bad" is purely subjective or arbitrary. It has no meaning in real or absolute terms.

Let us posit however, the existence of a transcendent, eternal, infinitely powerful, all-knowing Creator whom we will call God. Not only did this God bring the universe into existence, but the source of the very being of the world and its continued existence is only God's continuous *will* for it to be and exist. An approximate analogy would be a person daydreaming and picturing a scene in his head of a beautiful, pristine, tropical beach. The sun is shining overhead; the waves are gently lapping along the shore. Palm trees are swaying in the gentle breeze. Suddenly the phone rings and this person must answer the phone and discuss an urgent business problem. Where did the beach go? What happened to the ocean, the sun, and the palm trees? A moment ago they were there, and now they're gone. Was the scene real? It had to be real in some sense; after all, he had vividly experienced the scene in his head. The answer is that the beach was real. It just did not exist on the same *plane of reality* as the person himself and the world around him. It was a *contingent* reality. A reality that was totally and completely dependant on the will of the person thinking or dreaming about it. The beach had no independent reality of its own. When this person "withdrew" his will, or in this case simply became distracted and turned his attention elsewhere, the beach ceased to exist.

In a similar fashion, the universe came into existence and continues to exist because God sustains it with his will. Our existence is contingent; we do not have independent existence and reality. This is the meaning of the phrase in the Jewish morning prayer service, "He renews every day *constantly* the act of creation." God created the world by his will and constantly wills it to continue to exist.

Contingent Reality and Actual Reality

God is not like us. God in *actuality and reality* exists. Nothing caused or created him. We are created, along with time, space, matter, and energy. God *is;* we are **caused.** "Row, row, row your boat.....life is but a dream" is not just a nursery rhyme meant only for children. I think all human beings at one time or another are overwhelmed by a feeling of the "unreality" of our existence, that it seems like a dream; that our whole existence is just a "thought inside our head." I would suggest that these lurking feelings are our awareness at some primal level *that there is a plane of reality much greater than our own.* (I am not trying to prove the truth of this idea here; I am just trying to explain what it is and its implications.)

I Can't Get No Satisfaction – What does it mean that I want to "be" somebody

Rabbi Yaakov Weinberg has stated in this vein, "...the greatest need of a human being is to *"be."* [3] What does it mean when people say, "I want to *be* somebody," or I want *"more"* from my life? Give a cow hay, some shade and another cow for company, and it's happy forever. Human beings are always looking for "more." How many young and even not so young people "go on the road," to find this elusive something? What is there inside of us that elicits the almost universal identification with the adolescent Holden Caulfield, in *The Catcher in the Rye,* as he experiences the profoundly aching, bittersweet wonderment of self-discovery? Why do we ask ourselves who we are? What am I? Why am I here? It is not enough just to eat and breathe. That may satisfy those in the animal kingdom, but not us. As human beings, we constantly need and seek something besides the simple fact that that we are alive to justify our existence. This justification can be found in a particular career, a challenging avocation, raising a family, running a marathon, receiving awards and honors, achievement, success, etc. I would suggest to you that this "looking for more" and the burning desire to "be somebody" is really about the search for *actual being and existence, and we intuitively know that on our own we don't have it.* We seek a connection with something beyond ourselves and greater than ourselves to fulfill this need.

The only way a human being can find *true* being and existence is to "attach" himself to God and his absolute, eternal, infinite, and *actual* being and existence. If the created, contingently existent human can emulate, come close, and attach himself to the actual and real existence of God his creator; the human being in actuality and reality becomes *more.* He can "share," as it were, in God's actual being. *If this God actually exists,* then the closer I am to God and the deeper relationship I have with God, the more I am in absolute terms. I am, in objective reality, *more.* I am closer to the absolute, infinite, eternal existence that is God's being. Not only is there not anything more or greater than that, there isn't anything else period.

Why "Be Like Mike," when you can Be Like God?

The most profound attachment and intimacy one can have with God is to "be like him." Why do we all want to be independent and feel relentlessly goaded by a deep compulsion to make it on our own? Why do we feel less if we are dependent? Every parent has experienced even a toddler's fierce drive to be independent. What is the tremendous pleasure of individual achievement and standing on our own two feet? To be independent *is to be like God himself.* God is absolutely independent. His existence and being depend on nothing at all outside himself. He needs nothing from anyone else. I would suggest that we have been created with an innate drive to form a relationship with God, by striving to be like God. That is why a young child passionately and sometimes almost violently proclaims – *without anyone having taught him* – "I want to do it myself!"

- Why is it that we all agree that to be "strong" is better than to be "weak." (I am not necessarily referring to physical strength, although generally we admire that also.) God's strength is infinite. God's will is unfaltering and unstoppable. The stronger we are, the more like God we are.
- God's power is without limits. The more powerful we are, the more like God we are.
- God's knowledge and understanding are infinite. The more knowledge and understanding we have, the more like God we are.
- Since God needs nothing, the whole creation is a "gift" from God to his creatures. God, in this sense, is the ultimate "giver," he only gives and gets nothing in return. What could anyone possibly give him? "Giving" is being like God. The more we give, the more we are like God. (In truth, this is why Christopher Hitchens feels good giving blood.)
- In some sense the greatest emulation of God is to be creative; God is *the* Creator. The pleasure and exhilaration we experience when we feel strong, independent, powerful, knowledgeable, giving, and creative is the pleasure of being Godly. It is the ecstasy of "true being."

This then, is the only possible meaningful definition of "good" and "bad." The closer I come to the ultimate, infinite, actual being of God himself, the better I am. The further I move away from that absolute existence and reality which is his being, the worse I am. Connecting with God means connecting with what ultimately is the only thing that is real; distancing oneself from God means connecting to fantasy, hallucination, non-reality, *i.e., nothingness.* "Good or bad," "moral or immoral," are simply different ways to refer to, closeness to, or distance from, God. Outside of this context, moral and immoral can only have a purely subjective and/or arbitrary meaning.

When God commands us to "love your neighbor," it is not because it is "good" in the way atheists (and many others) use the word, which is simply some vague notion of pleasant deeds. With his commandments, God offers us a **relationship.** He is saying to us: If you want to emulate me, have a deeper relationship with me, and attach yourselves to my absolute, infinite being, then "love your neighbor." If you don't, you will be further away from me and my absolute, infinite, true being. "Thou shalt not murder" means that if you commit murder, you will be very, very far away from me. The more you approach me, the more of a "good" and "moral" person you are. If you choose to act in a way that moves you away from me, you are "bad," "immoral," and "evil." The significance of moral values can only be understood in the context of, and as a function of, a deep relationship with God.

The source of God's authority in this matter also becomes apparent. Only God himself knows what a human being must do in order to come close to God and what actions will cause a human being to become distant from God. Free will then, will ultimately boil down to this: Will one choose to be "more" and come close to God, or will one choose to be "less" and distance oneself from God. (In a general way, distancing oneself from God usually takes the form of choosing to live as part of the animal kingdom.)

The Euthyphro Argument Crumbles

In the context of Jewish theology (and I would imagine,

most monotheistic theologies), the Euth. Argument breaks down completely:

– Is "loving your neighbor" good because God commands it? – Obviously not, that would make it arbitrary.

– Does God command "love your neighbor" because it is good? *No, it is neither of these.* God commands us to love our neighbors so that we can choose to have a relationship with him, so that we can attach ourselves to his infinite and actual being; God himself is *the* good.

If this infinite being we call God actually exists, we have a real standard to determine a meaningful concept of moral truths. The standard is closeness to God, and the actual and absolute existence which is his being. This is what the Psalmist means when he proclaims, "To me, closeness to God *is* good." (*Psalms 73:28*)

On the other hand, if this God does not exist, we are left with nothing but 100% subjective human tastes, opinions, and social mores. Subjective human value systems, even if they come from a so-called "Professor of Ethics" at Princeton University, have no meaning at all outside of the heads of those who follow them. They are artificially constructed fantasies that give their adherents the illusion of purpose and meaning.

Who has greater Moral Authority: The Incredible Hulk or Zeus?

The Euthyphro Argument as a challenge to Monotheism is nothing more than philosophical smoke and mirrors. The only reason it has some superficial appeal at all is because the word "gods" is used, giving the impression of some authority above human beings. Plato's original argument, of course, involved the pagan gods of Greece. In fact, pagan gods have no more moral authority, nor moral credibility, than mortal humans. A pagan god is simply a human being projected to a large scale. He's just bigger, stronger, lives longer, and can even throw a few lightning bolts when needed. Pagan gods are no different than The Incredible Hulk, The Flash, or Superman (who as the old TV show told us had "powers far beyond those of mortal men!").

Formulating the Euthyphro Argument using pagan gods is exactly the same thing as saying: *Does The Incredible Hulk command it because it is good, or is it good because The Incredible Hulk commands it?* The moral proclamations of The Incredible Hulk, have no more or less significance, than the moral proclamations of Zeus, Mick Jagger, Jerry Seinfeld, Oprah Winfrey, or for that matter, any of the approximately 6,000,000,000 individuals living on this planet.

When stated this way, it becomes obvious how misguided and mistaken the whole argument was to begin with. What did you expect? Of course, pagan gods, superheroes, rock superstars, Jewish comedians, and even wildly successful talk show hosts – just like everyone else – can only tell us their totally subjective views on morality, or manufacture it arbitrarily.

Not so, the God of Abraham, the One God. The God of Monotheism is not a human being projected on a large scale. He is above time and space. He is above the physical. He is even above the spiritual. He *created* the spiritual. He is, as Rabbi Yaakov Weinberg has put it, "so totally and completely **other** than we are." [4] With the existence of the One God, greatness, goodness, meaning, and morality lie in front of us. They are within our grasp if we choose them. Without God, in the utterly empty void of the atheistic world, we are left with nothing but bleak despair, as expressed by the American novelist T.C. Boyle:

I am an atheist and a nihilist...I believe in nothing. And it causes me tremendous despair and heartbreak...there is nothing between us and the naked howling face of the universe. Nothing. [5]

Chapter 10

The Source of the Inborn
Moral Imperative: One God

Does Morality have actual metaphysical existence?

When all is said and done regarding God, morality, and atheism, we are left with only two intellectually consistent options:

> **A)** God does not exist and there are no moral boundaries whatsoever; only subjectively agreed upon, non-binding, pragmatically driven "social contracts."
>
> **B)** Morality is real and actual, and its source (as we discussed in Chapter Nine) is the absolute, infinite, and eternal being of God himself.

If there were a way to confirm that *morality* is not just an artificial human construct but has actual metaphysical existence, we would know beyond a reasonable doubt that God exists. There would be no other possible source for such a phenomenon. It is clear to me that not only is this possible, but it's relatively easy to understand, as long as the desire for truth is alive and well in a human being. In this chapter we will start by carefully examining the human need for self-esteem. This examination will lead us to a clarity regarding the metaphysical reality of our moral drive and to its source: The infinite, transcendent God of mankind.

The need for self-esteem transcends our need for life itself

We all have a deep inner need to see ourselves as important, valuable, and significant. According to Dr. Abraham Twerski, Director of the Gateway Rehabilitation Center (Aliquippa, PA) and a world renowned expert on alcoholism and addiction, issues of self-esteem are at the root of almost every psychological problem that are not the result of a purely biological cause or chemical imbalance.[1] Whether we express it as "feeling OK about ourselves," "having a positive self-image," or "a sense of self-worth," the human need for self-esteem is, along with our need for meaning, the most powerful of all human drives. Under certain circumstances, our need for self-esteem transcends our need for life itself. Below are a few examples that illustrate this principle.

Defending my family means more to me than my life

Your family home is attacked by terrorists and you are faced with the following two choices: A) Run quickly out the back door and escape, leaving your wife and children at the mercy of the terrorists, or B) Risk your own life by shooting at the terrorists in the front of the house, allowing your family to escape out the back. Which would you choose? There certainly are people who don't care about anyone and would save themselves. But for the majority who would fight (I would think an overwhelming majority), for what reason are they prepared to die defending their wives and children? For the simple reason that most men simply could not – and would not want to – live with themselves if they fled and abandoned their loved ones. They would see themselves as completely worthless cowards, *i.e.*, they would experience a total loss of self-esteem. They would literally risk their lives and die, if necessary, rather than live with the self-loathing that would result from the knowledge that they had not done everything within their power to save their families. (This judgment and assessment might not be made at a conscious level, but the split second decision to fight would ultimately be based on these factors.) Although for the sake of simplicity I used the example of a man defending his family, it goes without saying that this principle would apply to a woman in the same situation.

My honor means more to me than my life

An elected official is caught on camera taking a bribe, selling classified information to a foreign government, or buying child pornography. The video is shown on all the major networks and uploaded to YouTube. This humiliation is simply a public stripping of the person's self-worth. If this official committed suicide, all of us reading the news would understand why he did it. We are prepared to die under certain circumstances rather than face a loss of self-esteem. The agonizing feeling of worthlessness makes life unbearable.

We react to an attack on self-esteem as if in mortal danger

In a neighborhood with street gangs, a gang member is insulted publicly in front of a group of friends, or even worse, in front of a group of girls. It is not at all unlikely that this gang member would pull out a gun or knife and attempt to maim or kill the person who insulted him. In his mind the very essence of his identity and sense of self-worth were being attacked, and he reacts as if his very life had been threatened. This very same issue is usually the spark that ignites barroom brawls. Up until relatively recent times, a personal insult was grounds for a duel to the death among the aristocratic levels of society.

Murder by "Self-Esteem"

In the 1982 film *An Officer and a Gentleman,* Sid Worley (David Keith), is betrayed by his fiancé-to-be. He checks into a motel, swallows the engagement ring, and hangs himself in the motel bathroom where he is discovered by his friend Zack (Richard Gere). The cruel and heartless manner in which he is rejected sets the stage for this dramatic moment in the film. The only reason this scene works so effectively is because we understand it is possible to literally kill someone by destroying their sense of self-worth. Along with the loss of self-esteem comes the loss of the desire to go on living.

The Devil's Alternative

Imagine you are on a small cruise ship in the Mediterranean. Suddenly, terrorists board the ship and tie up all fifty passengers on deck. For some odd reason the leader of the terrorists takes a liking to you and offers you a deal to save your life. He hands you a hunting knife and says that if you kill all fifty passengers with this knife, he will set you free. There certainly are people who would not only take him up on this offer but would do it with glee. Thank God, I have been fortunate enough in my lifetime not to have met them. However, it is safe to say that nearly every single person reading this book would not be able to murder fifty people with a knife even in order to save their own lives. Why? What could possibly be more important than your own life? Remember, when you refuse, you will die and never experience all the wonderful things life has to offer. No more beautiful sunsets, no more glorious spring days. No more happiness, no more family, no more love. What internal force is compelling you to give it all up? The answer is obvious. Living with the knowledge that I had murdered fifty people would not be a life. I would rather be dead than have to live with myself as an evil person. Seeing oneself as "evil" is another way of describing the complete disintegration of self-esteem.

We disagree on what is "good", but we all agree on the need to "be good"

Although the need for self-esteem can be explored at many different levels, for our purposes the following statement is quite accurate: A person acquires self-esteem by being and doing those things which he considers to be good, meaningful, valuable, significant, or moral. Leaving aside issues of psychological pathology, it does not matter if those things that he considers to be good and valuable are objectively true or not. As long as the individual considers them to be true, generally speaking, they will nurture his sense of self-worth. It is self-evident that atheism and Christianity cannot possibly both be true. However, as long as atheists and Christians are firm in their convictions, loyalty to their respective ideologies will feed their sense of self-esteem.

It makes no difference what you consider to be good, moral, meaningful, or significant. Whatever it is that *you believe* fits into these categories – being popular with members of the opposite sex, getting high grades, success as an athlete, being a great warrior, acquiring wealth, being the toughest and most feared member of a gang, living an idealistic or spiritual life, being faithful to your religion – will be critical factors in determining your sense of self-worth and self-esteem. If I act in a way that I *myself* consider "immoral" or against my own values, I will suffer corresponding damage to my self-esteem. Pangs of conscience, guilt, feeling like a low-life, a nobody, a loser, or some other term all describe this shared human experience.

The amazing and fascinating conclusion that emerges from all this is that while there may be passionate and even violent disagreements on what actually is "good," everyone agrees that we need to "*be good*." Whether it is the German or Japanese soldier fighting for Emperor or Fatherland, or the Allied soldier fighting for freedom from tyranny; whether it be the evangelical pastor denouncing sinners, or the atheist denouncing the pastor; whether it is the idealistic doctor in a third world country, or the gang banger standing up for his machismo; whether it is the man defending his family, the betrayed lover who commits suicide, the humiliated politician, the kid who spends hours on the basketball court dreaming of making it in the NBA, or everyday people trying to do what they believe is right; every single one of them is driven by the same innate need for self-worth and self-esteem. The inescapable need is there; it's just a matter of which values or value system you will use to "fill in the blank."

We are born with the need and drive for self-esteem and morality

It is clear we are born with both the innate need for self-esteem and a moral drive, which are two sides of the same coin. Allow me to explain. The youngest babies are capable of processing certain all-important signals they receive from their parents or caregivers. Loving, caring behavior is processed by the infant as "I am loved, cared for, and important," *i.e., I am*

OK. If the parents convey the opposite, the infant processes that information as well – *I am not OK.*

> The foundations of self esteem are laid early in life...when adults readily respond to [infant's] cries and smiles, babies learn to feel loved and valued. ("How Can We Strengthen Children's Self-Esteem", Dr. Lillian Katz, Professor Emeritus of Early Childhood Education, University of Illinois Champaign-Urbana, Director of Education Resources Information Center) [2]

The infant certainly does not consciously understand what is happening, but there are built-in "receptors" that respond to, process, and store "you are OK" messages and "you are not OK" messages. In the younger stages of growth, it is the parents who are the primary formers of the child's self-image. As the child grows older, peer relationships also become an important factor: "As they grow, children become increasingly sensitive to the evaluations of their peers." [3] (Dr. L. Katz) General societal influences also kick in as the child develops and understands more about the world they are living in, "When children develop stronger ties with their peers...or around the neighborhood, they may begin to evaluate themselves differently from the way they were taught at home." [4] (Dr. L. Katz)

At some point in the development of a human being an almost miraculous transformation can occur. In what sometimes might be described as an epiphany, this person realizes:

> *I don't want to see myself as "good" or "OK," just because my parents, friends, teachers, and society approve of me and tell me I'm O.K. I refuse to continue on my path like a nameless sheep in the herd; I refuse to be just "another brick in the wall." I want to be **truly** "good." I want to feel a sense of self-worth because I'm doing the things that I feel are truly meaningful and valuable.*

With this realization, the individual has arrived at a psychological and spiritual crossroads. Different people can make radically different choices at this crucial instant.

The same inner need causes one person to embrace religion and another to reject it

At this point one person chooses to become deeply religious. Another heads in the opposite direction, abandons the faith of their youth, and embraces the "truth" of skepticism and atheism. At this point one person decides to leave his or her little home town, and go to the big city in order to "become someone and achieve something really important." Another, in his quest for true goodness joins a revolutionary cause. Another goes into the jungle to be a doctor for the underprivileged. There are countless different paths a human being can choose at this critical juncture but they are all driven by the same need; the need to do that which he or she consider to be truly significant, meaningful, good, and moral. The drive for self-esteem which compels a young child to crave his or her parents' approval, is the *same drive* which later in life might very well cause him or her to reject their parents' approval, and creates a powerful determination to achieve any one of the things described above. In other words, the inborn drive for self-esteem is the same drive that compels us, as we mature intellectually and emotionally, to seek true meaning, purpose, significance, and morality. It is also important to realize that every society forms some type of value system as a *response* to this inner need.

Self Esteem, the Inner Moral Imperative – Where does it come from?

There are only two possible sources for this inner inborn "moral imperative," this force which compels us to *crave self-esteem, be good, do what's right, and do what's important and significant even if it means (in certain cases) sacrificing our lives in the process.* We may be unclear or disagree on what the particulars are, but we are driven nonetheless.

This drive is either **A)** totally and wholly the function of some chemical, molecular, or genetic source and can be understood and explained as a purely physical process defined by the laws of chemistry and physics, or **B)** it is a genuine and authentic metaphysical need and drive that has been planted in us by God. As explained in Chapters 8 and 9, the only possible source for real (non-subjective) values and morality is from a transcendent God. That is to say, the reason I have an inner need to do what I believe is truly good is because there are, in absolute terms, values which *are* truly good. The reason I am prepared to die for certain values is because I have been hard-wired with an awareness that there are metaphysically existent values which actually are more important than my own life. (This awareness of values is only in a *general* sense. I do not think it is possible to support the assertion that the details of these values have been hard-wired into our souls. The details must be revealed to us by God.) God has programmed us to seek the absolute truths and values that will connect us to the infinite, eternal being of God himself (as was explained in Chapter Nine). If option **B**) is true, the "moral imperative" is ultimately the drive to seek a relationship with God. It is crucial to understand that there are no other choices or options; the source is either purely material or it is from God. (All joking aside, please remember that "something that no one has thought of yet" is in the category of *unreasonable* options)

We don't just want values; we want the truth

It is equally crucial to realize that the "inner moral imperative" is not to seek *"a"* value system, it is to seek *"the true"* value system. Richard Dawkins and I both agree that if our ideas and value systems are proved to be false beyond a reasonable doubt, we must abandon them. Why? We are not interested in an illusory system; only the truth will satisfy our inner need. This drive of which we have been speaking is also a drive *to seek the truth*; true meaning, true morality, true purpose, true value, true significance – a drive so strong we are prepared to die for it.

Self esteem is not a physical need

It should be obvious at this point that the source of our drive for self-esteem cannot possibly be physical because self-esteem itself is not a physical need. It is quite possible for someone in perfect physical health to be reduced to suicidal despair by attacking their sense of self-esteem. I cannot acquire self-esteem by ingesting a liquid, gas, or solid.* I need *values and ideas* that I believe in. I need values and ideas that I believe are the truth. I need *accomplishments* which I believe are truly significant. None of these are quantifiable by any physical or material measurement. The following scenarios are presented to drive this point home. Although the issues raised below have already been touched upon in Chapter Seven, they are worth repeating as we draw the final conclusions from our discussions and analysis of Morality, Spirituality, and Man's Search for Meaning.

1) My fiancé tells me she loves someone else. She informs me that she never wants to see me again. Is it the sound waves emanating from her mouth that devastate my self-esteem? Of course this is ridiculous. The same thing happens if I read the words in a letter. Do markings on a piece of paper cause the fluctuations in my heartbeat, brainwaves, and respiration? What if I plead with her to come back, and she says nothing, writes nothing, but makes an obscene gesture with a look of hatred and contempt on her face. Is it particular "body positions" that cause all the profound reactions we have been talking about? There is no physical, chemical, or molecular process to explain what caused this devastating reaction in the first place.

2) I consider myself to be a sincerely religious person. My entire understanding of who and what I am, my relations with others, and my sense of place in the universe, all revolve around the concepts and values that stem from certain religious principles. Imagine that I have just read a book which "proves" that my religious beliefs are false. I would no doubt experience a certain level of trauma. My sense of security has been shaken. Without question, monitors would have indicated profound changes in my body chemistry, heartbeat, respiration and brainwaves. What caused all this to happen? A purely physical, material, and clinical description would be roughly as follows: *After staring at printed symbols printed on bound pieces of paper, profound changes occurred in the subject's respiration, heartbeat, etc. Possible cause: chemicals in ink or on paper entered through pores on subject's skin causing reaction. No evidence found to support this hypothesis.*

---

* Psychiatric medications do not give a person self-esteem. At best they simply level the playing field by equalizing a chemical imbalance. The person must then go and create a life for himself just like all of us must do. If someone knew the chemical formula for self-esteem, they would patent it and instantly become the wealthiest person that ever lived.

Possible cause: subject swallowed piece of paper causing reaction. No evidence found to support this hypothesis. Possible cause: Unknown gas emanating from bound papers…No evidence to support this hypothesis.

Conclusion: Unable to detect any material link between bound papers with printed symbols and subject's internal bodily functions. Highly unlikely that bound papers containing printed symbols had any connection to detected changes. Can find no evidence of any physical cause whatsoever that explains fluctuations in monitored bodily functions.

The reason that an investigation would find no physical cause for my reaction is because there was no physical cause. Ideas, concepts, and information caused the reaction. Ideas and concepts exist in time but not space. They are not measurable, quantifiable, nor detectable by any material means. I repeat the assertion I made earlier: The burden of proof is on those who claim that every step, every action and reaction are definable in purely physical terms.

3) Recall the case we discussed earlier in Chapter Seven. At a family gathering someone reveals the terrible secret that you had hoped would stay hidden forever. You are engulfed by a burning, searing feeling of humiliation. Your face goes white with shame; your throat feels constricted; you have difficulty breathing. What happened to make your body react so violently? *Nothing at all changed in the physical universe.* How is it possible to destroy someone's self-esteem with cruel words and insults or revealing a secret? Are there tiny pieces of chemicals that enter into the person along with the offending words? How is it possible to lift somebody with a genuine compliment or kind words? Are there mysterious molecular structures that float through the air and enter in the person's body through their ears along with heartfelt praise and acknowledgement? I repeat what I said earlier: I defy any scientist to find a material, chemical, or molecular basis to explain why vicious or compassionate words, scrawled symbols on a piece of paper, or physical gestures can have such a profound effect on another human being.

4) After twenty years on the job, a man's boss regretfully informs him that the company has to let him go. He is completely devastated. What caused this "devastation"? The sound waves emanating from his boss' mouth? It beggars the imagination to attempt to explain what caused the turmoil going on inside this individual solely within the paradigms of physics and chemistry.

We have shown conclusively that the profound human need for self esteem cannot be explained or understood as a physical or material phenomenon. It clearly belongs to the spiritual dimension of our existence. The only possible source for this most potent of human drives is God himself. When we seek values and moral guidelines we are not seeking artificial human constructs; we are hard-wired to seek the absolute truths that will connect us to the infinite, eternal being of God. Uncovering the exact details of these moral truths and values is an altogether different undertaking, but this does not change the conclusions that we have reached thus far.

Summary of what we have learned until now about the atheistic worldview:

Atheism is based on leaps of faith, not rationality (Faitheism?)

• The atheist has no evidence that something as breathtakingly complex as a living cell could have emerged from non-life through an undirected naturalistic process. The world's leading scientists admit they are baffled. One non-believing scientist after the other finds himself unable to describe the wondrous and astonishing nature of the origin of life without using the word "miracle." Despite this, the skeptic denies even the *possibility* of the creation of life, not because it is in any way unreasonable, but because he has *faith* that scientists will one day find a naturalistic answer.

• The atheist boasts that in his willingness to embrace atheism – unlike the cowardly believer – he is bravely squaring up to reality; namely, that we are here for no particular reason at all and that there is no objective meaning and value to our existence. He then turns around and desperately seeks a *faith,* in the form of a "comforting fiction" which will give him the feeling that his life actually does have real meaning, purpose, and value.

• The atheist admits that the most fundamental aspect of our existence, which is our all-pervasive experience of a separate self, consciousness, and self-awareness, is an area about which, from a scientific perspective, he is completely ignorant and "has nothing relevant" to say. Nobel Prize winning biologist, George Wald, even went so far as to declare that consciousness is "wholly impervious to science." In admitting his ignorance on these issues, the skeptic implicitly admits that science has nothing relevant to say on the origin or ultimate nature of all those aspects of our lives that are inextricably linked with consciousness; namely, love, values, emotions, meaning, and morality. He hasn't the slightest idea how anything that is absolutely material (like a human being) could be conscious, self-aware, *and relentlessly be seeking transcendence and spirituality.* Despite this he confidently proclaims his *faith* that there is no spiritual dimension to our existence.

• Displaying a narrow-mindedness that is reminiscent of his attitude regarding the origin of life, the atheist refuses to even examine the *possibility* of a non-material soul. In order to maintain his *faith* in materialism he is prepared to accept the absurd notions that our "self," free will, thoughts and experiences, are all deterministic illusions manufactured by cerebral activity. He maintains this *faith* despite the ample evidence that the "illusory" self that he claims is nothing but a projection of neural processing, can through willful decisions actually turn around and change the physical configuration of the brain.

• The atheist admits that our ability to communicate with language is a "miracle" for which we have no material explanation, yet he maintains his *faith* that one day there will emerge a purely materialistic explanation for this incredible human faculty.

• Our drive for ultimate meaning and moral values, which has no chemical or molecular basis, transcends our drive for life itself. Despite this fact, which so clearly illustrates the essential spiritual nature of a human being and our irresistible compulsion to seek a relationship with a supreme being, the atheist continues to have *faith* that the disciples of Father Darwin will one day discover a naturalistic explanation for this mystery also.

• The atheistic philosopher openly acknowledges that "there are no grounds whatsoever for being good," that "morality is an illusion," that "nothing is intrinsically wrong," and that "in an objective sense" there is no reason not to rape, murder, and pillage. Dr. Joel Marks was even honest enough to admit that believers are correct when they proclaim that without God there is no morality and that as an intellectually consistent atheist he must "embrace amorality." Despite this, in a remarkable display of utter irrationality (a leap of *faith,* if you will), atheists obliviously continue to talk about atheistic "moral values," and Christopher Hitchens even gives a lecture absurdly entitled, "The Moral Necessity of Atheism."

If you hear God knocking, do not open the door!

Throughout this book I have been very careful not only to explain why I think that atheism is truly *nonsense of a high order* but to bring evidence and confirmation for my conclusions from the writings and statements of prominent atheists themselves. My assertion that atheism is a faith-based ideology will not be an exception, for unlike Diogenes of old who searched in vain for an honest man, in the person of Harvard geneticist Richard Lewontin I have found an honest atheist. It is clear from his remarkably candid confession – which appeared in an article by Lewontin in *The New York Review* – that regarding the *faith* of atheism all are in complete agreement:

> Our willingness to accept scientific claims that are *against common sense* is the key to an understanding of the real struggle between Science and the Supernatural. We take the side of science in spite of the patent absurdity of some of its constructs, in spite of its failure to fulfill many of its extravagant promises of health and life, in spite of the tolerance of the scientific community for unsubstantiated just-so stories, because we have a prior commitment, a commitment to naturalism. It is not that the methods and institutions of science somehow compel us to accept a material explanation of the phenomenal world, but, on the contrary, that we are forced by our a priori adherence to material causes to create an apparatus of investigation and a set of concepts that produce material explanation, no matter how counter-

intuitive, no matter how mystifying to the uninitiated. Moreover, that materialism is absolute, **for we cannot allow a Divine foot in the door.** [5]

We have now come full circle. Exhibiting bizarre Stockholm syndrome-like behavior, the skeptic has absorbed and regurgitated the most nonsensical attitudes of those believers whom he endlessly ridicules. *"Credo Quia Absurdum," I believe [in atheism] because it is absurd.* The razor sharp retort of Dr. David Berlinski to the statement above by Lewontin should probably be etched in stone at the National Academy of Sciences:

> If one is obliged to accept absurdities for fear of a Divine Foot, imagine what prodigies of effort would be required were the rest of the Divine Torso found wedged at the door and with some justifiable irritation demanding to be let in? [6]

Imagine, indeed. It is difficult to find a more appropriate description other than *Nonsense of a High Order* when we speak about a worldview that shamelessly suppresses and distorts rational thought and inquiry for no other purpose than to prevent the appearance of "a Divine foot in the door."

I heal you in the name of SCIENCE!

Nothing is more likely to elicit an aggrandized sense of superiority in the heart of the militant skeptic than when he has the opportunity to tauntingly wave the banner of Science in the face of the "primitive" and "backward" believer. What exactly are the parameters of this "Science" to which Lewontin and other card-carrying atheists have so faithfully pledged their allegiance and to which they are committed to defend, come what may?

- *Science has nothing to tell us about how life started.*
- *Science has no explanation for consciousness and our unique sense of identity.*
- *Science has no material explanation for our miraculous ability to communicate through spoken and written language.*
- *While Science can explain to us in great detail why we need*

*to eat and breathe, it gives us no meaningful insight into the burning human needs for ultimate meaning, purpose, accomplishment, and abstract moral values (in other words, those things which make us uniquely human). It offers no explanation (other than, of course, speculative theories), why every other form of life on earth continues thriving and reproducing perfectly well without any of the above, **while human beings are unable to live without them!***

In short, Science has nothing to tell us about who we are, where we came from, and where we are going. Then what *does* Science tell us? The simple truth is (this may be a shock to some people), that for the most part Science is preoccupied with describing and discovering *how the plumbing works*. This is not in any way meant to imply that Science is unimportant. Understanding how the "plumbing" works is critically important (every homeowner knows that a good plumber is worth his weight in gold). Not only are we in awe of scientific accomplishments, we are all profoundly grateful for the benefits that have been bestowed upon mankind by advances in science and technology, particularly in the area of medicine. However, despite the fact that scientific progress has saved countless lives, Science offers no insight at all into *why* a human life is so worth saving to begin with and what we are living *for* in the first place.

True devotees of naturalism

Talmudic sources describe the practices of an ancient pagan cult called *Ba'al Pe'or*. The adherents of this sect showed their devotion to their god by first defecating in front of his statue and then proceeding to engage in some of the more standard types of debauchery. Defecation as a form of worship might seem odd to us in the 21st century, but the obvious meaning behind this act was to proclaim the glorification of, and an exclusive devotion to the physical and material aspects of existence. If it were suggested that the above described scatology would be an appropriate expression of their own absolute commitment to naturalism and materialism, I imagine the reactions of Lewontin, Hitchens, Dawkins, Ruse, Dennet, Pinker, *et al.*, would be comically squeamish (although I don't rule out the possibility that they could surprise me). Despite that, my guess is they would still feel right at home in a post-worship philosophical discussion with the naturalist/materialist "theologians" of the *Ba'al Pe'or* seminary.

"Squaring up to reality" means accepting that we are seeking God

At this point it has become clear that not only is life itself the result of a Godly act of creation, but that our experiences of the rich spiritual dimensions of living – a soul that is separate from our physical bodies, our yearning for transcendent meaning and purpose, and our drive for moral truth – are not illusory, but are real and actual. Unless we are prepared to commit our hearts and souls to a "comforting fiction" – as Dawkins, Baggini, Harris, and other atheists clearly have – "squaring up to reality" means accepting the simple fact that we are seeking God, one way or another, with almost every move we make as human beings.

But doesn't that make so much more sense anyway? Doesn't it make more sense that these powerful, relentless inner longings and desires that drive us – longings and desires so powerful that they are greater than our desire for life itself – actually *are* connected to a reality that is much greater than ourselves? When Sam Harris, despite himself, writes of a "sacred dimension to life," when Dawkins speaks of a deep, tempting urge to "worship" a maker or creator, when Sartre exclaims that his "whole being cries out for God," isn't it the most simple and obvious explanation that these feelings reflect the truth of who and what we are? That there is a sacred dimension to life, that there is a Creator to worship, and that there is a God to cry out to?

What are we to make of the sublime experiential reality that in the face of a child we catch a glimpse of a splendor so brilliant and glorious that even if "all the earth were parchment and all the oceans ink" we still would be at a loss to capture it in words? Is the explanation for this indescribable radiance and preciousness to be found in the realization that a child reflects the infinite glory of his or her Creator, or is the explanation to be found in its having been descended from an ancient fish with a "peculiar fin anatomy?" Does the beauty and wonder of a child, and the depth and intensity of the love a parent feels for a child, bear witness to the words of Genesis that the human being was created "in the image of God," or does it bear witness to the proposition that mankind rose out of a pond of scum and was created not in the image of God, but evolved in the image of the bacterium and the cockroach? Is it true that it is beyond futile to attempt to define the value of a child in material terms; that the significance of one baby transcends the entire universe with its billions and billions of galaxies; or is the truth that a child is simply another "purposeless" arrangement of electrons and molecules, "bits of a star gone wrong," "a state of matter," a "carbon based bag of water," and that in objective reality there is no difference between burning 100 pounds of coal or a 100 pounds of babies? What is most incredible about this question is that *these are the only two choices.* Is there any honest, thinking human being alive to whom it is not obvious which of these two alternatives must be the answer?

For those prepared to embrace truth and follow wherever it leads, there can be no real doubt as to the actual existence of the One transcendent God who created life and the universe we live in, and whom we seek with an intensity and a passion that is so faithfully expressed by the Psalmist:

As the hart cries out in thirst for the springs of water, so does my soul cry out in thirst...for the living God... [7]

Part V

Closing Thoughts

———————

— Chapter 11 —

*What About Suffering
and Evil in the World?*

*What About Evil Committed
in the Name of Religion?*

*Does the Existence of Evil
Religious People Imply the
Non-Existence of God?*

Chapter 11

Closing Thoughts

What about Evil and Suffering in the world? What about Evil Committed in the Name of Religion? Does the Existence of Evil Religious People Imply the Non-Existence of God?

Evil and Suffering: Relevant factors in our relationship to God, not the existence of God

Living a Godly life consists of essentially two different stages. The first stage is attaining an intellectual and emotional clarity regarding the reality of God's existence; the second stage is seeking the true path that will lead an individual to a relationship with God. Unfortunately, after completing stage one, many people approach stage two employing less discretion and wisdom than they would in their search to buy a used car. How to go about finding a true path to a relationship with God is an entirely different undertaking than being certain in your mind and heart that God exists. It is also not the subject of this book. This is the reason why I did not make any lengthy attempts to address the issue of evil and suffering. Making sense out of evil and suffering is only necessary and meaningful as a function of building a relationship with an actually existent, infinite, transcendent God. In other words, if God exists, I need some kind of explanation for the terribly painful things that happen in life in order to properly relate to him. I will briefly elaborate.

The *One God* described in this book either exists or he does not. Either he created the universe or he did not. *The fact that the world is not exactly the way we would like it to be is not a factor in determining the existence or non-existence of God.* The truth of his existence or non-existence is independent of any subjective reactions we may have about the vicissitudes of life.

To suggest otherwise is as intellectually absurd as the notion that my negative evaluation of a particular corporation implies the non-existence of the CEO. The existence of the CEO has no connection whatsoever to my personal feelings about the corporation or the way it is run. If God does exist, it is clear that the gulf between the capabilities of the human mind and that of a donkey is trivial compared to the infinite gulf between the human being and God. It would be foolish to expect a donkey to understand everything that we do, and it is even more foolish for us to expect to understand everything that God does. If God does exist he will run his universe according to *his* will, purpose, and understanding, not ours. The reality of suffering and the existence of people who commit – what we consider to be – horrible crimes may very well interfere in our relationship with an existent God, but they do not determine, nor negate, his existence. Not only would this be an intellectually indefensible position, but even on an emotional level this approach would be invalid. There is no such thing as a "standard" emotional/spiritual response to a traumatically painful experience. There are those who *lose* their faith as a result of tragedy, there are those who *maintain or grow in* their faith during an encounter with tragedy, and incredibly enough, there are many who *find* their faith as a result of tragedy. In short, the question of suffering and evil in the world has to do with our *relationship* with God, not his existence. (On the other hand if God does not exist, the whole question ceases to have significance. The pain or pleasure of mankind turns out to be nothing more than the luck of the draw.)

Evil in the name of religion

Generally speaking, each of the major religions of the world – and I would imagine most of the minor ones also – claim to have a divinely revealed message for mankind. That is to say, each claims their Scripture does not just contain elements of truth and reality, but that only its Scripture expresses and represents *the* truth and reality. Despite the noble intentions of politically correct people everywhere, it is self-evident that every religion cannot be the truth. This is apparent even to those with only a superficial understanding of the theologies of the world's major religions. The commonly bandied about notion that "my beliefs are true for me, yours are true for you, and his are true for him", is in most cases a classic example of being so open minded that "your brains fall out."

If, for example, five different faiths each contain dogmas and tenets that theologically and philosophically exclude any of the other four from being the absolute God-given truth, then – to put it bluntly – we are stuck with only two possibilities: A) only one of them is *the* truth and the others are false, or B) none of them are *the* truth and they are *all* false. One could propose that they each contain aspects of truth, but that really doesn't solve this particular dilemma. You would now have to create a new religion containing all those little pieces of truth extracted from other sources, a religion which you would immediately proclaim as being the *real* truth. We would then of course be right back where we started from...with six religions instead of five. (It is important to understand that rejecting a religion's claim to truth does not preclude the practice of tolerance. Tolerance does not mean that I necessarily accept your ideas as being true or valid. It means that despite the fact that I disagree with you, I still respect your essential value as a human being and continue to relate to you with the sense of dignity and obligation due to someone created in the image of God.)

If you observe what you perceive to be evil behavior on the part of adherents of a particular faith or atrocities committed in the name of a particular religious belief, there are three possible explanations:

A) Their religion is false. What they claim is a divine message and a divinely commanded "moral code" is really nothing more than an imaginary human construct and their behavior reflects this falseness (it goes without saying that even if they behave in a way that one might find very pleasant, their religion *still* could be nothing more than a product of human imagination), *or*

B) Their religion or moral code is divinely revealed truth, but human beings through their own free will have chosen to do evil and distort what God intended *or*

C) Their religion is divinely revealed truth, they are essentially living the way God wants them to live, and *you* are the one who has a distorted sense of how human beings are really supposed to live and behave. Another possibility is that you have an improper or incomplete understanding of why the adherents of this faith are behaving in a certain way, or you might be lacking accurate information. It is also possible that what you perceive as an atrocity is not really an atrocity at all. Take for example, the destruction of Hiroshima by an atom bomb. Depending on one's perspective, it can be viewed as an absolutely justified, moral act that ultimately ended World War II and saved millions of lives, or it can be viewed as an unprecedented act of barbarism.

Does the existence of evil religious people imply the non-existence of God? Hardly; the fact that people may correctly and truthfully believe in God does not preclude the very real possibility that they have deluded themselves into thinking that their own particular code of behavior is divinely ordained. Human beings are also capable of choosing to do evil of their own free will despite what they outwardly proclaim to believe.

A Final Thought – Where does this leave us?

I would suggest that it is the responsibility of each individual to invest the time, effort, and energy necessary to discover the truth about the meaning and purpose of his or her own existence, which may very well include the investigation of various religious faith systems, and make their life decisions based on this truth. Otherwise, we are all faced with three equally lamentable alternatives: *1)* heedlessly following the path that our society has conditioned us to travel, *2)* manufacturing our own comforting illusion, or *3)* making ourselves "comfortably numb" and playing out our lives as aimless, rudderless pieces of driftwood following the path of least resistance.

I wish I had an easier answer for the reader, but there is no escaping the simple fact that no one can do your work for you. Let truth become your passion and your obsession. You must seek, investigate, question, contemplate, discover, evaluate, and ultimately make a decision as to what is true and what is false, what is real and what is fantasy. Your own mind, your own life, and your own soul are all you have. To allow yourself, out of laziness and distraction, to flounder in mindless insignificance and deception would be tragic beyond words. I urge the reader to consciously and resolutely choose to begin this, perhaps lengthy, journey and process without delay. The moment that choice is made, the *real* adventure of life begins.

Appendix

Taking the Next Step

(Neither of the lists below is in any way meant to be exhaustive)

(1) For those who are not Jewish and would like to find out more about what Judaism has to say about seeking a path to God, the following are recommended:

   A. *The Path of the Righteous Gentile, by Chaim Clorfene and Yaakov Rogalsky*

   B. *http://webpages.charter.net/chavurathbneinoach/index.html*

   C. *http://www.aish.com/w/nj/*

(2) For Jews who are interested in finding out more about the Torah and Judaism, the following are recommended (in no particular order)

   D. *Living Inspired, Worldmask, by Rabbi Dr. Akiva Tatz*
http://www.tatz.cc/bio.htm

   E. *The Informed Soul: Introductory Encounters with Jewish Thought, by Rabbi Dr. Dovid Gottlieb*
http://www.dovidgottlieb.com/

   F. *Rabbi David Aaron   http://www.isralight.org/*

   G. *http://www.partnersintorah.org/*

   H. *http://www.gatewaysonline.com/index.asp*

   I. *http://www.rabbiwein.com/*

   J. *http://lazerbrody.typepad.com/lazer_beams/*

   K. *http://www.aish.com/*

   L. *http://ohr.edu/*

   M. *http://jeffseidel.com/*

N. *Books by Rabbi Shimon Apisdorf,*
   http://www.allbookstores.com/author/
   Shimon_Apisdorf.html
O. *Rabbi Ari Kahn http://www.rabbiarikahn.com/*
P. *Books by Rabbi Aryeh Kaplan — The Sabbath: Day of*
   Eternity, Jerusalem: Eye of the Universe, The Infinite
   Light, If You Were God, Meditation and the Bible,
   Tefillin, Maimonides' Principles, A Call to the Infinite
Q. *Horeb, by Rabbi Samson Raphael Hirsch*
R. *Rabbi Lawrence Kelleman*
   http://www.lawrencekelemen.com/
S. *The Science of God: The Convergence of Scientific and*
   Biblical Wisdom, Dr. Gerald Schroeder
T. *Gateway to Judaism, by Rabbi Mordechai Becher*
U. *Why the Jews? The Reason for Anti-Semitism,*
   by Prager and Telushkin
V. *WorldPerfect: The Jewish Impact on Civilization,*
   by Ken Spiro
W. *The Living Torah (Rabbi Aryeh Kaplan's translation of*
   the Five Books of Moses)
X. *The Stone Edition of the Five Books of Moses*
   (Artscroll Publishers)

Endnotes

Chapter 1 — *Introduction to Modern Atheism 101*

1. *The God Delusion,* Richard Dawkins, (New York: Houghton Mifflin Co., First Mariner Edition, 2008) p. 52
2. *A History of the Jews,* Paul Johnson, (Harper and Rowe, New York, NY) p. 585
3. *The End of Faith: Religion, Terror, and the Future of Reason,* Sam Harris (W.W. Norton and Company, New York, NY, 2004) p. 72
4. *God: The Failed Hypothesis: How Science Shows That God Does Not Exist,* Victor Stenger, (Prometheus Books, Amherst, New York, 2007) p. 33
5. http://video.google.com/videoplay?docid=891776135764757633
6. *www.youtube.com*/watch?v=Zy6XaHpnkEg
7. *The Atheist's Bible,* Joan Konner, (New York: Harper Collins, 2007) p. 2
8. *The Quotable Atheist,* Jack Huberman (New York: Nation, 2007) p. 313
9. ibid, p. 98
10. *Broca's Brain: Reflections on the Romance of Science,* Carl Sagan, (Toronto: Ballantine Books, 1980) p. 341
11. *The Meaning of Evolution,* G. Gaylord Simpson, Paleontologist, Professor of Zoology at Columbia Univ. and influential evolutionary scientist, as cited by David Oderberg in *Real Essentialism,* (New York: Routledge, 2007) p. 241
12. http://en.wikiquote.org/wiki/H._L._Mencken
13. See note 5 above
14. http://chesterton.org/acs/quotes.htm (under *Government and Politics*)
15. see Chap. 8, note 10
16. *Letters of Sigmund Freud,* edited by Ernst Freud (New York: Basic Books, 1960) p. 436

17. *From Dreams of a Final Theory* as quoted by Dr. Stuart Kauffman http://www.edge.org/3rd_culture/kauffman06/ kauffman06_index.html

18. From an interview in the film, *Expelled: No Intelligence Allowed* http://www.youtube.com/ watch?v=vuVSIG265b4&feature=related

19. see note 5 above

Chapter 2 — *The Ground Rules – Guidelines for Discussing the Existence of God*

1. From "The Boxer", ©Paul Simon

2. Heard by the author in a lecture given by Rabbi Noah Weinberg

3. ibid

4. *The Counter Creationism Handbook,* Mark Isaak, (Berkely and Los Angeles: U. of California Press, 2007) p. 45

5. ibid

6. http://www.jewcy.com/dialogue/monday _why_are_atheists_so_angry_sam_harris

7. *God is not Great: How Religion Poisons Everything,* Christopher Hitchens, (Twelve, Hachette Book Group, New York, NY, 2009) p. 49

8. ibid, p. 54

9. From an article entitled "Is There a God?", by Bertrand Russell (1952) http://www.cfpf.org.uk/articles/religion/br/br_god.html

10. Heard by the author in a lecture given by Rabbi Yaakov Weinberg

11. *The God Delusion,* Dawkins, p. 164

Chapter 3 — *Yes Professor Dawkins, How Does Life Get Started?*

1. *The End of Science: Facing the Limits of Knowledge in the Twilight of the Scientific Age,* John Horgan, (Broadway Books, New York, NY, 1996) p. 138
2. *Evolution vs. Creationism – An Introduction,* Eugenie Scott (University of California Press, 2005 – Paperback Edition) p. 27
3. http://ncseweb.org/creationism/analysis/excursion-chapter-1-origin-life
4. *Climbing Mt. Improbable,* Richard Dawkins, (New York: Norton Paperback Edition, 1997), p. 282
5. *The God Delusion,* Dawkins, p. 164
6. ibid
7. www.spacedaily.com/news/life-04zzz.html
8. American Scientist Online –"The Beginnings of Life on Earth", Dr. Christian DeDuve, *American Scientist,* Sep/Oct 1995 http://www.americanscientist.org/issues/feature/the-beginnings-of-life-on-earth/1
9. http://ncseweb.org/creationism/analysis/excursion-chapter-1-origin-life
10. "The Origin of Life on Earth", Dr. Leslie Orgel, *www.geocities.com/capecanaveral/lab/2948/orgel.html?20077 (Scientific American, Oct. 1994)*
11. "A Simpler Origin for Life", Dr. Robert Shapiro, (*Scientific American, Feb. 12, 2007) www.sciam.com/article.cfm?id=a-simpler-origin-for-life&page=1*
12. "The Implausibility of Metabolic Cycles on the Prebiotic Earth", Leslie Orgel, published posthumously, (PlosBiology.org website, Jan. 22, 2008)
13. See note 10 above
14. "Self Organization Origin of Life Scenarios and Information Theory", (*Journal of Theoretical Biology,* Vol. 91, 1981), H.P. Yockey, physicist, information theorist
15. see note 48 below, pg. 249
16. *Seven Clues to the Origin of Life: A Scientific Detective Story,* Graham Cairns-Smith, (Cambridge, United Kingdom: Cambridge University Press, 1985), p. 46 ©1985 – Cambridge University Press, Reprinted with the permission

of Cambridge University Press

17. ibid
18. ibid
19. ibid
20. ibid
21. "More Big Questions – In Search of Eden", Dr. Paul Davies and Phillip Adams http://www.abc.net.au/science/more bigquestions/stories/s540242.htm
22. *Seven Clues to the Origin of Life,* G. Cairns-Smith, p. 44 ©1985 Cambridge University Press Reprinted with the permission of Cambridge University Press
23. *The Intelligent Universe,* Sir Fred Hoyle (New York: Holt, Rinehart, and Winston, 1983) p. 20-23
24. *Origins: A Skeptics Guide to the Creation of Life on Earth,* Dr. Robert Shapiro, (Summit Books, 1986) p. 105, 116
25. *From Primordial Soup to the Prebiotic Beach,* an interview with Dr. Stanley Miller, UC San Diego, *www.accessexcellence.org/WN/NM/miller.html*
26. see note 11 above
27. *The God Delusion,* Dawkins, p. 164
28. "Implications of Evolution," Dr. Gerald Kerkut, *International Series of Monographs on Pure and Applied Biology – Division: Zoology, Volume 4,* (Pergamon Press, 1960) p. 150
29. *The Creation of Life: Past, Future, Alien* Dr. Andrew Scott (Basil Blackwell: Oxford UK, 1986) p. 111-112
30. "Update on Genesis," Dr. Andrew Scott, (*New Scientist,* vol. 106, no. 1454, May 2, 1985)
31. ibid
32. See note 8 above
33. *The God Delusion,* Richard Dawkins, p. 164
34. *Life Itself: It's Origin and Nature,* Francis Crick (New York: Simon & Schuster, 1981) p.153
35. "Why Speculate", a lecture by Dr. Michael Crichton (4/26/02) http://www.michaelcrichton.net/speech-whyspeculate.html
http://bevets.com/equotesc.htm
36. *Life Itself,* Crick, p. 88
37. "A calculation of the probability of spontaneous biogenesis by

information theory", *Journal of Theoretical Biology* (1977), H.P. Yockey (http://www.americanvision.org/article/why-evolution-is-impossible/)

38. *Information Theory and Molecular Biology,* H.P. Yockey (Cambridge University Press, 1992) p. 336 (http://www.americanvision.org/article/why-evolution-is-impossible/)

39. *Beyond Reductionism: Reinventing the Sacred,* Stuart Kauffman, Nov. 13, 2006 *http://www.edge.org/3rd_culture/kauffman06/kauffman 06_index.html*

40. *The Fifth Miracle: The Search for the Origin and Meaning of Life,* Dr. Paul Davies (New York: Simon & Shuster, 2000) p. 17

41. ibid, p. 27

42. see note 4 above

43. "Can Thermodynamics explain biological order?", *Impact Of Science On Society,* Vol.23, No.3 (1973), Ilya Prigogine, p. 178

44. *The Fifth Miracle,* Davies, p. 29

45. ibid, p. 97-98

46. *www.pandasthumb.org/archives/2005/10/robert-shapiro.html*

47. *Genesis: The Scientific Quest for Life's Origin,* Dr. Robert Hazen, (Washington D.C.: Joseph Henry Press, 2005) p. 9

48. *Evolution: A Theory in Crisis,* Dr. Michael Denton, (Chevy Chase, MD: Adler & Adler, 1986) p. 234, 328

49. *Seven Clues to the Origin of Life,* G. Cairns-Smith, p. 14 ©1985 Cambridge University Press Reprinted with the permission of Cambridge University Press

50. ibid, p. 4

51. CNET News, December 7, 1999, "IBM to research proteins using supercomputer" by Stephen Shankland and Melanie Austria Farmer http://www.zdnetasia.com/news/hardware/ 0,39042972,13022659,00.htm

52. *Life Itself,* Crick, p. 51

53. *The God Delusion,* Dawkins, p. 165

54. *Origins,* Shapiro, p. 125-128

55. ibid, p. 168-169

56. "Life: What a Concept!", published by Edge, 2008, p. 100 *http://www.edge.org/documents/life/Life.pdf*

57. *Life Itself,* Crick, p. 51-52
58. see note 3 above
59. www.sciencemag.org/cgi/content/short/1167856v1
60. *Planetary Dreams: The Quest to Discover Life Beyond Earth,* Dr. Robert Shapiro (New York: John Wiley & Sons, Inc., 1999) p. 102-104
61. ibid
62. "NYU chemist Robert Shapiro decries RNA-first possibility", *Harvard Gazette,* 10/23/2008
63. *Of Flies, Mice and Men,* Francois Jacob (Harvard University Press, 1998, Translated by Giselle Weiss) p. 21
64. see Chap. 4, note 54
65. ibid
66. *36 Arguments for the Existence of God: A Work of Fiction,* Rebecca Goldstein (Random House, New York, NY, 2010) p. 355
67. see note 3 above
68. see Chap. 2, note 4
69. *The Fifth Miracle,* Davies, p. 31
70. *Life Itself,* Crick, p. 88
71. *Genesis,* Hazen, p. 17-18

Chapter 4 — *Objections to a Supernatural Creator*

1. *The Monkey Business: A Scientist Looks at Creationism,* Niles Eldredge (Washington Square Press, 1982) p. 27 http://bevets.com/equotese.htm
2. *Timeframes,* Niles Eldredge (Simon and Schuster, New York, NY, 1985) p. 46-47
3. "In the Mind of the Beholder", S. J. Gould, *Natural History,* Vol. 103 (February, 1994), p. 14 http://www.creationists.org/response-to-nas-science-evolution-creationism-book.html
4. Dr. Michael Crichton, from an essay, 1999 (http://www.newscientist.com/blogs/shortsharpscience/2008/11/so-long-and-thanks-for-all-the.html)
5. see Chap. 3, note 8

6. "In Search of Eden", Dr. Paul Davies and Phillip Adams http://www.abc.net.au/science/morebigquestions/stories/ s540242.htm
7. *Origins,* Shapiro, p. 119
8. *The Fifth Miracle,* Davies, p. 31
9. *Genesis,* Hazen, from the preface, xiii
10. ibid
11. ibid, xiii, xiv
12. ibid, p. 241
13. ibid
14. see note 11 above
15. see Chap. 3, note 10
16. *The Evolution of Life on Earth,* Stephen J. Gould (*Scientific American,* October, 1994) http://brembs.net/gould.html
17. http://ncseweb.org/creationism/analysis/excursion-chapter-1-origin-life
18. see Chap. 3, note 39
19. see Chap. 3, note 4
20. As quoted in "Evolution: The Next 200 Years", (*New Scientist,* Jan. 28, 2009)
21. ibid
22. "How Did Life Begin?", (NOVA, 7/1/04) http://www.pbs.org/wgbh/nova/beta/evolution/ how-did-life-begin.html
23. "The Origin of Life on Earth", Alonso Ricard and Jack Szostak, (*Scientific American,* September 2009) http://www.scientificamerican.com/article.cfm?id= origin-of-life-on-earth
24. As cited by Dr. Ada Yonath, 2009 Nobel Laureate in Chemistry http://scienceblogs.com/terrasig/2009/12/ada_ yonath_interview.php
25. "Isn't the origin of life highly improbable?", Dr. Darrel Falk, *The Biologos Forum http://biologos.org/the-questions/isnt-the-origin-of-life-highly-improbable/*
26. see Chap. 3, note 37
27. see Chap. 3, note 56, p. 101
28. see Chap. 3, note 56, p. 11
29. "Musings on the Origin of Life and Panspermia", Dr. Milton

Wainwright (*The Journal of Cosmology*, Jan. 31, 2010, Vol. 5, 1091-1100) http://journalofcosmology.com/SearchFor Life126.html

30. see Chap. 3, note 28
31. *The Creation of Life*, Scott, p. 112
32. see Chap. 3, note 8
33. see note 53 below, "Lessons of Life", Christian DeDuve, p. 5
34. see Chap. 3, note 63
35. *What is Life?*, Lynn Margulis (University of California Press, Berkley and Los Angeles, 1995) p. 57
36. ibid, p. 58-59
37. *The End of Science*, John Horgan (Addison Wesley Publishing Co., 1996) p. 140-141
38. see Chap. 3, note 36
39. As cited in "The Search for the Scum of the Universe", Robert Roy Britt (Space.com May 21, 2002) http://www.space.com/scienceastronomy/astronomy/ odds_of_et_020521-1.html
40. *Seven Clues to the Origin of Life*, G. Cairns-Smith, p. 4,15
41. "Revolution in Chemistry" – Priestley Medalist George Whitesides' Address – (*Chemical and Engineering News*, March 26, 2007, Vol 85, No.13, pg. 12-17) http://pubs.acs.org/cen/coverstory/85/8513cover1.html
42. *Genesis*, Hazen, preface xiv
43. ibid, p. 241
44. http://www.grc.org/programs.aspx?year=2010& program=origin
45. http://blogs.nature.com/boston/2009/03/09/the-origins-of- life-on-earth-really (Boston blog, a nature network blog, "The Origins of Life on Earth. Really.")
46. *Evolution vs. Creationism*, Scott p. 25-26
47. *www.pandasthumb.org/archives/2005/10/robert-shapiro.html*
48. *Planetary Dreams*, Shapiro, p. 26
49. see Chap. 3, note 56, p. 84
50. *The Fifth Miracle*, Davies, p. 29, 30, 17, 27
51. http://www.scripps.edu/news/press/20100316.html
52. *Bioinorganic Photochemistry*, G. Stochel, M. Brindell, W. Macyk, Z. Stasicka, K. Szacilowski (John Wiley and Sons,

Ltd., UK) p. 109

53. *Many Worlds,* (Templeton Foundation Press, Radnor, Pennsylvania, 2000) "Astrobiology: The Search for Life Beyond the Earth", Christopher Mckay, p. 49

54. "The Origins of the RNA World", Dr. Michael Robertson and Dr. Gerald Joyce (*Cold Spring Harbor Perspectives in Biology,* Cold Spring Harbor Laboratory Press, April 28,2010) p. 18 http://cshperspectives.cshlp.org/cgi/doi/10.1101/cshperspect.a003608

55. Dr. Klaus Dose http://www.pbs.org/wgbh/nova/beta/evolution/how-did-life-begin.html

56. Dr. Werner Arber, Nobel Laureate in Medicine, 1978 http://www.icr.org/article/werner-arber-nobel-laureate-darwin-skeptic/

57. "Bacteria harnessing complexity", E. Ben Jacob, Y. Aharonov, Y. Shapira (Biofilms, 2004, Cambridge University Press) http://star.tau.ac.il/~eshel/papers/Bacteria%20harnessing%20complexity.pdf

58. cited in the article, "In the Beginning…", by John Horgan (*Scientific American,* Feb, 1991)

59. see note 17 above

60. see Chap. 3, note 29

61. see note 12 above

62. *Life Itself,* Crick, p. 88

63. ibid, p. 51

64. *Seven Clues to the Origin of Life,* G. Cairns-Smith, p. 8

65. ibid, p. 30

66. see Chap. 3, note 11

67. *Origins,* Shapiro, p. 128

68. *The Young Earth,* Euan Nisbet, (Kluwer Academic Publishers, 1987) http://www2.glos.ac.uk/GDN/origins/life/index.htm

69. *The Fifth Miracle,* Davies, p. 98

70. ibid, p. 82

71. ibid, p. 93

72. *www.pandasthumb.org/archives/2005/10/robert-shapiro.html*

73. *Planetary Dreams,* Shapiro, p. 26

74. *www.edge.org/q2006/q06_9.html*

Chapter 5 — *Actually, the Watchmaker has 20/20 Vision*

1. see Chap. 3, note 3
2. *Atheism,* Baggini, p. 97
3. *Dialogues Concerning Natural Religion,* David Hume (Penguin Classics, 1970) p. 54
4. *God is Not Great: How Religion Poisons Everything,* Christopher Hitchens (Hachette Book Group, New York, 2007) p. 65
5. *The Blind Watchmaker: Why the Evidence of Evolution Reveals a Universe Without Design,* Richard Dawkins (New York: W.W. Norton & Company, Ltd., 1996) p. 5
6. ibid, p. 6
7. *River Out of Eden,* Richard Dawkins (New York: Basic Books, 1995) p. 19
8. *The Fifth Miracle,* Davies, p. 115
9. *The Road Ahead,* Bill Gates (Penguin, London, 1996) p. 228
10. "The Fear of Religion", Thomas Nagle (*The New Republic,* October 2006) http://www.tnr.com/article/the-fear-religion
11. *The Intelligent Universe,* Sir Fred Hoyle (Rinehart and Winston, 1983) p. 19
12. *The God Delusion,* Dawkins, p. 137-138
13. ibid, p. 145-146
14. *The Mind of God,* Paul Davies (Simon and Schuster, New York, NY, 1992), p. 50
15. *Origins,* Shapiro, p. 119
16. From the debate with Dr. John Lennox *www.dawkinslennoxdebate.com*
17. ibid
18. *Genesis,* Hazen, p. 241
19. *Planetary Dreams,* Shapiro, p. 26
20. see Chap. 4, note 41
21. *Seven Clues to the Origin of Life,* Cairns-Smith, p. 15
22. see Chap. 4, note 50
23. *http://www.youtube.com/watch?v=BoncJBrrdQ8*
24. see Chap. 4, note 39

Chapter 6 — *The Existence of a Personal God*

1. *Atheism: A Very Short Introduction,* Baggini, p. 10
2. *God: The Failed Hypothesis,* Stenger, p. 71
3. ibid, p. 256
4. *The Atheist's Bible,* Konner, p. 2
5. *The Letters of Sigmund Freud,* p. 436
6. From the lecture by Hitchens at Sewanee University, *www.youtube.com/watch?v=Zy6XaHpnkEg*
7. see Chap. 1, note 17
8. see note 2 above
9. *The God Delusion,* Dawkins, p. 126
10. see note 4 above
11. http://thinkexist.com/quotation/life_has_no_meaning_ the_moment_you_loose_the/210451.html
12. *Broca's Brain: Reflections on the Romance of Science,* Carl Sagan, (Ballantine Books, 1980) p. 341
13. see Chap. 1, note 11
14. http://en.wikipedia.org/wiki/Emil_Cioran http://www.brainyquote.com/quotes/authors/e/ emile_m_cioran_2.html
15. see Chap. 1, note 18
16. see Chap. 1, note 17
17. *The Atheist's Bible,* p. 42
18. ibid, p. 20
19. http://thinkexist.com/quotes/like/life-has-no-meaning-a-priori-before-you-come/397354/ http://en.wikiquote.org/wiki/June_21
20. *God: The Failed Hypothesis,* Stenger, p. 251
21. *Man's Search for Meaning,* Victor Frankl, (Simon and Schuster, Inc., 1985) p. 127
22. http://thinkexist.com/quotation/that_god_does_not_ exist-i_cannot_deny-that_my/189882.html http://atheisme.free.fr/Quotes/Sartre.htm
23. *The End of Faith,* Harris, p. 16
24. From the debate with Dr. John Lennox, www.dawkinslennoxdebate.com

Chapter 7 — *The World of Spirituality: "Spirits in the Sky"*

1. *Atheism: A Very Short Introduction*, Baggini, p. 30
2. ibid, pg. 6-7
3. *The God Delusion*, Dawkins, p. 34
4. *Beyond Reductionism: Reinventing the Sacred*, Dr. Stuart Kauffman http://www.edge.org/3rd_culture/kauffman06/kauffman06_index.html
5. *The Spiritual Brain: A Neuroscientist's Case for the Existence of the Soul*, Mario Beauregard and Denyse O'Leary (HarperCollins, New York, 2007) p. 115
6. "Consciousness Without Faith", Sam Harris, http://richarddawkins.net/articleComments, 497, Consciousness-Without-Faith,Sam-Harris-On-Faith, page 1 #16807
7. "The Mystery of Consciousness", Steven Pinker, (*Time Magazine*, 1/19/2007) http://www.time.com/time/magazine/article/0,9171,1580394-2,00.html (sec. 2)
8. *The Spiritual Brain*, Beauregard and O'Leary, p. 125
9. ibid, p. 30
10. *The Problem of Consciousness: Essays Towards a Resolution*, Colin McGinn (Blackwell Publishers, Cambridge, Massachusetts, 1993) p. 6
11. "Steven Pinker on the Ghost in the Machine, Soul, Free Will" http://www.youtube.com/watch?v=4A_r6_GGv3U
12. *The Spiritual Brain*, Beauregard and O'Leary, p. 3
13. "The Big Idea: Can There be a Science of Mind?", Jerry Fodor, *Times Literary Supplement*, July 3, 1992, p. 5
14. George Wald "The Cosmology of Life and Mind", in Harman, W. with Clark, J., eds. New Metaphysical Foundations of Modern Science. Institute of Noetic Sciences, (1994) p. 123-131
15. "Life and Mind in the Universe", George Wald, *International Journal of Quantum Chemistry* (April 16, 2008) http://www3.interscience.wiley.com/journal/118640345/abstract?CRETRY=1&SRETRY=0
16. see note 7 above
17. "Will the Mind Figure Out how the Brain Works?", Steven

Pinker, *TIME Magazine,* (April 10, 2000) http://www.time.
com/time/magazine/article/0,9171,996604,00.html

18. *The Large, the Small, and the Human Mind,* Sir Roger Penrose
(Cambridge University Press, UK, 1997) p. 98

19. *The Spiritual Brain,* Beauregard and O'Leary, p. 108

20. see note 11 above

21. ibid

22. *The Denial of Death,* Ernest Becker (Free Press Paperback,
Simon & Schuster, Inc., New York, NY 1997) p. 105

23. *The Meme Machine,* Susan Blackmore (Oxford University
Press, Oxford, England, 1999) p. 236-237

24. *The Spiritual Brain,* Beauregard and O'Leary, p. 30

25. *Objective Knowledge: An Evolutionary Approach,* Karl Popper,
(Oxford University Press, Oxford, England, 1972) p. 223

26. see note 6 above

27. *The Devil's Delusion: Atheism and Its Scientific Pretensions,*
David Berlinski (Crown Publishers, Random House,
New York, 2008) p. 8-9

28. see note 7 above

29. *The Spiritual Brain,* Beauregard and O'Leary, from the
Introduction, p. xiii

30. http://www.youtube.com/user/NatUrbanAlliance#p/u/4/
uXopVpQwivY

31. *The Spiritual Brain,* Beauregard and O'Leary, p. 126

32. As cited by Dr. Stephen Meyer in *Signature in the Cell: DNA
and the Evidence for Intelligent Design* (HarperCollins, New
York, 2009) p. 15

33. *The Language Instinct: How the Mind Creates Language,*
Steven Pinker (HarperCollins, New York, 1995), p. 1

34. *Black Robe,* a film directed by Bruce Beresford, 1991

35. "Life Transcending Physics and Chemistry", Michael Polanyi
(*Chemical and Engineering News,* Vol. 45, No. 35, August 21,
1967)

Chapter 8 — *The Amoral World of Atheism*

1. "The Meaning of Evolution", G. Gaylord Simpson, Paleontologist, Professor of Zoology at Columbia Univ. and influential evolutionary scientist, as cited by David Oderberg in *Real Essentialism*, (Routledge, 2007) p. 241
2. *The Notebooks of Samuel Butler*, (Paperback Edition, Biblio-Bazaar, 2006) p. 48
3. As quoted by Prager and Telushkin in *The Nine Questions People Ask about Judaism*, (New York: Simon & Schuster, Inc., 1986) p. 22
4. "An Amoral Manifesto, Part 1", Joel Marks, (*Philosophy Now*, Aug./Sep. 2010) http://www.philosophynow.org/issue80/80marks.htm
5. *Atheism: A Very Short Introduction*, Julian Baggini, (Oxford University Press, USA, 2003) p. 2
6. ibid, p. 3
7. See Chapter 1, note 5
8. *The Descent of Man and Selection in Relation to Sex*, Charles Darwin (2nd Edition, London: John Murray, 1882) p. 133-134
9. *Anticipations of the Reactions of Mechanical and Scientific Progress upon Human Life and Thought*, H.G. Wells, 1902
10. *Prefaces*, George Bernard Shaw (London: Constable and Co., 1934)
11. Dr. Konrad Lorenz, from *The Legacy of Malthus: The Social Costs of the New Scientific Racism*, A. Chase, (Alfred Knopf, 1980) p. 349
12. Havelock Ellis, from an essay entitled "The Control of Population" as cited in *Breeding Superman*, Dan Stone, (Liverpool Univ. Press, 2002) p. 76
13. *The Portable Atheist: Essential Readings for the Non-Believer*, Christopher Hitchens, from the Introduction (Philadelphia, PA: DeCapo Press, 2007)
14. http://citador.pt/quotes/citador.php?cit=1&op=7&author=19&firstrec=0
    http://www.brainyquote.com/quotes/quotes/j/jeanpauls118277.html

http://thinkexist.com/quotation/it_disturbs_me_no_more_
to_find_men_base-unjust-or/211342.html

15. *The Quotable Atheist,* Jack Huberman, p. 313

16. *The Portable Atheist,* Hitchens, from the Introduction

17. "A Brief History of Infanticide", Dr. Larry Milner (1998),
The Society for the Prevention of Infanticide
http://www.infanticide.org/history.htm

18. "Why They Kill Their Newborns", Dr. Steven Pinker, (*The
New York Times,* November 2, 1997, Magazine Desk Section)
http://www.rightgrrl.com/carolyn/pinker.html

19. *The Histories* by Cornelius Tacitus, The Jews (Book Five,
paragraph 5) http://civilizationis.com/smartboard/shop/
tacitusc/histries/chap18.htm

20. heard in a lecture given by Rabbi Yaakov Weinberg

21. http://en.wikipedia.org/wiki/File:Himmler_Posen_Speech
_-_Extermination_of_the_Jews_excerpt,_Oct_4,_1943.ogg

22. *The God Delusion,* Dawkins, p. 315

23. *Webster's Quotationary,* Leonard Roy Frank, (Random House
Information Group, 2001) p. 524

24. ibid, p. 247

25. ibid, p. 715

26. *The End of Faith: Religion, Terror, and the Future of Reason,*
Sam Harris (New York: First Edition, W.W. Norton, Inc.,
2004) p. 12

27. "Why I Am An Unbeliever", an essay by Carl Van Doren
(http://www.skeptically.org/thinkersonreligion
/id10.html)

28. *The Portable Atheist,* Hitchens, p. 133

29. Christopher Hitchens as cited in *The Atheist's Bible,* p. 82

30. *The End of Faith,* Harris p. 175

31. ibid, p. 173

32. http://www.thedarwinpapers.com/oldsite/number12/
Darwinpapers12HTML.htm (see footnote 13 at this website)

33. *Mein Kampf,* Vol. I, Chapter 11

34. http://www.youtube.com/watch?v=gAhAlbsAbLM&
feature=related

35. Richard Dawkins, "River of Eden", *Scientific American* 1995,
as cited by Victor Stenger in *God: The Failed Hypothesis* –

How Science Shows that God Does Not Exist, (Amherst, NY: Prometheus Books, 2007) p. 71

36. *www.edge.org/q2006/q06_9.html*

37. Jean Paul Sartre, from a lecture entitled: Existentialism is a Humanism, 1946
(*http://www.marxists.org/reference/archive/sartre/works/exist/sartre.htm*)

38. "God is dead. Long live morality", Michael Ruse, *The Guardian* (U.K.) March 15, 2010
http://www.guardian.co.uk/commentisfree/belief/2010/mar/15/morality-evolution-philosophy

39. *Atheism: A Very Short Introduction,* Baggini, p. 44

40. ibid, p. 56

41. *http://www.youtube.com/watch?v=vuVSIG265 b4&feature=related* (from an interview with Ben Stein in the film, Expelled: No Intelligence Allowed)

42. "An Amoral Manifesto, Part I", Joel Marks, (*Philosophy Now,* August/Sep. 2010)
http://www.philosophynow.org/issue80/80marks.htm

43. Jeffrey Dahmer, from an interview with Stone Phillips on *Dateline, NBC,* November 29, 1994
http://scienceblogs.com/insolence/2007/10/evolution_made_me_do_it.php

44. "Where do Atheists Get Their Morality From?"
http://www.mwillett.org/atheism/moralsource.htm

Chapter 9 — Euthyphro: A Philosophical Dinosaur

1. *Atheism: A Very Short Introduction,* Baggini, p. 56

2. ibid, p. 38

3. heard in a lecture given by Rabbi Yaakov Weinberg

4. ibid

5. *The Quotable Atheist,* p. 50

Chapter 10 — *The Source of Self Esteem and the Moral Drive:*
One God

1. *Addictive Thinking: Understanding Self-Deception,* 2nd ed.,
   Abraham Twerski, M.D. (Center City, Minnesota: Hazelden,
   1977) p. 24
2. *www.Kidsource.com/kidsource/content2/strengthen_children*
   _self.html
3. ibid
4. ibid
5. "Billions and Billions of Demons", Richard Lewontin
   (*New York Times Book Reviews,* January 9, 1997)
   http://www.drjbloom.com/Public%20files/Lewontin
   _Review.htm
6. *The Devil's Delusion,* Berlinski, p. 15
7. *Psalms,* 42: 2-3

Made in the USA
Lexington, KY
23 March 2012